Memori⟨

By Admiral of the Fleet, Lord Fisher

Baron John Arbuthnot Fisher Fisher

Alpha Editions

This edition published in 2023

ISBN : 9789357389587

Design and Setting By
Alpha Editions
www.alphaedis.com
Email - info@alphaedis.com

Contents

PREFACE

NOT long ago a gentleman enclosed me the manuscript of his book, and asked me for a preface. I had never heard of him. He reminded me of Mark Twain in a similar case—the gentleman in a postscript asked Mr. Twain if he found fish good for the brain; he had been recommended it, he said. Twain replied, Yes! and he suggested his correspondent having whales for breakfast!

One gentleman sent me a cheque for two thousand guineas, and asked me to let him have a short article, on any subject. I returned the cheque—I had never heard of him either. I have had some most generous offers from publishers.

Sir George Reid said to me: "Never write an Autobiography. You only know one view of yourself—others see you all round." But I don't see any harm in such "Memories" as I now indite! In regard to Sir G. Reid's observation, there's one side no one else can see, and that's "*the inside!*"

Nothing in this Volume in the least approaches the idea of a Biography. Facts illumined by letters, and the life divided into sections, to be filled in with the struggles of the ascent, seems the ideal sort of representation of a man's life. A friend once wrote me the requisites of a biographer. Three qualifications were:

(*a*) Plenty of time for the job.
(*b*) A keen appreciation of the work done.
(*c*) A devotion to the Hero.

And, as if it didn't so much matter, he added—the biographer should possess a high standard of literary ability.

But yet I believe that the vindication of a man's lifework is almost an impossible task for even the most intimate of friends or the most assiduous and talented of Biographers, simply because they cannot possibly appreciate how great deeds have been belittled and ravaged by small contemporary men. These yelping curs made the most noise, as the empty barrels do! and it's only long afterwards that the truth emerges out of the mist of obloquy and becomes history.

Remember it's only in this century that Nelson has come into his own.

FISHER.

*   *   *   *   *

"Sworn to no Party—Of no Sect am I!

I can't be silent and I will not lie!"

* * * * *

"Time and the Ocean and some Guiding Star
In High Cabal have made us what we are!"

———————————

CHAPTER I
KING EDWARD VII

KING EDWARD had faith in me, and so supported me always that it is only natural I should begin this book with the remarks about him which I privately printed long since for use at my death; but events have occurred to alter that decision and induce me to publish this book.

There are more intimate touches than those related here, which I forbear to publish. There is a limit to those peculiar and pregnant little exhibitions of a kind heart's purpose being put in print. They lose their aroma.

In the *Dictionary of National Biography* there is a Marginal Heading in the Life of King Edward as follows:

"HIS FAITH IN LORD FISHER."

It is the only personal marginal note! I now descant upon it, not to be egotistical, but to exemplify one of the finest traits in King Edward's noble character—without doubt I personally could not be of the very least service to him in any way, and yet in his belief of my being right in the vast and drastic reforms in the Navy he gave me his unfaltering support right through unswervingly, though every sycophantic effort was exhausted in the endeavour to alienate him from his support of me. He quite enjoyed the numberless communications he got, and the more outrageous the calumnies the more he revelled in my reputed wickedness! I can't very well put some of them on paper, but the Minotaur wasn't in it with me! Also I was a Malay! I was the son of a Cingalese Princess—hence my wicked cunning and duplicity! I had formed a syndicate and bought all the land round Rosyth before the Government fixed on it as a Naval Base—hence my wealth! How the King enjoyed my showing him my private income as given to the Income Tax Commissioners was £382 6s. 11d. after the legal charges for income tax, annuities, etc., were subtracted from the total private income of £750!2

But King Edward's abiding characteristic was his unfailing intuition in doing the right thing and saying the right thing at the right time. I once heard him on the spur of the moment make a quite impromptu and totally unexpected speech to the notabilities of Malta which was simply superb! Elsewhere I have related his visit to Russia when I accompanied him. As Prince Orloff said to me, swept away by King Edward's eloquence, *"Your King has changed the atmosphere!"*

King Edward, besides his wonderful likeness to King Henry the Eighth, had that great King's remarkable attributes of combining autocracy with almost a socialistic tie with the masses. I said to His Majesty once: "Sir, that was a real low form of cunning on your Majesty's part sending to ask after Keir

Hardie's stomach-ache!" By Jove, he went for me like a mad bull! and replied: "You don't understand me! I am the King of *ALL* the People! No one has got me in their pockets, as some of them think they have!" and he proceeded with names I can't quote!

Acting on Sir Francis Knollys's example and advice I burnt all his letters to me, except one or two purely personal in their delightful adherence to Right and Justice! but even these I won't publish ever—they were not meant to be seen by others. What anointed cads are those who sell Nelson's letters to Lady Hamilton! letters written out of the abundance of his heart and the thankfulness of an emotional nature full of heartfelt gratitude to the sympathising woman who dressed his wounds, his torn-off scalp after the Nile, and his never-ceasing calamity of what is now called neuritis, which was for ever wasting his frail body with pain and anguish of spirit as it so unfitted him for exertion.

Here is a letter to King Edward, dated March 14th, 1908:

"With Sir John Fisher's humble duty to your Majesty and in accordance with your Majesty's orders, I saw Mr. Blank as to the contents of the secret paper sent your Majesty, but I did not disclose what makes it so valuable—that it came from a Minister of Foreign Affairs, whose testimony is absolutely reliable.

"I told Mr. Blank and asked him to forgive my presumption in saying it, that we were making a hideous mistake in our half measures, which pleased no one and thus we perpetuate the fable of 'Perfidious Albion,' and that we ought to have thrown in our lot with Russia and completely allowed her to fortify the Aland Islands as against Sweden and Germany.

"For a Naval War against Germany we want Russia with us, and we want the Aland Islands fortified.

"Germany has got Sweden in her pocket, and they will divide Denmark between them in a War against Russia and England, and unless our Offensive is quick and overwhelming Germany will close the Baltic just as effectually as Turkey locks up the Black Sea with the possession of the Dardanelles.

"*Russia and Turkey are the two Powers, and the only two Powers, that matter to us as against Germany, and that we have eventually to fight Germany is just as sure as anything can be, solely because she can't expand commercially without it.*

"I humbly trust your Majesty will forgive my presumption in thus talking Politics, but I know I am right, and I only look at it because if we fight we want Russia and Turkey on our side against Germany.

"With my grateful thanks for your Majesty's letter,

"I am your Majesty's humble servant,
"J. A. FISHER."

*   *   *   *   *

March 14th, 1908.

Note.—This letter to King Edward followed on a previous long secret conversation with his Majesty in which I urged that we should "Copenhagen" the German Fleet at Kiel *à la* Nelson, and I lamented that we possessed neither a Pitt nor a Bismarck to give the order. I have alluded to this matter in my account of Mr. Beit's interview with the German Emperor, and the German Emperor's indignation with Lord Esher as signified in the German Emperor's letter to Lord Tweedmouth that Sir John Fisher was the most dreaded man in Germany from the Emperor downwards.

It must be emphasized that at this moment we had a mass of effective Submarines and Germany only had three, and we had seven Dreadnoughts fit to fight and Germany had none!

This proposal of mine having been discarded, all that then remained for our inevitable war with Germany was to continue the concentration of our whole Naval strength in the Decisive Theatre of the War, in Northern Waters, which was so unostentatiously carried out that it was only Admiral Mahan's article in *The Scientific American* that drew attention to the fact, when he said that 88 per cent. of England's guns were pointed at Germany.

I mention another excellent illustration of King Edward's fine and magnanimous character though it's to my own detriment. He used to say to me often at Big Functions: "Have I missed out anyone, do you think?" for he would go round in a most careful way to speak to all he should. Just then a certain Admiral approached—perhaps the biggest ass I ever met. The King shook hands with him and said something I thought quite unnecessarily loving to him: when he had gone he turned on me like a tiger and said: "You ought to be ashamed of yourself!" I humbly said, "What for?" "Why!" he replied, "when that man came up to me your face was perfectly demoniacal! Everyone saw it! and the poor fellow couldn't kick you back! You're First Sea Lord and he's a ruined man! You've no business to show your hate!" and the lovely thing was that then a man came up I knew the King did perfectly hate, and I'm blessed if he didn't smile on him and cuddle him as if he was his long-lost brother, and then he turned to me afterwards and said with joyful revenge, "*Well! did you see that?*" Isn't that a Great Heart? and is it to be wondered at that he was so Popular?

An Australian wrote a book of his first visit to England. He was on a horse omnibus sitting alongside the 'Bus Driver—suddenly he pulled up the horses with a jerk! The Australian said to him, "What's up?" The Driver said, "Don't you see?" pointing to a single mounted policeman riding in front of a one-horse brougham. The Australian said, "What is it?" The 'Bus Driver said, "It's the King!" The Australian said, "Where's the escort?" thinking of cavalry and outriders and equerries that he had read of! The 'Bus Driver turned and looked on the Australian with a contemptuous regard and said: "Hescourt? 'e wants no Hescourt! Nobody will touch a 'air of 'is 'ead!" The Australian writes that fixed him up as regards King Edward!

His astounding memory served King Edward beautifully. Once he beckoned me up to him, having finished his tour round the room, to talk about something and I said: "Sir, the new Japanese Ambassador is just behind you and I don't believe your Majesty has spoken to His Excellency." The King instantly turned round and said these very words straight off. I remember them exactly; he took my breath away: "My dear Ambassador, do let me shake you by the hand and congratulate you warmly on the splendid achievement yesterday of your wonderful country in launching a 'Dreadnought' so completely home-produced in every way, guns, armour engines, and steel, etc. Kindly convey my admiration of this splendid achievement!"

I remembered then that in the yesterday's paper there had been an account of the great rejoicings in Japan on the launch of this "Dreadnought." The sequel is good. The Japanese Ambassador sought me later in the evening and said: "Sir John! it was kind of you to remind the King about the 'Dreadnought' as it enables me to send a much coveted recognition to Japan in the King's words!" I said: "My dear Ambassador, I never said a word to the King, and I am truly and heartily ashamed that as First Sea Lord it never occurred to me to congratulate you on what the King has truly designated as a splendid feat!"

I expect the Ambassador spent a young fortune in sending out a telegram to Japan, and do you wonder that King Edward was a Cosmopolitan Idol?

Another occasion to illustrate his saying out of his heart always the right thing at the right time. I was journeying with His Majesty from Biarritz to Toulon—I was alone with him in his railway carriage, there was a railway time table before him. The train began unexpectedly to slow down, and he said "Hulloa! why are we stopping?" I said, "Perhaps, your Majesty, the engine wants a drink!" so we stopped at a big station we were to have passed through—the masses of people shouted not "Vive le Roi!" but "EDOUARD!" (As the Governor of the Bank of France said to a friend of mine, "If he stays in France much longer we shall have him as our King! When's he going?"). Sir Stanley Clarke I saw get out and fetch the Prefect and the General in Command to the King—the King got out, said something sweet to the Prefect and then turned to the General and said with quite unaffected delight, "Oh, Mon Général! How delightful to meet you again! how glorious was that splendid regiment of yours, the —th Regiment of Infantry, which I inspected 20 years ago!" If I ever saw Heaven in a man's face, that General had it! He was certainly a most splendid looking man and not to be forgotten, but yet it was striking the King coming out with his immediate remembrance of him. Well! that incident you may be sure went through the French Army, and being a conscript nation, it went into every village of France! Do you wonder he was loved in France? And yet the King had the simplicity and even the weaknesses of a child, and sometimes the petulance thereof. He gave me a lovely box of all sizes of rosettes of the Legion of Honour adapted to each kind of uniform coat, and he added, "Always wear this in France—I find it aids me very much in getting about!" As if he wasn't as well known in all France as the Town Pump!

These are the sweet incidents that illustrate his nature!

He went to a lunch at Marienbad with some great swells who were there who had invited His Majesty to meet a party of the King's friends from Carlsbad, where I was—I wasn't asked—being an arranged snub! A looker-on described the scene to me. The King came in and said "How d'ye do" all round and then said to the Host, "Where's the Admiral?" My absence was apologised for—lunch was ready and announced. The King said, "Excuse me a moment, I must write him a letter to say how sorry I am at the oversight," so he left them stewing in their own juice, and His Majesty's letter to me was lovely—I've kept that one. He began by d——ing the pen and then the blotting paper!—there were big blots and smudges! He came back and gave the letter to my friend and said, "See he gets it directly you get back to Carlsbad to-night."

Once at a very dull lunch party given in his honour I sat next King Edward and said to His Majesty: "Pretty dull, Sir, this—hadn't I better give them a song?" He was delighted! (*he always did enjoy everything!*) so I recited (but, of course, I can't repeat the delicious Cockney tune in writing, so it loses all its aroma!). Two tramps had been camping out (as was their usual custom) in Trafalgar Square. They appear on the stage leaning against each other for support!—too much beer! They look upwards at Nelson on his monument, and in an inimitable and "beery" voice they each sing:

"We live in Trafalgar Square, with four Lions to guard us,

Fountains and statues all over the place!

The 'Metropole' staring us right in the face!

We own it's a trifle draughty—but we don't want to make no fuss!

What's *good e-nough* for Nelson is good *e-nough* for us!"

On another occasion I was driving with him alone, and utterly carried away by my feelings, I suddenly stood up in the carriage and waved to a very beautiful woman who I thought was in America! The King was awfully angry, but I made it much worse by saying I had forgotten all about him! But he added, "Well! find out where she lives and let me know," and he gave her little child a sovereign and asked her to dinner, to my intense joy!

On a classic occasion at Balmoral, when staying with King Edward, I unfolded a plan, much to his delight (now that masts and sails are extinct), of fusing the Army into the Navy—an "Army and Navy co-operative society." And my favourite illustration has always been the magnificent help of our splendid soldiers at the Battle of Cape St. Vincent, where a Sergeant of the 69th Regiment was the first to board the Spanish three-decker, "San Josef," and he turned then round to help Lord Nelson, who, with his one arm, found it difficult to get through the stern port of the "San Josef" again. In Lord Howe's victory two Regiments participated—the Queen's Royal West Surrey Regiment (formerly the 2nd Foot) and the Worcestershire Regiment (formerly the 29th and 36th Regiment). Let us hope that the Future will bring us back to that good old practice! This was the occasion when I was so carried away by the subject that I found myself shaking my fist in the King's face!

Lord Denbigh, in a lecture he gave at the Royal Colonial Institute, related an incident which he quite correctly stated had hitherto been a piece of diplomatic secret history, and it is how I got the Grand Cordon of the Legion of Honour, associated with a lovely episode with King Edward of blessed memory.

In 1906, at Madeira, the Germans first took an hotel; then they wanted a Convalescent Home; and finally put forth the desire to establish certain vested interests. They imperiously demanded certain concessions from Portugal. The most significant of these amounted to a coaling station isolated and fortified. The German Ambassador at Lisbon called on the Portuguese Prime Minister at 10 o'clock one Saturday night and said that if he didn't get his answer by 10 o'clock the next night he should leave. The Portuguese sent us a telegram. That night we ordered the British Fleet to move. The next morning the German Ambassador told the Portuguese Prime Minister that he had made a mistake in the cipher, and he was awfully sorry but he wasn't going; it was all his fault, he said, and he had been reprimanded by his Government. (As if any German had ever yet made a mistake with a telegram!)

To resume about the Grand Cordon of the Legion of Honour. The French Official statement when conveying to me the felicitations of the President of the French Republic was that I had the distinction of being at that time the only living Englishman who had received this honour, but the disaster that had been averted by the timely action of the British Fleet deserved it. So that evening, on meeting King Edward, I told His Majesty of the quite unexpected honour that I had received, and that I had been informed that I was the only Englishman that had got it, on which the King said: "Excuse me I've got it!" Then, alas, I made a *faux pas* and said "Kings don't count!" And no more do they! He got it because certainly they all loved him in the first place, and secondly, President Loubet couldn't help it, while if it hadn't been for the British Fleet on this occasion the Germans would have been in Paris in a week, and if the Germans had known as much as they do now they would have been!

I don't mean to urge that King Edward was in any way a clever man. I'm not sure that he could do the rule of three, *but he had the Heavenly gift of Proportion and Perspective!* Brains never yet moved the Masses—but Emotion and Earnestness will not only move the Masses, but they will remove Mountains! As I told Queen Alexandra on seeing his dear face (dead) for the last time, his epitaph is the great words of Pascal in the "Pensées" (Chapter ix, 19):

"Le cœur a ses raisons

Que la raison ne connaît point."

("The heart has reasons that reason knows nothing about"!)

He was a noble man and every inch a King! God Bless Him! I don't either say he was a Saint! I know lots of cabbages that are saints!—they couldn't sin if they wanted to!

Postscript.

It suddenly occurred to me to send these notes on King Edward to Lord Esher as he had peculiar opportunities of realizing King Edward's special qualities as a King, and realized how much there was in him of the Tudor gift of being an autocrat and yet being loved of the people!

Lord Esher to Lord Fisher

ROMAN CAMP,
CALLANDER, N.B.
July 30, 1918.

MY DEAR ADMIRAL,

The pages are wonderful, because they are *you*.

Not a square inch of pose about them.

Tears! that was the result of reading what you have to say about King Edward. But do you recollect our talk with him on board the Royal Yacht about France and Germany? Surely that was worth recording.

I have kept many of his letters. They show him to have been one of the "cleverest" of men. He had never depended upon book-learning—why should he?

He read, not books—but men and women—and jolly good reading too!

But he knew everything that it was requisite a King should know—unless Learning prepares a man for action, it is not of much value in this work-a-day world: and no Sovereign since the Tudors was so brave and wise in action as this King!

Your anecdotes of him are splendid. Add to them all that you can remember.

It was a pleasure to be scolded by the King for the sake of the smile you subsequently got.

The most awful time I ever had with him was at Balmoral when I refused to be Secretary of State for War. But I beat him on that, thank God!

Ever yours,
My beloved Admiral,
ESHER.

Letter from Lord Redesdale

1 KENSINGTON COURT, W.
May 24, 1915.

MY DEAR FISHER,

Do me the favour of accepting this little attempt to render justice to the best friend you ever had. (King Edward the Seventh.)

You and he were worthy of one another. Your old and very affectionate friend,

REDESDALE.

The following letter, written in 1907, would never have been penned but for the kindly intimacy and confidence placed and reposed in me by King Edward; it therefore rightly comes in these remarks about him; and so does the subsequent explanatory note on "Nelson and Copenhagen."

EXTRACT FROM A LETTER FROM SIR JOHN FISHER TO KING EDWARD

I have just received Reich's book. It is one unmitigated mass of misrepresentations.

In March this year, 1907, it is an absolute fact that Germany had not laid down a single "Dreadnought," nor had she commenced building a single Battleship or Big Cruiser for eighteen months.

Germany has been paralysed by the "Dreadnought."

The more the German Admiralty looked into her qualities the more convinced they became that they must follow suit, and the more convinced they were that the whole of their existing Battle Fleet was utterly useless because utterly wanting in gun power! For instance, half of the whole German Battle Fleet is only about equal to the English Armoured Cruisers.

The German Admiralty wrestled with the "Dreadnought" problem for eighteen months, and did nothing. Why? Because it meant their spending twelve and a half million sterling on widening and deepening the Kiel Canal, and in dredging all their harbours and all the approaches to their harbours, because if they did not do so it would be no use building German "Dreadnoughts" because they could not float! But there was another reason never yet made public. It is this: Our Battleships draw too much water to get close into the German Coast and harbours (we have to build ours big to go all over the world with great fuel endurance). But the German Admiralty is going, is indeed obliged, to spend twelve and a half million sterling in dredging so as to allow these existing ships of ours to go and fight them in their own waters when before they could not do so. It was, indeed, a Machiavellian interference of Providence on our behalf that brought about the evolution of the "Dreadnought."

To return to Mr. Reich. He makes the flesh of the British public creep at page 78 *et seq.*, by saying what the Germans are going to do. He does not say what they have done and what we have done.

Now this is the truth: England has seven "Dreadnoughts" and three "Dreadnought" Battle Cruisers (which last three ships are, in my opinion, far better than "Dreadnoughts"); total, ten "Dreadnoughts" built and building, while Germany, in March last, had not begun even one "Dreadnought." It is doubtful if, even so late as May last, a German "Dreadnought" had been commenced. It will therefore be seen, from this one fact, what a liar Mr. Reich is.

Again, at page 86, he makes out the Germans are stronger than we are in torpedo craft, and states that England has only 24 fully commissioned Destroyers.

Again, what are the real facts? As stated in an Admiralty official document, dated August 22nd, 1907: "We have 123 Destroyers and 40 Submarines. The Germans have 48 Destroyers and 1 Submarine."

The whole of our Destroyers and Submarines are absolutely efficient and ready for instant battle and are fully manned, except a portion of the Destroyers, which have four-fifths of their crew on board. Quite enough for instant service, and can be filled up under an hour to full crew. And they are all of them constantly being exercised.

There is one more piece of information I have to give: Admiral Tirpitz, the German Minister of Marine, has just stated, in a secret official document, that the English Navy is now four times stronger than the German Navy. Yes, that is so, and we are going to keep the British Navy at that strength, *vide* ten "Dreadnoughts" built and building, and not one German "Dreadnought" commenced last May. But we don't want to parade all this to the world at large. Also we might have Parliamentary trouble. A hundred and fifty members of the House of Commons have just prepared one of the best papers I have ever read, shewing convincingly that we don't want to lay down any new ships at all because we are so strong. My answer is: We can't be too strong. Sir Charles Dilke, in the *United Service Magazine* for this month, says: "Sir George Clarke points out that the Navy is now, in October, 1907, stronger than at any previous time in all History," and he adds that Sir George Clarke, in making this printed statement, makes it with the full knowledge of all the secrets of the Government, because, as Secretary of the Committee of Imperial Defence, he, Sir George Clarke, has access to every bit of information that exists in regard to our own and foreign Naval strength.

KING EDWARD VII. (WHO DIED MAY 6TH, 1910) SAYING GOOD-BYE TO LORD FISHER, FIRST SEA LORD, 1910.

(Lord Fisher 69, so also the King.)

N.B.—The King thought the 1841 vintage very good. Certainly good men were born that year!

In conclusion, a letter in *The Times* of September 17th, 1907, should be read. The writer of the letter understates the case, as the British Home Fleet is twenty per cent. stronger than he puts it.

As regards Mr. Reich's Naval statements, they are a *réchauffé* of the mendacious drivel of a certain English newspaper. I got a letter last night from a trustworthy person *à propos* of these virulent and persistent newspaper attacks as to the weakness of the Navy, stating that the recent inspection of the Fleet by Your Majesty has knocked the bottom out of the case against the Admiralty.

I don't mean to say that we are not now menaced by Germany. Her diplomacy is, and always has been, and always will be, infinitely superior to ours. Observe our treatment of the Sultan as compared with Germany. The Sultan is the most important personage in the whole world for England. He lifts his finger, and Egypt and India are in a blaze of religious disaffection.

That great American, Mr. Choate, swore to me before going to the Hague Conference that he would side with England over submarine mines and other Naval matters, but Germany has diplomatically collared the United States absolutely at The Hague.

The only thing in the world that England has to fear is Germany, and none else.

We have no idea, at the Foreign Office, of coping with the German propaganda in America. Our Naval Attaché in the United States tells me that the German Emperor is unceasing in his efforts to win over the American Official authorities, and that the German Embassy at Washington is far and away in the ascendant with the American Government.

I hope I shall not be considered presumptuous in saying all this. I humbly confess I am neither a diplomatist nor a politician. I thank God I am neither. The former are senile, and the latter are liars. But it all does seem such simple common sense to me that for our Army we require mobile troops as against sedentary garrisons, and that our military intervention in any very great Continental struggle is unwise, remembering what Napoleon said on that point with such emphasis and such sure conception of war, and that great combined Naval and Military expeditions should be our rôle. In the splendid words of Sir Edward Grey: "The British Army should be a projectile to be fired by the British Navy."

The foundation of our policy is that the communications of the Empire must be kept open by a predominant Fleet, and *ipso facto* such a Fleet will suffice to allay the fears of the "old women of both sexes" in regard to the invasion of England or the invasion of her Colonies.

NELSON'S COPENHAGEN

In May, 1907, England had seven "Dreadnoughts" ready for battle, and Germany had not one. And England had flotillas of submarines peculiarly adapted to the shallower German waters when Germany had none.

Even in 1908 Germany only had four submarines. At that time, in the above letter I wrote to King Edward, I approached His Majesty, and quoted certain apposite sayings of Mr. Pitt about dealing with the probable enemy before he got too strong. It is admitted that it was not quite a gentlemanly sort of thing for Nelson to go and destroy the Danish Fleet at Copenhagen without notice, but "la raison du plus fort est toujours la meilleure."

Therefore, in view of the known steadfast German purpose, as always unmitigatedly set forth by the German High Authority that it was Germany's set intention to make even England's mighty Navy hesitate at sea, it seemed to me simply a sagacious act on England's part to seize the German Fleet when it was so very easy of accomplishment in the manner I sketched out to His Majesty, and probably without bloodshed. But, alas! even the very whisper of it excited exasperation against the supposed bellicose, but really peaceful, First Sea Lord, and the project was damned. At that time, Germany was peculiarly open to this "peaceful penetration." A new Kiel Canal, at the cost of many, many millions, had been rendered necessary by the advent of the "Dreadnought"; but worse still for the Germans, it was necessary for them to spend further vast millions in deepening not only the approaches to the German Harbours, but the Harbours themselves, to allow the German "Dreadnoughts," when built, to be able to float. In doing this, the Germans were thus forced to arrange that thirty-three British pre-"Dreadnoughts" should be capable of attacking their shores, which shallow water had previously denied them. Such, therefore, was the time of stress and unreadiness in Germany that made it peculiarly timely to repeat Nelson's Copenhagen. Alas! we had no Pitt, no Bismarck, no Gambetta! And consequently came those terrible years of War, with millions massacred and maimed and many millions more of their kith and kin with piercèd hearts and bereft of all that was mortal for their joy.

QUEEN ALEXANDRA, LORD KNOLLYS, and SIR DIGHTON PROBYN.

At the end of these short and much too scant memories of him whom Lord Redesdale rightly calls in the letter I printed above

"The best friend you ever had,"

I can't but allude to a Trio forming so great a part of his Glory. Not to name them here would be "King Edward—an Unreality." I could not ask Queen Alexandra for permission either to print her Letters or her Words, but I am justified in printing how her steadfast love, and faith, and wonderful loyalty and fidelity to her husband have proved how just is the judgment of Her Majesty by the Common People—"the most loved Woman in the whole Nation."

And then Lord Knollys and Sir Dighton Probyn, those two Great Pillars of Wisdom and Judgment, who so reminded me, as they used to sit side by side in the Royal Chapel, of those two who on either side held up the arms of Moses in fighting the Amalekites:

"And Aaron and Hur stayed up his hands,

The one on the one side, and the other on the other side;

And his hands were steady until the going down of the sun."

Yes! King Edward's hands were held steady till the setting of his sun on May 6th, 1910, and so did he "discomfit his enemies by their aid."

For over forty years Lord Knollys played that great part in great affairs which will occupy his Biographer with Admiration of his Self-Effacement and unerring Judgment. Myself I owe him gratitude inexpressible.

For myself, those Great Three ever live in my heart and ever will.

There are no such that I know of who are left to us to rise in their place.

CHAPTER II
"THE MOON SWAYS OCEANS AND PROVOKES THE HOUND."

THE hound keeps baying at the moon but gets no answer from her, and she continues silently her mighty influence in causing the tides of the earth, such a mighty influence as I have seen in the Bay of Fundy, and on the coast of Arcadia where the tide rises some 40 feet—you see it like a high wall rolling in towards you on the beach! It exalts one, and the base things of earth vanish from one's thoughts. So also may the contents of this book be like-minded by a mighty silence against baying hounds! I hope to name no living name except for praise, and even against envy I hope I may be silent. Envy caused the first murder. It was the biggest and nastiest of all Cæsar's wounds:

"See what a rent the *envious* Casca made."

My impenetrable armour is Contempt and Fortitude.

Well, yesterday September 7th, 1919, we completed our conversations for the six articles in *The Times*, and to-day we begin this book with similar talks.

My reluctance to this book being published before my death is increasingly definite; but I have put my hand to the plough, because of the overbearing argument that I cannot resist, that I shall be helping to

(*a*) Avoid national bankruptcy.

(*b*) Avert the insanity and wickedness of building a Navy against the United States.

(*c*) Establish a union with America, as advocated by John Bright and Mr. Roosevelt.

(*d*) Enable the United States and British Navies to say to all other Navies "If you build more, we will fight you, here and now. We'll 'Copenhagen' you, without remorse."

This is why I have consented, with such extreme reluctance, to write letters to *The Times* and dictate six articles; and having thus entered into the fight, I follow the advice of Polonius—*Vestigia nulla retrorsum*. And so, to-day, I will begin this book—not an autobiography, but a collection of memories of a life-long war against limpets, parasites, sycophants, and jellyfish—at one time there were 19½ millions sterling of 'em. At times they stung; but that only made me more relentless, ruthless and remorseless.

Why I so hate a book, and those articles in *The Times*, and even the letters, is that the printed word never can convey the virtue of the soul. The *aroma* is not there—it evaporates when printed—a scentless product, flat and stale like a bad bottle of champagne. It is like an embalmed corpse. Personality, which is the soul of man, is absent from the reader. It is a man's personality that is the living thing, and in the other world that is the thing you will meet. I have often asked ecclesiastics—"What period of life will the resurrected body represent?" It has always been a poser for them! There will not be any bodies, thank God! we have had quite enough trouble with them down below here. St. Paul distinctly says that it is a spiritual body in the Resurrection. It is our Personalities that will talk to each other in Heaven. I don't care at what age of a man's life, even when toothless and decrepit and indistinguishable as he may then be, yet like another Rip Van Winkle, when he speaks you know him. However, that's a digression.

What I want to rub in is this: The man who reads this in his armchair in the Athenæum Club would take it all quite differently if I could walk up and down in front of him and shake my fist in his face.

(It was a lovely episode this recalls to my mind. King Edward—God bless him!—said to me once in one of my moments of wild enthusiasm: "Would you kindly leave off shaking your fist in my face?")

I tried once, so as to make the dead print more lifelike, using different kinds of type—big Roman block letters for the "fist-shaking," large italics for the cajoling, small italics for the facts, and ordinary print for the fool. The printer's price was ruinous, and the effect ludicrous. But I made this compromise and he agreed to it—whenever the following words occurred they were to be printed in large capitals: "Fool," "Ass," "Congenital Idiot." Myself, I don't know that I am singular, but I seldom read a book. I look at the pages as you look at a picture, and grasp it that way. Of course, I know what the skunks will say when they read this—"Didn't I tell you he was superficial? and here he is judged out of his own mouth." I do confess to having only one idea at a time, and King Edward found fault with me and said it would be my ruin; so I replied: "Anyhow, I am stopping a fortnight with you at Balmoral, and I never expected that when I entered the Navy, penniless, friendless, and forlorn!" Besides, didn't Solomon and Mr. Disraeli both say that whatever you did you were to do it with all your might? You can't do more than one thing at a time with all your might—that's Euclid. Mr. Disraeli added something to Solomon—he said "there was nothing you couldn't have if only you wanted it enough." And such is my only excuse for whatever success I have had. I have only had one idea at a time. *Longo intervallo*, I have been a humble, and I endeavoured to be an unostentatious, follower of our Immortal Hero. Some venomous reptile (his name has disappeared—I tried in vain to get hold of it at Mr. Maggs's bookshop only the other day) called Nelson "vain and egotistical." Good God! if he seemed so, how could he help it? Some nip-cheese clerk at the Admiralty wrote to him for a statement of his services, to justify his being given a pension for his wounds. His arm off, his eye out, his scalp torn off at the Nile—that clerk must have known that quite well but it elicited a gem. Let us thank God for that clerk! How this shows one the wonderful working of the Almighty Providence, and no doubt whatever that fools are an essential feature in the great scheme of creation. Why!—didn't some geese cackling save Rome? Nelson told this clerk he had been in a hundred fights and he enumerated his wounds; and his letter lives to illumine his fame.

The Almighty has a place for nip-cheese clerks as much as for the sweetest wild flower that perishes in a day.

It is really astounding that Nelson's life has not yet been properly written. All that has been written is utterly unrepresentative of him. The key-notes of his being were imagination, audacity, tenderness.

He never flogged a man. (One of my first Captains flogged every man in the ship and was tried for cruelty, but being the scion of a noble house he was promoted to a bigger ship instead of being shot.) It oozed out of Nelson that he felt in himself the certainty of effecting what to other men seemed rash and even maniacal rashness; and this involved his seeming vain and egotistical. Like Napoleon's presence on the field of battle that meant 40,000 men, so did the advent of Nelson in a fleet (this is a fact) make every common sailor in that fleet as sure of victory as he was breathing. I have somewhere a conversation of two sailors that was overheard and taken down after the battle of Trafalgar, which illustrates what I have been saying. Great odds against 'em—but going into action the odds were not even thought of, they were not dreamt of, by these common men. Nelson's presence was victory. However, I must add here that he hated the word Victory. What he wanted was Annihilation. That Crowning Mercy (as Cromwell would have called it), the battle of the Nile, deserves the wonderful pen of Lord Rosebery, but he won't do it. Warburton in "The Crescent and the Cross" gives a faint inkling of what the glorious chronicle should be. For two years, that frail body of his daily tormented with pain (he was a martyr to what they now call neuritis— I believe they called it then "*tic douloureux*"), he never put his foot outside his ship, watching off Toulon. The Lord Mayor and Citizens of London sent him a gold casket for keeping the hostile fleet locked up in Toulon. He wrote back to say he would take the casket, but he never wanted to keep the French Fleet in harbour; he wanted them to come out. But he did keep close in to Toulon for fear of missing them coming out in darkness or in a fog.

In his two years off Toulon Nelson only made £6,000 of prize money, while it was a common thing for the Captain of a single man-of-war off the Straits of Gibraltar to make a haul of £20,000, and Prize-Money Admirals in crowds basked in Bath enriched beyond the dreams of avarice. Nelson practically died a pauper.

Now this is another big digression which I must apologise for, but that's the damnable part of a book. If one could walk up and down and talk to someone, it never strikes them as incongruous having a digression.

I wind up this chapter, as I began it, with the fervent intention of avoiding any reference to those who have assailed me. I will only print their affectionate letters to me, for which I still retain the most affectionate feelings towards them. I regret now that on one occasion I did so far lose my self-control as to tell a specific Judas to take back his thirty pieces of silver and go and hang himself. However, eventually he did get hanged, so it was all right.

CHAPTER III
ADMIRAL VON POHL AND ADMIRAL VON TIRPITZ

YESTERDAY, September 8th, 1919 (I must put this date down because yesterday in a telegram I called von Tirpitz a liar) I got an enquiry whether it was correct that in 1909, as stated by Admiral von Tirpitz, I, as First Sea Lord of the Admiralty, engineered a German Naval Scare in England in order to get bigger British Naval estimates—and that I had said this to the German Naval Attaché. I replied "Tell Tirpitz—using the immortal words of Dr. Johnson—'you lie Sir, and you know it!'" Now, first of all, could I possibly have told the German Naval Attaché such a thing if I possessed the Machiavellian nature which is inferred by Tirpitz?

Secondly, there was a vast multitude of acute domestic enemies too closely watching me to permit any such manœuvre.

This affords an opportunity of telling you some very interesting facts about Tirpitz. They came to be known through the widow of Admiral von Pohl (who had been at the German Admiralty and commanded the German High Sea Fleet) interviewing a man who had been a prisoner at Ruhleben. He relates a conversation with Frau von Pohl, and he mentions her being an intimate friend of the German ex-Crown Princess, and as being extremely intelligent. Frau von Pohl had been reading Lord Jellicoe's book, and said to the ex-Ruhleben prisoner: "How strange is the parallel between Germany and Britain, that in both Navies the Admirals were in a stew as to the failings of their respective fleets." So much so on the German side, she said, that the German Fleet did not consider itself ready to fight till two months before the battle of Jutland, and the Germans till then lived in a constant fever of trepidation. These were the questions she heard. "'Why do the English not attack? Will the English attack to-morrow?'3 These questions we asked ourselves hourly. We felt like crabs in the process of changing their shells. Apparently our secret never oozed out." She put the inefficiency of the German Fleet all down to Tirpitz, and said that if any man deserved hanging it was he. Admiral von Pohl was supposed to have committed suicide through dejection. If all this be true, how it does once more illuminate that great Nelsonic maxim of an immediate Offensive in war! Presumably Frau von Pohl had good information; and she added: "The only reason Tirpitz was not dismissed sooner was lest the British should suspect from his fall something serious was the matter, and attack at once."4 Part of her interview is of special interest, as it so reminded me of my deciding on Scapa Flow as the base for the fleet. For as Frau von Pohl states, its speciality was that the German Destroyers could not get to Scapa Flow and back at full speed. Their fuel arrangements were inadequate for such a distance. "My husband," she said, "was called out by the Emperor to put things right, but was in a constant state of trepidation." Alas! trepidation was on our side also, for in a book written by a Naval Lieutenant he says how a German submarine was supposed to have got inside Scapa.5 As a matter of fact, it was subsequently discovered that a torpedo had rolled out of its tube aboard one of our Destroyers and passed close to H.M.S. "Leda," who quite properly reported "a torpedo has passed under my stern." This caused all the excitement.

Admiral von Pohl succeeded Admiral von Ingenohl as Commander-in-Chief of the German High Sea Fleet. It has not much bearing on what I have been saying, but it is interesting that Frau von Pohl said that the wife of the German Minister of the Interior had told her that her husband, on November 6th, five days before the Armistice, had talked to the Emperor of the truth as to the German inferiority. The Emperor listened, first with amazement, and then with incredulity, and ultimately in a passion of rage called him a madman and an arrogant fool, and turned him out in fury from his presence. This is not quite on all fours with Ludendorff, but Ludendorff may have been confining himself strictly to the fighting condition of the Army; and without doubt he was right there, for General Plumer told me himself he had the opportunity of bearing personal testimony to the complete efficiency of the German Army at the moment of the Armistice. Plumer was, it may be observed, rightly accorded the honour of leading the British Army into Cologne.

The man who contemplates all the things that may be somewhat at fault and adds up his own war deficiencies with that curious failure of judgment to realise that his enemy has got as many if not more, has neither the Napoleonic nor the Nelsonic gift of Imagination and Audacity. We know, now, how very near—within almost a few minutes of total destruction (at the time the battle-cruiser "Blucher" was sunk)—was the loss to the Germans of several even more powerful ships than the "Blucher," more particularly the "Seydlitz." Alas! there was a fatal doubt which prevented the continuance of the onslaught, and it was indeed too grievous that we missed by so little so great a "Might Have Been!" Well, anyhow, we won the war and it is all over. But I for one simply abominate the saying "Let bygones be bygones." I should shoot 'em now! And seek another Voltaire.

SIR JOHN FISHER IN "RENOWN," 1897.

I get the following from Lord Esher:—"In January, 1906, King Edward sent me to see Mr. Beit, who had been recently received by the German Emperor at Potsdam. The Emperor said to Beit that 'England wanted war: not the King—not, perhaps, the Government; but influential people like Sir John Fisher.' He said Fisher held that because the British Fleet was in perfect order, and the German Fleet was not ready, England should provoke war. Beit said he had met Fisher at Carlsbad, and had long talks with him, and that what he said to him did not convey at all the impression gathered by His Imperial Majesty. The Emperor replied: 'He thinks it is the hour for an attack, and I am not blaming him. I quite understand his point of view; but we, too, are prepared, and if it comes to war the result will depend upon the weight you carry into action—namely, a good conscience, and I have that.... Fisher can, no doubt, land 100,000 men in Schleswig-Holstein—it would not be difficult—and the British Navy has reconnoitred the coast of Denmark with this object during the cruise of the Fleet. But Fisher forgets that it will be for me to deal with the 100,000 men when they are landed.'"

The German Emperor told another friend of mine the real spot. It was not Schleswig-Holstein—that was only a feint to be turned into a reality against the Kiel Canal if things went well. No, the real spot was the Pomeranian Coast, under a hundred miles from Berlin, where the Russian Army landed in the time of Frederick the Great. Frederick felt it was the end and sent for a bottle of poison, but he didn't take it, as the Russian Empress died that night and peace came.

Long before I heard from Lord Esher, I had written the following note about Beit:—

A mutual friend at Carlsbad introduced me to Mr. Beit, the great South African millionaire. He adored Cecil Rhodes, and so did I. Beit, so I was told, had got it into his head that I somewhat resembled his dead friend, and he talked to me on one occasion about Rhodes until 3 a.m. after dining together. Beit begged me to come and see him on my return to London at his house in Park Lane, just then finished, but I never did for I was vastly busy then. I was troubled on all sides, like St. Paul.

"Without were fightings, and within were fears." Fighting outside the Admiralty, and fears inside it.

He really was a dear man, was Beit.

Of course I don't know anything about his business character. Apparently there is a character a man puts on in business, just as a man does in politics, and it may be quite different from his character as a gentleman.

Beit every year made a pilgrimage to Hamburg, to see his old mother, who lived there, and it much touched me, his devotion to her. But our bond of affection was our affection for Rhodes.

The German Emperor sent for Beit, for I gathered that Beit saw how peace was threatened. I don't know if this was the reason of the interview. In this Imperial conversation my name turned up as Lord Esher had made a statement that by all from the German Emperor downwards I was the most hated man in Germany. The German Emperor did say to Beit that I was dangerous, and that he knew of my ideas as regards the Baltic being Germany's vulnerable spot, and he had heard of my idea for the "Copenhagening" of the German Fleet. But this last I much doubt. He only said it because he knew it was what we ought to have done.

With regard to saying anything more of that interview I prefer to keep silent. In an Italian book, printed at Brescia in A.D. 1594, occur these words of Steven Guazzo;

"They should know," says Anniball, "that it is no lesse admirable to know how to holde one's peace than to know how to speake. For, as wordes well uttered shewe eloquance and learning, so silence well kept sheweth prudence and gravitie!"

I wish Beit could have read Stead's splendid appreciation of Cecil Rhodes, who describes him as a Titan of intrinsic nobility and sincerity, of innate excellence of heart, and immense vitality of genius, and describes the splendid impulsiveness of his generous nature. I am told that Rhodes's favourite quotation was from Marcus Aurelius:

"Take care always to remember you are a Roman, and let every action be done with perfect and unaffected gravity, humanity, freedom and justice."

Stead's opinion was that Rhodes was a practical mystic of the Cromwell type. Stead was right. Rhodes was a Cromwell. He was Cromwellian in thoroughness, he was Napoleonic in audacity, and he was Nelsonic in execution.

"Let us praise famous men." (*Ecclesiasticus*, chapter 44, verse 1).

From Lord Fisher to a Friend

36, BERKELEY SQUARE.

MY DEAR FRIEND,

I was asked yesterday: Could I end the War?

I said: "Yes, by one decisive stroke!"

"What's the stroke?" I was asked.

I replied: "Never prescribe till you are called in."

But I said this: "Winston once told me, 'You can see Visions! That's why you should come back.'"

For instance, even Jellicoe was against me in sending the Battle Cruisers to gobble up von Spee at the Falkland Islands! (All were against me!) Yes! and all were against me in 1904! when the Navy was turned inside out—ships, officers and men. "A New Heaven and a New Earth!" 160 ships put on the scrap heap because they could neither fight nor run away! *Vide* Mr. Balfour's speech at Manchester about this "Courageous stroke of the pen!"

We now want another Courageous Stroke! And the Stroke is ready! It's the British Navy waiting to strike! And it would end the War!

This project of mine sounds an impossibility! but so did von Spee's annihilation! Pitt said "I walk on Impossibilities." All the old women of both sexes would squirm at it! They equally squirmed when I did away with 19½ millions sterling of parasites in ships, officers and men, between 1904 and 1910! They squirmed when, at one big plunge, we introduced the Turbine in the Dreadnought (the Turbine only before having been in a penny steamboat). They squirmed at my introduction of the water tube Boiler, when I put the fire where the water used to be and the water where the fire used to be! And now 82 per cent. of the Horse Power of the whole world is Turbine propulsion actuated by water tube Boilers!

They squirmed when I concentrated 88 per cent. of the British Fleet in the North Sea, and this concentration was only found out by accident, and so published to the ignorant world, by Admiral Mahan in an article in *The Scientific American*!

And they squirm now when I say at one stroke the War could be ended. It could be!

Yours, etc.
(Signed) FISHER.

Lord Fisher to a Privy Councillor

36, BERKELEY SQUARE,
LONDON,
Dec. 27, 1916.

MY DEAR FRIEND,

You've sent me a very charming letter, though I begged you not to trouble yourself to write, but as you have written and said things I am constrained to reply, lest you should be under false impressions. I have an immense regard for Jellicoe.... Callaghan I got where he was—he was a great friend of mine—but Jellicoe was better; and Jellicoe, in spite of mutinous threats, was appointed Admiralissimo on the eve of war. I just mention all this to show what I've done for Jellicoe because I knew him to be a born Commander of a Fleet! Like poets, Fleet Admirals are born, not made! *Nascitur non fit!* Jellicoe is incomparable as the Commander of a Fleet, but to prop up an effete Administration he allowed himself to be cajoled away from his great post of duty. I enclose my letter to him.

I need hardly say how private all this is, but you are so closely associated with all the wonders we effected from October 21, 1904, onwards, that I feel bound to take you into my inmost confidence. Jellicoe retorted I had praised

Beatty—*so I had!* See my reply thereon. I told the Dardanelles Commission (why they asked me I don't know!) that Jellicoe had all the Nelsonic attributes except *one*—he is totally wanting in the great gift of Insubordination. Nelson's greatest achievements were all solely due to his disobeying orders! But that's another story, as Mr. Kipling would say. Wait till we meet, and I'll astonish you on this subject! Any fool can obey orders! But it required a Nelson to disobey Sir John Jervis at the Battle of Cape St. Vincent, to disregard the order to retire at Copenhagen, to go into the Battle of the Nile by night with no charts against orders, and, to crown all, to enter into the Battle of Trafalgar in a battle formation contrary to all the Sea orders of the time! BLESS HIM! Alas! Jellicoe is saturated with Discipline! He is THE ONE MAN to command the Fleet, BUT he is not the man to stand up against a pack of lawyers clothed with Cabinet garments, and possessed with tongues that have put them where they are!

David was nodding when he said in the Psalms: "A man full of words shall not prosper on the Earth." *They are the very ones that* **DO** *prosper!* For War, my dead Friend, you want a totally differently constituted mind to that of a statesman and politician! There are great exemplars of immense minds being utter fools! They weigh everything in the Balance! I know great men who never came to a prompt decision—men who could talk a bird out of a tree!

War is Big Conceptions and Quick Decisions. Think in Oceans. Shoot at Sight! The essence of War is Violence. Moderation in War is Imbecility. All we have done this war is to imitate the Germans! We have neither been Napoleonic in Audacity nor Cromwellian in Thoroughness nor Nelsonic in execution. Always, always, always "TOO LATE"!

I could finish this present German submarine menace in a few weeks, but I must have POWER! My plans would be emasculated if I handed them in. I must be able to say to the men I employ: "*If you don't do what I tell you, I'll make your wife a widow and your house a dunghill!!!*" (*and they know I would!*)

Don't prescribe till you're called in! Someone else might put something else in the pill!

Heaven bless you!

When people come and sympathise with me, I always reply, with those old Romans 2,000 years ago expelled:

"Non fugimus:

Nos fugamur."

"We are not Deserters,

We are Outcasts."

Yours, etc.

(Signed) FISHER.

From a Privy Councillor to Lord Fisher

Jan. 8th, 1917.

MY DEAR FISHER,

I have always thought Jellicoe one of those rare exceptions to the general rule that no great commander is ever a good administrator. I knew you had picked him out long ago to command the Grand Fleet if war came, and it is in my mind that you had told me years ago your opinion of him as a Sea Commander so that it was what I was expecting and hoping for at the time, though I was sorry for Jellicoe superseding Callaghan when the war broke out, but I remembered your old saying, "Some day the Empire will go down because it is Buggins's turn"! At the same time, I'm not sure that any man can stand the strain of active command under present conditions for more than 2½ years. I see no sign of tiredness about Jellicoe now, but it must be almost impossible to keep at high tension so long without losing some of the spring and dash, and it did look as if a stronger man than Jackson was wanted as First Sea Lord at the Admiralty. Of course when you were First Sea Lord and Jellicoe with the Grand Fleet it was absolutely the right combination, but as they haven't brought you back to the Admiralty I feel Jellicoe is the man to be where he is, provided his successor is the right man too. I don't know Beatty, so can only go by what I hear of him. I can only pray that when his day of trial comes he will come up to your high standard.

I largely agree with all you say about the politicians. No doubt our great handicap in this war is that nearly all the party leaders get their positions through qualities which serve them admirably in peace time, but are fatal in war. The great art in politics in recent years has always seemed to me to be to pretend to lead, when you are really following the public bent of the moment. All sense of right and wrong is blunted, and no one stands up for what he honestly believes in but which may not at the moment be popular. If he does, he is regarded as a fool, and a "waster," and may get out. A habit of mind is thus formed which is wholly wanting in initiative, and in war the initiative is everything. I agree with you absolutely:—"*Make up your mind, and strike! and strike hard and without mercy.*" We have thrown away chance upon chance, and nothing saves us but the splendid fighting material at our disposal. I doubt whether the recent changes will bring about any great change. I trust they may, but, whatever happens, neither side can go on indefinitely. Everything points to Germany's economic condition being very bad, and there may come a crash, *but meantime the submarine warfare is most serious, and no complete answer to it is yet available.*

Yours very sincerely,

_____

CHAPTER IV
ECONOMY IS VICTORY

MR. GLADSTONE stood by me last night. Mr. McKenna was by his side. I am not inventing this dream. It is a true story. (It is Godly sincerity that wins—not fleshly wisdom!)

A gentleman, such as you, was by way of interviewing Mr. Gladstone. Mr. Gladstone was castigating me. I was a Public Department. He said to you, who were interviewing him, that he was helpless against all the Public Departments, for he was fighting for Economy, and he gave a case to you worse than either Chepstow or Slough. I am sorry to say it was the War Office he was illustrating, as I am devoted to Mr. Churchill and would not hurt him for the world—even in a dream. It is too puerile to describe in print, but what Mr. Gladstone pointed to I have told you in conversation.

Now, the above is an Allegory.

Imagine! nearly a year after the Armistice and yet we are spending two millions sterling a day beyond an absolutely fabulous income—beyond any income ever yet produced by any Empire or any Nation!

Sweep them out!

Dr. Macnamara, a few days since, in his *apologia pro vita sua* excuses his Department to the public by saying that on the very day of the Armistice the Board of Admiralty sat on Economy! *So they did!* They *sat* on it!

Economy! To send Squadrons all over the globe that were not there before! The globe did without them during the War—why not now? "Oh my Sacred Aunt!" (as the French say when in an extremity). "Showing the flag," I suppose, for that was the cry of the "baying hounds" in 1905 when we brought home some 160 vessels of war that could neither fight nor run away—and whose Officers were shooting pheasants up Chinese rivers and giving tea parties to British Consuls. How those Consuls did write! And how agitated was the Foreign Office! I must produce some of these communications directly "DORA" is abolished. Well, that's what "showing the flag" means.

Sweep 'em out!

Gladstone was hopeless against Departments—so is now the Nation.

Dr. Macnamara may not know it, but Mr. Herbert Samuel was to have had his place. I did not know either of them, but I said to the Prime Minister "Let's have the 'Two Macs'!" Mind, I don't class him with the Music Hall artist. (*Tempus*: Death of Campbell-Bannerman)—that epoch—I cannot forget Mr. Asquith's kindness to me. He had telephoned to me from

Bordeaux after seeing the King at Biarritz, asking me to meet him on his arrival home next night at 8.30 p.m. at 40 Cavendish Square. His motor car was leaving the door as I arrived. He told me he had seen the King, and had proposed Mr. McKenna as First Lord of the Admiralty. The King seemed to have some suspicion that I should not think Mr. McKenna a congenial spirit. I made no objection—I thought to myself that if Mr. McKenna were hostile then *Tempus edax rerum*. I don't think Jonathan and David were "in it," when Mr. McKenna and I parted on January 25th, 1910—my selected day to go and plant roses in Norfolk. I blush to quote the Latin inscription on the beautiful vase he gave me;

Joanni Fisher
Baroni Kilverstonæ
Navarchorum Principi, Ensis, Linguæ,
Stili Valde Perito,
Vel in Concilio vel in Praelio insigni,
Nihil Timenti,
Inflexibili, Indomitabili, Invincibili,6
Pignus Amicitiæ Sempiternae,
Dederunt Reginaldus et Pamela McKenna.

To
John
Lord Fisher of Kilverstone
First of Admirals
Skilled of Sword, Tongue & Pen
Brilliant in Council and Battle
Dreading Nought
Inflexible, Indomitable, Invincible6
This Token of Enduring Friendship
a Gift from
Reginald & Pamela McKenna

And, even now, when time and absence might have deadened those feelings of affection, he casts himself into the burning fiery furnace, bound with me in a trusteeship of a huge estate with only 3*s*. 4*d*. in the £ left—all that the spendthrifts leave us. "Showing the flag" and presumably resuscitating the same old game of multitudinous dockyards to minister to the ships that are "showing the flag"; and so more Chepstows and more Sloughs! And these multitudes of shipwrights superfluous in Government Dockyards who ought to be in day and night shifts making good at Private Yards the seven millions sterling of merchant vessels that Dr. Macnamara's Government associates supinely allowed to be sent to the bottom! Those political and professional associates, who, instead of using the unparalleled British Navy of the moment as a colossal weapon for landing Russian Armies in Pomerania and Schleswig-Holstein, aided by the calm and tideless waters of the Baltic, were led astray to follow the road that led to conscription and an army of Four Million Soldiers, while the Navy was described in the House of Commons as "a subsidiary service." How Napoleon must now be chortling at his prognostication coming true, that he put forth at St. Helena, as described on page 177 of Lord Rosebery's "Last Phase," that the day we left the sea would be our downfall!

But this chapter is on "Economy"; and I have to tell a story here about my dear friend McKenna. He was Secretary of the Treasury; he, and an almost equal friend of mine—Mr. Runciman—were, as we all know, extremely cunning at figures. Lots of people were then looking after me—Kind friends! For instance, I remember my good friend John Burns at one Cabinet Committee meeting instructing me on a piece of blotting paper how to deal with a hostile fleet. I don't mean to say that John Burns would not have been a first-class Admiral. To be a good Admiral, a man does not need to be a good sailor. That's a common mistake. He wants good sailors under him. He is the Conceptionist. However, to resume. At that time I was "Pooh-Bah" at the Admiralty; the First Lord was in a trance, and the Financial Secretary had locomotor ataxy. I was First Sea Lord, and I acted for both the Financial Secretary and the First Lord in their absence. I wasn't justified, but I did it. So I was the *tria juncta in uno*; and I referred, as First Sea Lord, a matter to the Financial Secretary for his urgent and favourable consideration, and he favourably commended it to the First Lord, who invariably cordially approved. It was all over in about a minute. *Business buzzed!*

(I'm doubtful whether this ought to come out before Dora's abolished. That's why I wanted these papers to be edited in the United States by some indiscreet woman, where no action for libel lies. Colonel House did ask me to go to America when I saw him in Paris last May. There is a great temptation, for the climate goes from the Equator to the Pole, and a dear American Admiral friend of mine expatiated to me on the joy of laying hold of the hand of the summer girl at Palm Beach in Florida and never letting it go until you get to Bar Harbour in the State of Maine. I have had endless invitations and most hearty words from Florida to Maine, and from Passedena to Boston, and I have as many American dear friends as I have English.)

Well! the Treasury could not make out how all those submarines were being built—where the devil the money was coming from; so these ferrets came over. I led a dog's life, or rather a rabbit's life, chased from hole to hole. Nothing came of it; and as an outcome of that time I left the Admiralty with 61 good submarines and 13 building. The Germans, thank God! had gone to the bottom with their first submarine, which never came up again, and the few more they had at that time were not much use.

I must tell a story now. Mind! I don't want to run down the Treasury. The Treasury is an absolutely necessary affliction.

There was once a good Parsee ship-owner with a good Captain. But this Captain *would* charge his owner with the cost of his carriage from his ship to the office. Not being far, the old Parsee thought the Captain ought to walk, and if he didn't walk then he ought to pay for the cab himself. They call the carriages "buggies" at Bombay. However, when the old Parsee had to pay the bill next month—there it was: "Buggy—so many rupees." He told his Captain he would pay that once but never again; and not finding it in the items of the bill presented the following month he gave the Captain his cheque. As the Captain put it in his pocket he said: "Buggy's there!" That's what happened to the Treasury and the submarines.

I had a friend in the Accountant-General's Department called "The Mole." He taught me how to hide the money. I may observe I was called a "Mole." It wasn't a bad name. I was not seen or heard, but I was recognised by upheavals—"There is that damned fellow Fisher again, I will swear to it!" But, as David said, "Let us be abundantly satisfied" that we have such among us as McKennas and Runcimans. I should like to let those ferrets loose now. However, "Out of Evil Good comes." Now comes a pardonable digression, I think.

Here's a letter I got yesterday, September 9th, 1919, coming from Russia. Now suppose we had not made the very damnedest mess of Russia ever made in this world—with Lord Milner first going there and then Mr. Henderson, the head of the Labour Party, ambassadoring (as least, he says so) and this nation in every possible conceivable way alienating the Russian people—then I never could have had this magnificent letter from Russia to give you. Just observing, before I quote it: Supposing a French Army landed at Dover to help us subjugate Ireland? I guess we should all forget whether we were Tories or Carsons or Smillies, and unite to get this French army out of our Archangel, and the Entente Cordial would be "in the cart," as the vulgar say. Well, this is the letter which does my heart good. It is from a young lad in an English man-of-war, now off St. Petersburg. He is writing of the recent defeat of the Russian fleet there:—

"There has been such a fight. I was only a looker-on. I was furious. Kronstadt was attacked by our motor boats each carrying two torpedoes" [by the way, I was vilified for introducing motor boats] "and seaplanes with destroyers backing them up" [isn't it awful! I introduced destroyers also]. "Two Russian battleships, a Depôt ship and a Destroyer Leader were torpedoed.

"Our motor boats were MAGNIFICENT!

"I nearly cried with pride at belonging to the same Race.

"There has been nothing like it in the whole War.

"I would rather take part in a thing like that than be Prime Minister of England. You would have been so proud if you could have seen them."

The letter is to the boy's mother. On it is written, by him who sends it me, "The Nelson touch, I think!"

NATIONAL SERVICE OR THE NAVY?

SIR JOHN FISHER AND LORD ROBERTS, 1906.

CHAPTER V
THE DARDANELLES

"UNTIL THIS DAY REMAINETH THE SAME VAIL UNTAKEN AWAY"

2 Corinthians, iii, 14.

I COMPARED this morning early what I had formerly written on the subject of Personalities with what I said to you yesterday on the same subject in my peripatetic dictation—I can't recognise what is in type for the same as what I spoke.

This morning I get a letter from Lord Rosebery. Lord Rosebery is, I think, in a way attached to me. In fact he must be, or I should not have drunk so much of his splendid champagne! Now *you* don't call me "frisky" when I walk up and down talking to you; and although he reads the actual living words I say to you, yet when he sees the beastly thing in print he calls me "frisky"! I keep on saying this *ad nauseam*, to keep on hammering it not only into you but into the public at large who happen to read these words—that no printed effusion can ever represent what, when face to face, cannot help conveying conviction to the hearer. And so we come to the same old story, that the written word is an inanimate corpse. You want to have the Soul of the Man pouring out to you his personality.

And here again, when I contrasted the notes which I spoke from with what I said, again I find I don't recognise them—Well! enough of that!

Now if anyone thinks that in this chapter they are going to see Sport and that I am going to trounce Mr. Winston Churchill and abuse Mr. Asquith and put it all upon poor Kitchener they are woefully mistaken. It was a Miasma that brought about the Dardanelles Adventure. A Miasma like the invisible, scentless, poisonous—*deadly* poisonous—gas with which my dear friend Brock, of imperishable memory and Victoria Cross bravery, wickedly massacred at Zeebrugge, was going (in unison with a plan I had) to polish off not alone every human soul in Heligoland and its surrounding fleet sheltered under its guns from the Grand Fleet, but every rabbit. It was much the same gas the German put into the "Inflexible" (which I commanded), in 1882 to light the engine-room. When it escaped it was scentless; instead of going up, as it ought to have done, it went down, and permeated the double-bottom, and we kept hauling up unconscious men like poisoned miners out of a coalpit. Gas catastrophe—Yes! Brock was lost to us at the massacre of Zeebrugge—lost uselessly; for no such folly was ever devised by fools as such an operation as that of Zeebrugge divorced from military co-operation on land. What were the bravest of the brave massacred for? Was it glory? Is the British Navy a young Navy requiring glory? When 25 per cent. of our Officers were killed a few days since, sinking two Bolshevik battleships, etc., and heroic on their own element, the sea, we all thank God, as we should do, that Nelson, looking down on us in Trafalgar Square, feels his spirit is still with us. But for sailors to go on shore and attack forts, which Nelson said no sailor but a lunatic would do, without those on shore of the military persuasion to keep what you have stormed, is not only silly but it's murder and it's criminal. Also by the time Zeebrugge was attacked, the German submarine had got far beyond a fighting radius that required this base near the English coast. As Dean Inge says: "We must hope that in the Paradise of brave men the knowledge is mercifully hid from them that they died in vain."

Again, this is a digression—but such must be the nature of this book when speaking *ore rotundo* and from the fulness of a disgusted heart, that such Lions should be led by such Asses. The book can't convey my feelings, however carefully my good friend the typewriter is taking it down. All the quill drivers, the ink spillers, and the Junius-aping journalists will jeer at you as the Editor, and say, "Why didn't you stop him? Where's the argument? Where's the lucid exposition? Where's the subtle dialectician who will talk a bird out of a tree? Where is this wonderful personality I'm told of, who fooled King Edward, and ravished virgins, and preached the Gospel (so he says)? Like Gaul, he is divided into three parts; we don't see one of them."

We'll get along with the Dardanelles now. All this will make pulp for paper for the *National Review*.

"Imperial Cæsar dead and turned to clay

Now stops a hole to keep the wind away."

Well, I left off at the "Miasma" that, imperceptibly to each of them in the War Council, floated down on them with rare subtle dialectical skill, and proved so incontestably to them that cutting off the enemy's big toe in the East was better than stabbing him to the heart in the West; and that the Dardanelles was better than the Baltic, and that Gallipoli knocked spots off the Kiel Canal, or a Russian Army landed by the British Fleet on the Baltic shore of Schleswig-Holstein.

Without any doubt, the "beseechings" of the Grand Duke Nicholas in the Caucasus on January 2nd, 1915,7 addressed to Kitchener in such soldierly terms, moved that great man's heart; for say what you will, Kitchener was a great man. But he was a great deception, all the same, inasmuch as he couldn't do what a lot of people thought he could do. Like Moses, he was a great Commissariat Officer, but he was not a Napoleon or a Moltke; he was a Carnot *in excelsis*, and he was the facile dupe of his own failings. But "Speak well of those who treat you well." I went to him one evening at 5 p.m., with Mr. Churchill's knowledge, and said to him as First Sea Lord of the Admiralty that if his myrmidons did not cease that same night from seducing men from the private shipyards to become "Cannon-fodder" I was going to resign at 6 p.m. I explained to him the egregious folly of not pressing on our shipbuilding to its utmost limits. He admitted the soft impeachment as to the seduction; and there, while I waited, he wrote the telegram calling off the seducers. If only that had been stuck to after I left the Admiralty, we shouldn't be rationed now in sugar nearly a year after the Armistice, nor should we be bidding fair to become a second Carthage. We left our element, the sea, to make ourselves into a conscript nation fighting on the Continent with four million soldiers out of a population of forty millions. More than all the other nations' was our Army.

The last words of Mr. A. G. Gardiner's article about him who is now dictating are these: "He is fighting his last great battle. And his foe is the veteran of the rival service. For in his struggle to establish conscription Lord Roberts's most formidable antagonist is the author of the 'Dreadnought.'"

Well, once more resuming the Dardanelles story. These side-lights really illuminate the situation. These Armies we were raising incited us to these wild-cat expeditions. I haven't reckoned them up, but there must have been a Baker's Dozen of 'em going on. Now, do endeavour to get this vital fact into your mind. We are an Island. Every soldier that wants to go anywhere out of England—a sailor has got to carry him there on his back.

Consequently, every soldier that you raise or enlist, or recruit, or whatever the proper word is, unless he is absolutely part of a Lord Lieutenant's Army, never to go out of England and only recruited, like the Militia—that splendid force!—to be called up only in case of invasion—as I say, every soldier that is recruited on any other basis means so much tonnage in shipping that has to be provided, not only to take him to the Continent; but it's got to be kept ready to bring him back, in case of his being wounded, and all the time to take him provisions, ammunition, stores. Those vessels again have to have other vessels to carry out coal for those vessels, and those colliers have again to be supplemented by other colliers to take the place of those removed from the normal trade, and the coal mines themselves necessitate more miners or the miners' working beyond the hours of fatigue to bring forth the extra coal; or else the commercial work of the nation gets diminished and your economic resources get crippled, and that of itself carried *in extremis* means finishing the war. As a matter of fact, it *has* nearly finished the English Nation—the crippling of our economic resources by endeavouring to swell ourselves out like the Frog in Æsop's Fables, and become a great continental

Power—forgetting the Heaven-sent gift of an incomparable Navy dating from the time of Alfred the Great, and God's providing a breakwater 600 miles long (the British Islands) in front of the German Coast to stop the German access to the ocean, and thus by easy blockade killing him from the sea as he was killed eventually. Alas! what happened? In the House of Commons the British Navy is called a subsidiary Service. And then Lord Rosebery doesn't like my "frisking"; and cartoons represent that I want a job; and fossil Admirals call me immodest!

Mr. Churchill was behind no one both in his enthusiasm for the Baltic project, and also in his belief that the decisive theatre of the war was beyond doubt in Northern waters; and both he and Mr. Lloyd George, the Chancellor of the Exchequer, magnificently responded to the idea of constructing a great Armada of 612 vessels, to be rapidly built—mostly in a few weeks and only a few extending over a few months—to carry out the great purpose; and I prepared my own self with my own hands alone, to preserve secrecy, all the arrangements for landing three great armies at different places—two of them being feints that could be turned into a reality. Also I made all the preparations, shortly before these expeditions were to start, to practise them embarking at Southampton and disembarking at Stokes Bay, so that those who were going to work the Russian Armies would be practised in the art, having seen the experiment conducted on a scale of twelve inches to the foot with 50,000 men.

(We once embarked 8,000 soldiers on board the Mediterranean Fleet in nineteen minutes, and the fleet steamed out and landed them at similar speed. Old Abdul Hamid, the Sultan, heard of it, and he complimented me on there being such a Navy. That was the occasion when a red-haired, short, fat Major, livid with rage, complained to me on the beach that a bluejacket had shoved him into the boat and said to him "Hurry up, you bloody lobster, or I'll be 'ung!" I explained to the Major that the man *would* have been hanged; he was responsible for getting the boat filled and shoved off in so many seconds.)

I remember that at the War Council held on January 28th, 1915, at 11.30 a.m., Mr. Churchill announced that the real purpose of the Navy was to obtain access to the Baltic, and he illustrated that there were three naval phases. The first phase was the clearing of the outer seas; and that had been accomplished. The second phase was the clearing of the North Sea. And the third phase was the clearing of the Baltic. Mr. Churchill laid stress on the importance of this latter operation, because Germany always had been and still was very much afraid of being attacked in the Baltic. For this purpose special vessels were needed and the First Sea Lord, Lord Fisher, had designed cruisers, etc., etc., meaning the Armada. Mr. Lloyd George said to me at another meeting of the War Council, with all listening: "How many battleships shall we lose in the Dardanelles?" "A dozen!" said I, "but I prefer to lose them elsewhere." In dictating this account I can't represent his face when I said this.

Here I insert a letter on the subject which I wrote to Lord Cromer in October, 1916:—

36, BERKELEY SQUARE,
October 11th, 1916.

DEAR LORD CROMER,

To-day Sir F. Cawley asked me to reconcile Kitchener's statement of May 14th at the War Council that the Admiralty proposed the Dardanelles enterprise with my assertion that he (Kitchener) did it. Please see question No. 1119. Mr. Churchill is speaking, and Lord Kitchener said to him *"could we not for instance make a demonstration at the Dardanelles?"*

I repeat that before Kitchener's letter of Jan. 2nd to Mr. Churchill there was no Dardanelles! Mr. Churchill had been rightly wrapped up in the splendid project of the British Army sweeping along the sea in association with the British Fleet. See Mr. Churchill at Question No. 1179.

"The advance of the (British) Army along the Coast was *an attractive operation, but we could not get it settled.* Sir John French wanted very much to do it, but it fell through."

See Lord Fisher, *War Council of Jan. 13th*! Sir John French then present—(*3 times he came over about it*)—"Lord Fisher demurred to any attempt to attack Zeebrugge without the co-operation of the British Army along the coast."

As to the *Queen Elizabeth*, Mr. Churchill is right in saying there was great tension between Kitchener and myself. He came over to the Admiralty and when I said *"if the 'Queen Elizabeth' didn't leave the Dardanelles that night I should!"* he got up from the table and he left! and wrote an unpleasant letter about me to the Prime Minister! *Lucky she did leave!!* The German submarine prowling around for a fortnight looking for her (*and neglecting all the other battleships*) blew up her duplicate wooden image.

Yours, etc.,
(Signed) FISHER.

Mr. Churchill is quite correct. I backed him up till I resigned. *I would do the same again!* He had courage and imagination! He was a War Man!

If you doubt my dictum that the Cabinet Ministers only were members of the War Council and the rest of us voice tubes to convey information and advice, ask Hankey to come before you again and state the status!

Otherwise the experts would be the Government! Kindly read what Mr. Asquith said on Nov. 2nd, 1915, in Parliament. (See p. 70.)

(We had constructed a fleet of dummy battleships to draw off the German submarines. This squadron appeared with effect in the Atlantic and much confused the enemy.)

Mr. Asquith also was miasma-ed; and it's not allowable to describe the discussion that he, I, and Mr. Churchill had in the Prime Minister's private room, except so far as to observe that Mr. Churchill had been strongly in favour of military co-operation with the fleet on the Belgian Coast, and Sir John French, on three different visits to the War Council, had assented to carrying out the operation, provided he had another Division added to his Force. This project—so fruitful as it would have been in its results at the early stage of the war—was, I understand, prevented by three deterrents: (1) Lord Kitchener's disinclination; (2) The French didn't want the British Army to get into Belgium; (3) The Dardanelles came along.

I objected to any Naval action on the Belgian Coast without such military co-operation. Those flat shores of the Belgian coast, enfiladed by the guns of the accompanying British Fleet, rendered that enterprise feasible, encouraging and, beyond doubt, deadly to the enemy's sea flank. Besides preventing Zeebrugge from being fortified and the Belgian Coast being made use of as a jumping-off place for the air raids on London and elsewhere, with guns capable of ranging such an enormous distance as those mounted in the Monitors, we could have enfiladed with great effect all attacks by the Germans.

When we got to the Council table—the members having been kept waiting a considerable time—the Prime Minister gave the decision that the Dardanelles project must proceed; and as I rose from the Council table Kitchener followed me, and was so earnest and even emotional8 that I should return that I said to myself after some delay: "Well, we can withdraw the ships at any moment, so long as the Military don't land," and I succumbed. I was mad on that Armada of 612 vessels, so generously fostered by Mr. Lloyd George and Mr. Churchill and sustained by the Prime Minister. They were of all sorts and sizes—but alas! as they reached completion they began to be gradually perverted and diverted to purposes for which they were unfitted and employed in waters to which they were unsuited. Nevertheless they made (some of them) the Germans flee for their lives, and with such a one as the gallant Arbuthnot or the splendid Hood, who gave their lives for nothing at Jutland, we might have had another Quiberon.

To resume: I gave Lord Cromer, the Chairman of the Dardanelles Commission a précis of the Dardanelles case. It doesn't appear in the Report of the Dardanelles Commission. I forgive him that, because, when in his prime, he did me a good deed. It is worth relating. I entreated him to cut a channel into Alexandria Harbour deep enough for a Dreadnought; and he did it, though it cost a million sterling, and thus gave us a base of incalculable advantage in certain contingencies.

I will now shortly pass in review the Dardanelles statement that I gave Lord Cromer. Those who will read this book won't want to be fooled with figures. I give a figurative synopsis. Of course, as I told the Dardanelles Commission (Cromer thought it judicious to omit my comment, I believe), the continuation of the Dardanelles adventure beyond the first operations, confined solely to the ships of the fleet which could be withdrawn at any moment and the matter ended—the continuation, I explained to the Dardanelles Commission, was largely due to champion liars. It must ever be so in these matters. I presume that's how it came about that two Cabinet Ministers—no doubt so fully fed up with the voice tube, as it has been described—told the nation that we were within a few yards of victory at the Dardanelles, and so justified and encouraged a continuance of that deplorable massacre. However, no politician regards truth from the same point of view as a gentleman. He puts on the spectacles of his Party. The *suppressio veri* and the *suggestio falsi* flourish in politics like the green baize tree.

Sworn to no Party—of no Sect am I:

I can't be silent and I will not lie.

Before the insertion of the following narrative prepared by me at the time of the Dardanelles Commission I wish to interject this remark: When sailors get round a Council Board they are almost invariably mute. The Politicians who are round that Board are not mute; they never would have got there if they had been mute. That's why for the life of me I can't understand what on earth made David say in the Psalms "A man full of words shall not prosper on the Earth." They are the very ones who do prosper! It shows what a wonderful fellow St. Paul was; he was a bad talker and yet he got on. He gives a bit of autobiography, and tells us that his bodily presence was weak and his speech contemptible, though his letters were weighty and powerful. However, in that case, another Gospel was being preached, where the worldly wise were confounded by the worldly foolish.

While my evidence was being taken before the Dardanelles Commission, the Secretary (Mears) was splendid in his kindness to me, and my everlasting gratitude is with the "Dauntless Three" who broke away from their colleagues and made an independent report. They were Mr. Fisher—formerly Prime Minister of Australia, (a fellow labourer), Sir Thomas

Mackenzie (High Commissioner for New Zealand), and Mr. Roch, M.P. Their Report was my life-buoy; a précis of their Report, so far as it affects me and which I consider unanswerable, establishes that it is the duty of any Officer, however highly placed, to subordinate his views to that of the Government, unless he considers such a course so vitally antagonistic to his Country's interests as to compel him to resign. I know of no line of action so criminally outrageous and subversive of all discipline as that of public wrangling between a subordinate and his superior, or the Board of Admiralty and an Admiral afloat, or the War Office and their Commander-in-Chief in the Field.

This Dardanelles Commission reminds me of another "cloudy and dark day," as Ezekiel would describe it, when five Cabinet Ministers, at the instigation of an Admiral recently serving, held an enquiry absolutely technical and professional on matters about which not one of them could give an authoritative opinion but only an opinion which regarded political opportunism—an enquiry neither more nor less than of my professional capacity as First Sea Lord of the Admiralty. The trained mind of Mr. McKenna only just succeeded in saving me from being thrown to the wolves of the hustings. But it has inflicted a mortal wound on the discipline of the Navy. Hereafter no mutinous Admiral need despair (only provided he has political and social influence) of obtaining countenance for an onslaught against his superiors; and we may yet lose the decisive battle of the world in consequence.

The following is my narrative of my connexion with the Dardanelles Operations.

"The position will not be clear and, indeed, will be incomprehensible, if it be not first explained how very close an official intimacy existed between Mr. Winston Churchill and Lord Fisher for very many years previous to the Dardanelles episode, and how Lord Fisher thus formed the conviction that Mr. Churchill's audacity, courage, and imagination specially fitted him to be a War Minister.

"When, in the autumn of 1911, Mr. Winston Churchill became First Lord of the Admiralty, Lord Fisher had retired from the position of First Sea Lord which he had occupied from October 21st, 1904, to January 25th, 1910, amidst great turmoil all the time. During Lord Fisher's tenure of office as First Lord, vast Naval reforms were carried out, including the scrapping of some 160 ships of no fighting value, and great naval economies were effected, and all this time (except for one unhappy lapse when Mr. Churchill resisted the additional 'Dreadnought' building programme) Mr. Winston Churchill was in close association with these drastic reforms, and gave Lord

Fisher all his sympathy when hostile criticism was both malignant and perilous. For this reason, on Mr. Churchill's advent as First Lord of the Admiralty in the autumn of 1911, Lord Fisher most gladly complied with his request to return home from Italy to help him to proceed with that great task that had previously occupied Lord Fisher for six years as First Sea Lord, namely, the preparation for a German War which Lord Fisher had predicted in 1905 would certainly occur in August, 1914, in a written memorandum, and afterwards also personally to Sir M. Hankey, the Secretary of the Committee of Imperial Defence, necessitating that drastic revolution in all things Naval which brought 88 per cent. of the British Fleet into close proximity with Germany and *made its future battle ground in the North Sea its drill ground*, weeding out of the Navy inefficiency in ships, officers, and men, and obtaining absolute fighting sea supremacy by an unparalleled advance in types of fighting vessels.

"Mr. Churchill then at Lord Fisher's request did a fine thing in so disposing his patronage as First Lord as to develop Sir John Jellicoe into his Nelsonic position. So that when the day of war came Sir John Jellicoe became admiralissimo in spite of great professional opposition....

"This increased Lord Fisher's regard for Mr. Churchill, and on July 30th, 1914, at his request, Lord Fisher spent hours with him on that fifth day before war was declared and by his wish saw Mr. Balfour to explain to him the Naval situation. This is just mentioned to show the close official intimacy existing between Mr. Churchill and Lord Fisher, and when, on October 20th, 1914, Mr. Churchill asked Lord Fisher to become First Sea Lord he gladly assented to co-operating with him in using the great weapon Lord Fisher had helped to forge.

THE KINGFISHER.

"This bird has a somewhat long bill and is equipped with a brilliant blue back and tail; the latter not of sufficient length to be in the way. Its usual cry is much like the typical cry of the family, but besides this it gives a low, hoarse croak from time to time when seated in the shadows. Although exclusively a water bird, it is not unfrequently found at some distance from any water. It is very wary, keeping a good look-out, and defends its breeding place with great courage and daring."—*Zoological Studies.*

"Mr. Churchill and Lord Fisher worked in absolute accord until it came to the question of the Dardanelles, when Lord Fisher's instinct absolutely forbade him to give it any welcome. But finding himself the one solitary person dissenting from the project in the War Council, and knowing it to be of vital importance that he should personally see to the completion of the great shipbuilding programme of 612 vessels initiated on his recent advent to the Admiralty as First Sea Lord, also being confident that all these vessels could only be finished rapidly if he remained, Lord Fisher allowed himself to be persuaded by Lord Kitchener on January 28th, 1915, to continue as First Sea Lord. That point now remains to be related in somewhat greater detail.

"To begin with:—When exactly 10 years previously Lord Fisher became First Sea Lord, on October 20th, 1904, that very day occurred the Dogger Bank incident with Russia, and the Prime Minister made a speech at Southampton that seemed to make war with Russia a certainty; so Lord

Fisher, as First Sea Lord, immediately looked into the Forcing of the Dardanelles in the event of Russia's movements necessitating British action in the Dardanelles. He then satisfied himself that, even with military co-operation, it was mighty hazardous, and he so represented it at that time. The proceedings of the Committee of Imperial Defence, however, will furnish full details respecting the Dardanelles, especially Field-Marshal Lord Nicholson's remarks when Director of Military Operations, and also those of Sir N. Lyttelton when Chief of the General Staff.

"But Lord Fisher had had the great advantage of commanding a battleship under Admiral Sir Geoffrey Phipps Hornby when, during the Russo-Turkish War, that celebrated Flag Officer lay with the British Fleet near Constantinople, and Lord Fisher listened at the feet of that Naval Gamaliel when he supported Nelson's dictum that no sailor but a fool would ever attack a fort! Nevertheless, Nelson did attack Copenhagen—was really beaten, but he bluffed the Danish Crown Prince and came out ostensibly as victor. Nelson's Commander-in-Chief, Sir Hyde Parker, knew Nelson was beaten and signalled to him to retreat, but Nelson disobeyed orders as he did at St. Vincent and the Nile, and with equal judgment.

"We might have done the same bluff with the Turks, had promptitude and decision directed us, but procrastination, indecision, and vacillation dogged us instead. The 29th Division oscillated for weeks between France and Turkey. (*See* below my notes of the War Council Meetings of February 19th and 24th.)

"*Note.—See* Mr. Churchill's statement at the 19th Meeting of the War Council on May 14th, 1915, that had it been known three months previously that an English army of 100,000 men would have been available for the attack on the Dardanelles, *the naval attack would never have been undertaken.*

"The War Council met on May 14th, 1915, and certain steps proposed to be taken by Mr. Churchill immediately afterwards, decided Lord Fisher that he could no longer support the Dardanelles operations. He could not go further in this project with Mr. Churchill, and was himself convinced that we should seize that moment to give up the Dardanelles operations. So Lord Fisher went.

"Lord Fisher's parting with Mr. Churchill was pathetic, but it was the only way out. When the Prime Minister read to Lord Fisher Lord Kitchener's letter to the Prime Minister attacking Lord Fisher for withdrawing the 'Queen Elizabeth' from certain destruction at the Dardanelles, Lord Fisher then realised how splendid had been Mr. Churchill's support of him as to her withdrawal. A few days afterwards the German submarine that had been hovering round the British Fleet for a fortnight blew up the wooden image of the super-Dreadnought we had sent out there as a bait for the German submarines, showing how the Germans realised the 'Queen Elizabeth's' value in letting all the other older battleships alone for about a fortnight till they thought they really had the 'Queen Elizabeth' in this wooden prototype!

"It must be emphasised on Mr. Churchill's behalf that he had the whole Naval opinion at the Admiralty as well as the Naval opinion at the Dardanelles with him—Lord Fisher was the only dissentient.

"It must be again repeated that though Lord Fisher was so decidedly against the Dardanelles operations from the very first, yet he was very largely influenced to remain because he was convinced it was of vital importance to the nation to carry out the large building programme initiated by him, which was to enable the Navy to deal such a decisive blow in the decisive theatre (in Northern Waters) as would shorten the war—by the great projects alluded to by Mr. Churchill at the 9th meeting of the War Council on January 28th, 1915, when he described the Three Naval phases of the War, leading to our occupation of the Baltic as being the supreme end to be attained.

"Had Lord Fisher maintained his resignation on 28th January, 1915, the Dardanelles enterprise would certainly still have gone on, because it was considered a matter of vital political expediency (*see* Mr. Balfour's memorandum of 24th February, 1915), but those 612 new vessels would not have been built, or they would have been so delayed as to be useless. As it was, by Lord Fisher's leaving the Admiralty even so late as May 22nd, 1915, there was great delay in the completion of the five fast Battle Cruisers and in the laying down of further Destroyers and Submarines, and, in fact, four large Monitors (some of which had been advanced one thousand tons) that had been considerably advanced were stopped altogether for a time and the further building of fast Battle Cruisers was given up. Lord Fisher had prepared a design for a very fast Battle Cruiser carrying six 20-inch guns, and the model was completed. She was of exceptionally light draught of water and of exceptionally high speed. He had arranged for the manufacture of these 20-inch guns.

"It has also to be emphasised that that programme of new vessels owed its inception to a great plan, sketched out in secret memoranda, which it can be confidently asserted would have produced such great military results as would certainly have ended the war in 1915.

"These plans were in addition to that concurred in by Sir John French in his three visits to the War Council in November, 1914, for joint action of the British Army and the British Fleet on the Belgian Coast.

"*Note.*—*See* Note to 8th meeting of the War Council on January 13th, 1915, where Lord Fisher demurs to any Naval action without the co-operation of the British Army along the coast."

I quote here a report of the opinion of Mr. Andrew Fisher, the High Commissioner of Australia, and formerly Prime Minister of Australia; a member of the Dardanelles Commission, on the duty of departmental advisers:—

"I am of opinion it would seal the fate of responsible government if servants of the State were to share the responsibility of Ministers to Parliament and to the people on matters of public policy. The Minister has command of the opinions and views of all officers of the department he administers on matters of public policy. Good stewardship demands from Ministers of the Crown frank, fair, full statements of all opinions of trusted experienced officials to colleagues when they have direct reference to matters of high policy." *I give prominence to this because Ministers, and Ministers only, must be responsible to the democracy.*

If they find themselves in conflict with their expert advisers *they should sack the advisers or themselves resign.* An official, whether a Sea Lord or a junior clerk—having been asked a question by his immediate chief and given his answer and the chief acts contrary to advice—should not be subjected to reprimand for not stating to the board of directors that he disagrees with his chief or that he has given a reluctant consent. *If there is blame it rests with the Minister and not with his subordinates.*

"*I dissent in the strongest terms," says Mr. Fisher in his Minority Report, "from any suggestion that the Departmental Adviser of a Minister in his company at a Council meeting should express any views at all other than to the Minister and through him unless specifically invited to do so.*"

Sir Thomas Mackenzie expresses exactly the same view.

Mr. Asquith, in the House of Commons on November 2, 1915, said:—

"It is the duty of the Government—of any Government—to rely very largely upon the advice of its military and naval counsellors; but in the long run, a Government which is worthy of the name, which is adequate in the discharge of the trust which the nation reposes in it, must bring all these things into some kind of proportion one to the other, and sometimes it is not only expedient, but necessary, to run risks and to encounter dangers which pure naval or military policy would warn you against."

The Government and the War Council knew my opinion—as I told the Dardanelles Commission, it was known to all. It was known even to the charwomen at the Admiralty. It was my duty to acquiesce cheerfully and do my best, but when the moment came that there was jeopardy to the Nation I resigned.

Such is the stupidity of the General Public—and such was the stupidity of Lord Cromer—that it was not realized there would be an end of Parliamentary Government and of the People's will, therefore, being followed, if experts were able to override a Government Policy. Sea Lords are the servants of the Government. Having given their advice, then it's their duty to carry out the commands of the political party in power until the moment comes when they feel they can no longer support a policy which they are convinced is disastrous.

Here follows a summary for the Chairman of the Dardanelles Commission of my evidence (handed to Lord Cromer, but not circulated by him or printed in the Report of the Commission):—

"Mr. Churchill and I worked in absolute accord at the Admiralty until it came to the question of the Dardanelles.

"I was absolutely unable to give the Dardanelles proposal any welcome, for there was the Nelsonic dictum that 'any sailor who attacked a fort was a fool.'

"My direct personal knowledge of the Dardanelles problem dates back many years. I had had the great advantage of commanding a battleship under Admiral Sir Geoffrey Phipps Hornby when, during the Russo-Turkish War, that celebrated flag officer took the Fleet through the Dardanelles.

"I had again knowledge of the subject as Commander-in-Chief of the Mediterranean Fleet for three years during the Boer War, when for a long period the Fleet under my command lay at Lemnos off the mouth of the Dardanelles, thus affording me means of close study of the feasibility of forcing the Straits.

"When I became First Sea Lord on October 20th, 1904, there arrived that very day the news of the Dogger Bank incident with Russia.

"In my official capacity, in view of the possibility of a war with Russia, I immediately examined the question of the forcing of the Dardanelles, and I satisfied myself at that time that even with military co-operation the operation was mighty hazardous.

"Basing myself on the experience gained over so many years, when the project was mooted in the present War my opinion was that the attempt to force the Dardanelles would not succeed.

"I was the only member of the War Council who dissented from the project, but I did not carry my dissent to the point of resignation because I understood that there were overwhelming political reasons why the attempt at least should be made.

"Moreover, I felt it to be of vital importance that I should personally see to the completion of the great shipbuilding programme which was then under construction, which had been initiated by me on my advent to the Admiralty, and which included no less than 612 vessels.

"The change in my opinion as to the relative importance of the probable failure in the Dardanelles began when the ever-increasing drain upon the Fleet, as the result of the prosecution of the Dardanelles undertaking, reached a point at which in my opinion it destroyed the possibility of other naval operations which I had in view, and even approached to jeopardising our naval supremacy in the decisive theatre of the War.

"I may be pressed with the question why did I not carry my objections to the point of resignation when the decision was first reached to attack the Dardanelles with naval forces.

"In my judgment it is not the business of the chief technical advisers of the Government to resign because their advice is not accepted, unless they are of opinion that the operation proposed must lead to disastrous results.

"The attempt to force the Dardanelles, though a failure, would not have been disastrous so long as the ships employed could be withdrawn at any moment, and only such vessels were engaged, as in the beginning of the operations was in fact the case, as could be spared without detriment to the general service of the Fleet.

"I may next be asked whether I made any protest at the War Council when the First Lord proposed the Dardanelles enterprise, or at any later date.

"Mr. Churchill knew my opinion. I did not think it would tend towards good relations between the First Lord and myself nor to the smooth working of the Board of Admiralty to raise objections in the War Council's discussions. My opinion being known to Mr. Churchill in what I regarded as the proper constitutional way, I preferred thereafter to remain silent.

"When the operation was undertaken my duty from that time onwards was confined to seeing that the Government plan was carried out as successfully as possible with the available means.

"I did everything I could to secure its success, and I only resigned when the drain it was making on the resources of the Navy became so great as to jeopardise the major operations of the Fleet.

"On May 14th, 1915, the War Council made it clear to me that the great projects in Northern waters which I had in view in laying down the Armada of new vessels were at an end, and the further drain on our naval resources foreshadowed that evening convinced me that I could no longer countenance the Dardanelles operations, and the next day I resigned.

"It seemed to me that I was faced at last by a progressive frustration of my main scheme of naval strategy.

"Gradually the crowning work of war construction was being diverted and perverted from its original aim. The Monitors, for instance, planned for the banks and shallows of Northern waters, were sent off to the Mediterranean where they had never been meant to operate.

"I felt I was right in remaining in office until this situation, never contemplated at first by anyone, was accepted by the War Council. I felt right in resigning on this decision.

"My conduct and the interpretation of my responsibility I respectfully submit to the judgment of the Committee. Perhaps I may be allowed to say that as regards the opinion I held I was right.

FISHER,
October 7th, 1916."

This is a letter which I wrote to Colonel Sir Maurice Hankey, Secretary of the War Council:—

September 1st, 1916.

DEAR HANKEY,

In reply to your letter in which you propose to give only one extract concerning my hostility to the Dardanelles enterprise, do you not think that the following words in the official Print of Proceedings of War Council should be inserted in your report in justice to me?

"*19th Meeting of the War Council, May 14th, 1915.*—Lord Fisher reminded the War Council that he had been no party to the Dardanelles operations. When the matter was first under consideration he had stated his opinion to the Prime Minister at a private interview."

The reason I abstained from any further pronouncement was stated.

Yours, etc.,
(Signed) *Fisher.*

I note you will kindly testify to the accuracy of my statement that I left the Council table with the intention of resigning, but yielded to Kitchener's entreaty to return.

Have you the letter I wrote on January 28th, 1915, to Mr. Asquith, beginning:—

"I am giving this note to Colonel Hankey to hand to you ...," because in it occur these following words:—"At any moment the great crisis may occur in the North Sea, for the German High Sea Fleet may be driven to fight by the German Military Headquarters, as part of some great German military operation."

It looks as if Hindenburg might try such a coup now.

I heard from Jellicoe a few days since that the Zeppelins now made the German submarines very formidable, and by way of example he pointed out that the "Falmouth" was torpedoed even when at a speed of 25 knots and zigzagging every five minutes.

        *   *   *   *   *

In some notes compiled on this matter I find it recorded that I was present at the meeting on the 13th January, when the plan was first proposed and approved in principle, and was also present at the meeting on the evening of the 28th January, when Mr. Churchill announced that the Admiralty had decided to push on with the project. On the morning of the 28th January I said that I had understood that this question would not be raised to-day, and that the Prime Minister was well aware of my own views in regard to it.

After the failure of the naval attack on the Narrows on the 18th March, I remarked at the meeting on the 19th March that I had always said that a loss of 12 battleships must be expected before the Dardanelles could be forced by the Navy alone, and that I still adhered to this view.

Also, at the meeting held on the 14th May, I reminded the War Council that I had been no party to the Dardanelles operations. When the matter was under consideration I had stated my opinion to the Prime Minister at a private interview.

Some light is perhaps thrown on my general attitude towards naval attacks by the following remark, made at the meeting held on the 13th January, which related, not to the Dardanelles project, but to a proposed naval attack on Zeebrugge:—

I said that the Navy had only a limited number of battleships to lose, and would probably sustain losses in an attack on Zeebrugge. I demurred to any attempt to attack Zeebrugge *without the co-operation of the Army along the coast.*

This note is here inserted because the Dardanelles operation interfered with the project of certain action in the Decisive Theatre of the War explained in a Memorandum given to the Prime Minister on January 25th, 1915, but it has been decided to be too secret for publication even now, so it is not included in these papers.

A Memorandum was also submitted by me on General Naval Policy, deprecating the use of Naval Force in Coast Operations unsupported by Military Force and emphasising the supreme importance of maintaining the unchallengeable strength of the Grand Fleet in the Decisive Theatre.

LORD FISHER TO COLONEL SIR MAURICE HANKEY

September 6th, 1916.

DEAR HANKEY,

I have only just this very moment received your letter, dated September 4th, and its enclosure, for I had suddenly to leave the address you wrote to on important official business....

The Prime Minister and Kitchener knew from me on January 7th or January 8th that I objected to the Dardanelles enterprise, but I admit this does not come under your official cognisance as Secretary of the War Council, consequently I cannot press you in the matter.

If I ever am allowed hereafter to see what you have prepared for Lord Cromer's Committee of Inquiry I shall be better able to judge of its personal application to myself.

I was told yesterday by an influential Parliamentary friend that the likelihood was that *all* would emerge from the Dardanelles Inquiry as free from blame, except one person only—Lord Fisher! That really would be comic! considering that I was the only sufferer by it, by loss of office and of an immense certainty in my mind of Big Things in the North Sea and Baltic by the unparalleled Armada we were building so marvellously quickly, *e.g.*, submarines in five months instead of 14, and destroyers in nine months instead of 18! and immense fast Battle Cruisers with 18-inch and 15-inch guns in 11 months instead of two years! *Why, it was the desolation of my life to leave the Admiralty at that moment!* Knowing that once out I should never get back! The "wherefore" you know!

Yours, etc.,
(Signed) FISHER,
6th September, 1916.

LORD FISHER TO THE RIGHT HON. WINSTON CHURCHILL.

"The Baltic a German Lake."

MY DEAR WINSTON,

I am here for a few days longer before rejoining my "Wise men" at Victory House—

"The   World   forgetting,
By the World forgot!"

but some Headlines in the newspapers have utterly upset me! Terrible!!

"The German Fleet to assist the Land operations in the Baltic."

"Landing the German Army South of Reval."

We are five times stronger at Sea than our enemies and here is a small Fleet that we could gobble up in a few minutes playing the great vital Sea part of landing an Army in the enemies' rear and probably capturing the Russian Capital by Sea!

This is "Holding the ring" with a vengeance!

Are we really incapable of a big Enterprise?

I hear that a new order of Knighthood is on the tapis—O.M.G. (Oh! My God!)—Shower it on the Admiralty!!

Yours,
FISHER.
9/9/17.

P.S.—In War, you want—"SURPRISE."

To beget "SURPRISE" you want "IMAGINATION" to go to bed with "AUDACITY."

Admiral von Spee's first words at the Falkland Islands when he saw the British Battle Cruisers were

"Oh, what a surprise"!

And he went to the bottom with 3,000 men and 11 ships, and not one man killed or wounded on board the "Invincible."

LORD FISHER'S NOTES OF HIS OWN SPECIAL INTERVENTIONS AT WAR COUNCIL MEETINGS

Notes.—The first two meetings of the War Committee took place on August 5th and August 6th, 1914.

Lord Fisher was appointed First Sea Lord on October 30th, 1914.

The third meeting of the War Council (being the first after Lord Fisher's appointment) took place on November 25th, 1914.

3rd Meeting of the War Council, November 25th, 1914.

Lord Fisher asked whether Greece might not attack Gallipoli in conjunction with Bulgaria.

It was pointed out Bulgaria blocked the way.

(*Note.*—From his experience of three years as Commander-in-Chief of the Mediterranean Fleet, Lord Fisher had formed the conviction that Bulgaria was the key of the situation, and this he had pointed out to Lord Kitchener personally at the War Office.)

4th Meeting of War Council, December 1st, 1914.

Lord Fisher pressed for the adoption of the Offensive.

The Defensive attitude of the Fleet was bad for its morale, and was no real protection from enemy submarines.

The suggestion of seizing an island off the German coast was adjourned.

7th Meeting of War Council, January 8th, 1915.

ZEEBRUGGE.

Asked whether the bombardment of Zeebrugge would materially lessen the risks to transports and other ships in the English Channel, Lord Fisher replied that he thought not. In his opinion the danger involved in the operation (in loss of ships) would outweigh the results.

8th Meeting of War Council, January 13th, 1915.

ZEEBRUGGE.

Lord Fisher said that the Navy had not unlimited battleships to lose, and there would probably be losses in any attack on Zeebrugge. He objected to any attack on Zeebrugge *without the co-operation of the Army along the coast.*

The Dardanelles was mentioned, Mr. Churchill stating that he had exchanged telegrams with Admiral Carden as to the possibilities of a naval attack on the Dardanelles. He had taken this step because Lord Kitchener, in a letter to him, dated January 3rd, had urged instant naval action at the Dardanelles to relieve the pressure on the Grand Duke Nicholas in the Caucasus.

9th Meeting of War Council, January 28th, 1915, 11.30 a.m.

(*Note.*—Before this meeting the Prime Minister discussed with Mr. Churchill and Lord Fisher the proposed Dardanelles operations and decided in favour of considering the project in opposition to Lord Fisher's opinion.)

THE DARDANELLES.

Mr. Churchill asked if the War Council attached importance to the proposed Dardanelles operations, which undoubtedly involved risks.

Lord Fisher said that he had understood that this question was not to be raised at this meeting. The Prime Minister knew his (Lord Fisher's) views on the subject.

The Prime Minister said that, in view of what had already been done, the question could not be left in abeyance.

(*Note.*—Thereupon Lord Fisher left the Council table. He was followed by Lord Kitchener, who asked him what he intended to do. Lord Fisher replied to Lord Kitchener that he would not return to the Council table, and would resign his office as First Sea Lord. Lord Kitchener then pointed out to Lord Fisher that he (Lord Fisher) was the only dissentient, and that the Dardanelles operations had been decided upon by the Prime Minister; and he urged on Lord Fisher that his duty to his country was to go on carrying out the duties of First Sea Lord. After further talk Lord Fisher reluctantly gave in to Lord Kitchener and went back to the Council table.9)

THE FIRST SEA LORD. By William Nicholson.

Mr. Churchill stated *that the ultimate object of the Navy was to obtain access to the Baltic.* There were, he said, three Naval phases:—

1st phase.—The clearing of the outer seas (this had been accomplished).

2nd phase.—The clearing of the North Sea.

3rd phase.—The clearing of the Baltic.

Mr. Churchill laid stress on the importance of the third phase and said this latter operation was of great importance, as Germany always had been, and still was, very nervous of an attack from the Baltic. For this purpose special vessels were required, and the First Sea Lord (Lord Fisher) had designed cruisers, &c., &c.10 The meeting was adjourned to 6.30 the same evening.

10th Meeting of War Council (same day), January 28th, 1915, at 6.30 p.m.

The plan of a naval attack on Zeebrugge was abandoned and the Dardanelles operations were decided upon.

11th Meeting of War Council, February 9th, 1915.

Mr. Churchill reported that the Naval attack on the Dardanelles would take place on February 15th. (This was afterwards postponed until February 19th.)

12th Meeting of War Council, February 16th, 1915.

Agreed that the 29th Division should be sent to the Dardanelles and other arrangements made to support the Naval attack on the Dardanelles.

The Admiralty were authorised and pressed to build or obtain special craft for landing 50,000 men wherever a landing might be required.

13th Meeting of War Council, February 19th, 1915.

Transports ordered to be got ready:—

1. To convey troops from Egypt to the Dardanelles;

2. To convey the 29th Division from England to the Dardanelles,

but no final decision to be taken as to 29th Division.

14th Meeting of War Council, February 24th, 1915.

General Birdwood selected to join Admiral Carden before the Dardanelles.

The decision as to sending 29th Division postponed.

15th Meeting of War Council, February 26th, 1915.

Mr. Churchill said he could not offer any assurance of success in the Dardanelles attack.

16th Meeting of War Council, March 3rd, 1915.

The future of Constantinople was discussed, and what should be the next step after the Dardanelles. Lord Lansdowne and Mr. Bonar Law, besides Mr. Balfour, were present.

17th Meeting of War Council, March 10th, 1915.

The War Office was directed to prepare a memorandum on the strategical advantages of Alexandretta.

18th Meeting of War Council, March 19th, 1915.

The sinking of the battleships "Irresistible," "Ocean," and "Bouvet," the running ashore of "Gaulois" and the disablement of "Inflexible," were discussed.

The continuance of naval operations against Dardanelles was authorised if the Admiral at the Dardanelles agreed.

Lord Fisher said that it was impossible to explain away the sinking of four battleships. *He had always said that a loss of 12 battleships must be expected before the Dardanelles could be forced by the Navy alone.* He still adhered to this view.

Note.—There was no meeting of the War Council from March 19th to May 14th.

19th Meeting of War Council, May 14th, 1915.

Mr. Churchill reported that one, or perhaps two, German submarines had arrived in the Eastern Mediterranean, *and that the attack on the Dardanelles had now become primarily a military rather than a naval operation.* It had been decided to recall the "Queen Elizabeth." Mr. Churchill stated that if it had been known three months ago that an army of from 80,000 to 100,000 men would now be available for the attack on the Dardanelles the naval attack would never have been undertaken.

Lord Fisher reminded the War Council that he had been no party to the Dardanelles operations. When the matter was first under consideration he had stated his opinion to the Prime Minister at a private interview.

Conclusion.—Lord Kitchener to send a telegram to Sir Ian Hamilton asking what military force he would require in order to ensure success at the Dardanelles.

Note.—On the evening of this day Mr. Churchill drafted orders for further naval reinforcements for the Dardanelles, a course to which Lord Fisher could not assent.

(This led to Lord Fisher leaving the Admiralty.)

A Note on the Dardanelles Operations.

Major-General Sir Chas. Caldwell, K.C.B., was Director of Military Operations at the War Office during the whole period of the inception, incubation and execution of the Dardanelles adventure, and in an article in the "Nineteenth Century" for March, 1919, he completely disposes of the criticisms of Mr. G. A. Schreiner in his book "From Berlin to Bagdad," and of those of Mr. H. Morgenthau, the late United States Ambassador at Constantinople, in his recent book, "The Secrets of the Bosphorus." Both these works convey the impression that the general attack by the Fleet upon the Defences of the Narrows on March 18th, 1915, very nearly succeeded. This verdict is not justified by the facts as certified by Sir C. Caldwell. He proves incontestably that, even in the very unlikely case of indirect bombardment really effecting its object in putting the batteries out of action, there would still be the movable armament of the Turks left to worry and defeat the mine-sweepers, and there would still be the drifting mines and possibly the torpedoes fired from the shore to imperil the battleships. When peace did come it occupied the British Admiral a very long time to sweep up the mines. The damaging effect of Naval Bombardment was over-estimated—the extent to which the enemy's movable armament would interfere with mine-sweeping was not realised, and the extent and efficiency of the minefields were unknown and unheeded. Sir Charles Caldwell says:

"The whole thing was a mistake, quite apart from the disastrous influence which the premature and unsuccessful operation exerted over the subsequent land campaign."

It is also most true what Sir C. Caldwell says that "the idea at the back of the sailors' minds (who so reluctantly assented to the *political* desire of getting possession of the Straits) was that it was an experiment which could always be instantly stopped if the undertaking were to be found too difficult." But alas! *"the view of the War Council came to be that they could not now abandon the adventure."*

*　　　*　　　*　　　*　　　*

Marshal Liman von Sanders, who had charge of the defence of the Dardanelles, said:

"The attack on the Straits by the Navy alone I don't think could ever have succeeded. I proposed to flood the Straits broadcast with mines, and it was my view that these were the main defences of the Dardanelles, and that the function of the guns of the forts was simply to protect the minefields from interference."

The evidence given by Captain (now Rear-Admiral Sir) William Reginald Hall, R.N., Director of Naval Intelligence, at the Dardanelles Inquiry, conflicts with the facts as afterwards made known to us; and no doubt this led to such official speeches as were made of our being so near victory at the Dardanelles—speeches which caused the further great sacrifice of life which took place after General Sir Charles Munro, the present Commander-in-Chief in India, had definitely and without any equivocation officially reported that the Evacuation of the Gallipoli Peninsula should immediately take place.

Field Marshal Lord Nicholson asked Captain Hall, R.N., how far the Gallipoli Peninsula was under German control; and his answer was that it was known that the defences had been inspected by a German and that many Germans were arriving there, whereas it is a matter of fact stated by General Liman von Sanders and confirmed from other sources that the Germans were in complete control; and it took the British Admiral many weeks after the Armistice, helped by the Turks, to clear a way through the mines for his Flagship to take him to Constantinople. At question 4930 Captain Hall stated his spies made him convinced that he could have pushed through with only the loss of one or more ships and got to Constantinople on March 18th.

AN EPISODE OF THE WAR.

A friend asking me yesterday (this was written in 1917) about the replacement of Tonnage destroyed by the German Submarines, and telling me how quite ineffectual had been the course pursued up to the present when really we are in measurable distance of starvation or else an ignoble peace, I ventured to send him the enclosed account (*written at the time*) of how 612 Vessels were hustled! As in all other War matters, it is Personality that is required, even more than Brains!

STATEMENT OF NEW SHIPBUILDING INAUGURATED BY LORD FISHER.

Note.—The following Memoranda are inserted as vital to the explanation of Lord Fisher's reluctance to resign on the Dardanelles question. It will be seen that Mr. Churchill had given him sole charge of the creation of this armada of new ships, *intended for great projects in the Baltic and North Sea.*

Tuesday, November 3rd, 1914.

(*Note.*—Lord Fisher had joined the Admiralty as First Sea Lord four days before this meeting.)

The First Sea Lord (Lord Fisher) presided at a Conference this day at the Admiralty.

Present:

- Second Sea Lord.

- Third Sea Lord.

- Additional Civil Lord.

- Parliamentary and Financial Secretary.

- Secretary.

- Naval Secretary to First Lord.

- Engineer-in-Chief.

- Assistant Director of Torpedoes and another representative of the Director of Naval Ordnance.

- Commodore (S) and Assistant.

- Naval Assistant to First Sea Lord.

- Director of Naval Construction and an Assistant.

- Superintendent of Contract Work.

- Superintending Electrical Engineer.

- Director of Dockyard Work.

- Director of Naval Contracts and an Assistant.

Lord Fisher explained to those present that this Conference had been summoned with the approval of Mr. Churchill, primarily with the object of expediting the delivery of 20 submarines which were to be at once commenced,

but in the second place a big further building programme for a special purpose had been decided on.

The question of placing orders for submarines had been under consideration for some time past. The First Lord, however, had assented to the cancellation of all existing papers on this subject, *and a fresh start was to be made immediately on the lines of a special war routine.* All red-tape methods—very proper in time of peace—were now to be abandoned, and *everything must be entirely subordinated to rapidity of construction.* It was desired to impress upon all present the necessity of avoiding "paper" work, and of proceeding in the manner indicated in the secret memorandum which would be circulated next day in regard to the matter. Arrangements would be made in due course to obtain additional vessels of other types in a similar manner.

Note.—After this, a meeting of all the shipbuilding firms of the United Kingdom took place at the Admiralty under the presidency of Lord Fisher, and the programme mentioned above in italics was parcelled out there and then.

BUILDING PROGRAMME.

Meeting on November 3rd, 1914, four days after Lord Fisher became First Sea Lord.

- 5 Battle Cruisers of 33 knots speed of light draught.

- 2 Light Cruisers.

- 5 Flotilla Leaders.

- 56 Destroyers.

- 64 Submarines.

- 37 Monitors.

- 24 River Light Gunboats.

- 19 Whaling Steamers.

- 24 Submarine Destroyers.

- 50 Seagoing Patrol Boats.

- 200 Motor Barges, oil engines.

- 90 Smaller Barges.

- 36 Sloops.

- 612 Total.

MEMORANDUM BY LORD FISHER, DATED NOVEMBER 3RD, 1914, ON LAYING DOWN FURTHER NUMBERS OF SUBMARINES.

There is no doubt that at this moment the supply of additional submarine boats in the shortest time possible is a matter of urgent national importance. They will not be obtained unless the whole engineering and shipbuilding resources of the country are enlisted in the effort, and the whole of the peace paraphernalia of red-tape routine and consequent delay are brushed on one side. I have carefully studied the submarine question during my retirement and have had many opportunities of keeping in touch with the present position and future possibilities, and am convinced that 20 submarines can be commenced at once, and that the first batch of these should be delivered in nine months, and the remainder at short intervals, completing the lot in 11 or 12 months.

NOTE.—*A dozen more were actually delivered in five months, and made the voyage alone from America to the Dardanelles.*

To do this, however, cheapness must be entirely subordinated to rapidity of construction, and the technical departments must have a free hand to take whatever steps are necessary to secure this end without any paper work whatever. Apparently this matter has been under consideration at the Admiralty already for a considerable time, but

nothing has yet been ordered,

and the First Lord has concurred that a fresh start be made independently of former papers,

and the matter placed under my sole supervision, without any other officers or departments intervening between me and the professional officers.

I will give instructions as to the work, and direct that

if any difficulties are met with, they be brought to me instantly to be overcome.

The professional officers' reports as to acceptances of tenders or allocation of work must be immediately carried out by the branches.

Only in this way can we get the boats we require. To ensure the completion of the 20 boats, steps to be immediately taken to order the parts for the engines for 25 boats. We know from experience that it is in the machinery parts that defects and failures occur in manufacture of castings, forgings, etc., causing great delay. The parts for the extra five sets of engines will be available for these replacements, and eventually the five extra sets can be fitted in five further hulls. I propose to review the progress being made once a fortnight in the hope that it may be feasible to order still further submarines beyond these 20 now to be commenced at once.

The training of sufficient officers and men for manning these extra boats must obviously be proceeded with forthwith, and those responsible must see to it that the officers and crews are ready.

FISHER.

November 3rd, 1914.

NOTE by Lord Fisher.—I gave personal orders on this day to the Director of Mobilization to enter officers, men, and boys to the utmost limit regardless of present or supposed prospective wants, so when he left the Admiralty last week to be Captain of the *Renown* he wrote me we wanted for nothing in the way of personnel!

FISHER.

August 15th, 1916.

CHAPTER VI
ABDUL HAMID AND THE POPE

Be to my virtues very kind,

Be to my faults a little blind.

TWO great Personalities came across my path when I commanded the Mediterranean Fleet for three years—the Sultan Abdul Hamid and Pope Leo XIII. They each greatly admired the astuteness of the other. Wily as Abdul was, the Pope was the subtler of the two. I did not have the interviews with the Pope which I might have had. There was no real occasion for it, as was the case with Abdul Hamid; and also, though by the accident of birth I was of the Church of England (nearly everybody's religion is the accident of his birth), yet by taste and conviction I was a Covenanter, and therefore dead against the Pope. I would have loved to participate in the fight against Claverhouse at the battle of Drumclog.

I happen to be looking at the battlefield of Drumclog now, and I hope to be buried in Drumclog Church—that is, if I die here; or in the nearest Church to my death bed. I am particular to say this, as it avoids so much trouble; and I don't have any more feeling for a cast-off body than for a cast-off suit of clothes. The body, after he's left it at death, is not the man himself, any more than his cast-off clothes. The only thing I ask for is a white marble tablet made by Mr. Bridgman of Lichfield (if he's still alive), with the inscription on it to be found in Croxall Church as written of herself by my sainted Godmother, of whom Byron wrote so beautifully: "She walks in beauty like the night." She deserved his poem.

That was a big digression; but being dictated, as it is, this is a conversation book and not a classic. Classics are dry. Conversation, taking no account of grammar or sequence, is more interesting. However, that's a matter of opinion. To talk is easy, but to write is terrific. Even Job thought so, that patient man.

To resume Abdul Hamid and the Pope.

Neither rats nor Jews can exist at Malta. The Maltese are too much for either. A Maltese can't get a living in the Levant. The Levantine is too much for the Maltese. No Levantine has ever been seen in Armenia. His late Majesty, Abdul Hamid, was an Armenian. He massacred more Armenians than had ever been massacred before. I've no doubt that can be explained. It is supposed that the Armenian coachman of the previous Sultan was his father. He certainly was not a bit like his presumed father, the Sultan. When I dined several times with the Sultan, his father's picture hung behind him and he used to ask people if they traced the likeness—there wasn't even a resemblance.

The Sultan paid me a very special honour in sending his most distinguished Admiral with his Staff down to the British Fleet lying at Lemnos, to escort me up to Constantinople. This Admiral was known to me; and it afforded me an opportunity, in the passage up the Dardanelles, of making a thorough inspection of the Forts and all the particulars connected with the defence of the Dardanelles. Nothing was kept back from me; and incidentally it was through this inspection I became on such terms with the Pashas that a most amicable arrangement was reached between us as to our ever having to work in common. A very striking incident occurred illustrating Kiamil Pasha's remark to me of how every Turk in the Turkish Empire trusted the English when they trusted no one else. Kiamil's argument was that such trust was only natural after the Crimean War, and after the war with Russia—when Russia was at the gates of Constantinople, and the British Fleet, coming up under Admiral Hornby in a blinding snowstorm, encountering great risks and not knowing but what the Forts, bribed by Russia, might open fire— that British Fleet, by its opportune arrival, hardly a minute too soon, effectually banged, barred and bolted the gates of Constantinople against the Russians and produced peace. And Kiamil's emphasis was that, notwithstanding all these wonderful things that England had done for Turkey, England never asked for the very smallest favour or concession in return, whereas other nations were all of them notoriously always grabbing; and I told Kiamil Pasha that I felt very proud indeed, as a British Admiral, that England had this noble character and deserved it. The incident I referred to was this: Upon an observation being made to the Turkish Commander-in-Chief in the Dardanelles as to whether some written document wouldn't be satisfactory to him, he replied he wanted no such document—if a British Midshipman brought him a message, the word of a British Midshipman was enough for him.

The views I formed at that period of the impregnability of the Dardanelles stood me in good stead when the Dogger Bank incident became known on Trafalgar Day, 1904—the very day I assumed the position of First Sea Lord of the Admiralty. We were within an ace of war with Russia; the Prime Minister's speech at Southampton, if consulted, will show that to be the case; and I then drew up a secret memorandum with respect to the Dardanelles, which I alluded to at the War Council when the attack on the Dardanelles was being discussed, also in my official memorandum to Lord Cromer, the Chairman of the Dardanelles Commission, and in my evidence before the Commission.

Personally I had a great regard for Abdul Hamid. Our Ambassadors had not. One who knew of these matters considered Abdul Hamid the greatest diplomat in Europe. I have mentioned elsewhere how greatly he resented Lord Salisbury throwing over the traditional English Alliance with Turkey and Lord Salisbury saying in a memorable speech that in making that alliance in past years we had backed the wrong horse. For were not (was Abdul Hamid's argument) England and Turkey the two greatest Mahomedan nations on Earth—England being somewhat the greater? Kiamil—the Grand Old Man of Turkey—told me the same. He had been many times Grand Vizier, and I went especially with the Mediterranean Fleet to Smyrna to do him honour. He was the Vali there. His nickname in Turkey was "The Englishman"; he was so devoted to us. He lamented to me that England had had only one diplomatist of ability at Constantinople since the days of Sir Stratford Canning, whom he knew. His exception was a Sir William White, who had been a Consul somewhere in the Balkan States. No other English Ambassador had ever been able to cope with the Germans. I remonstrated with Kiamil by saying that Ambassadors now were only telegraph instruments—they only conveyed messages, and quite probably from some quite young man at the Foreign Office who had charge of that Department. I venture to remark here in passing what I have very frequently urged to those in authority—that the United States system is infinitely better than ours. Their diplomatic representatives are all fresh from home, with each change of President; ours live all their lives abroad and practically cease to be Englishmen, and very often, like Solomon, marry foreign wives. Another thing I've urged on Authority is that some Great Personage should annually make a tour of inspection of all the Diplomatic and Consular Agents (exactly as the big Banks have a travelling Inspector), who would ask how much he had increased the trade of the great British Commonwealth of Nations; and if it weren't more than five per cent. would give him the sack. This Great Travelling Personage must be a man independent in means and station of any Government connexion and undertake the duty as Sir Edward (now Lord) Grey goes to Washington. The German Ambassador at Constantinople used to go round selling beetroot sugar by the pound! The English Ambassador said to me at a Garden Party he gave by those lovely sweet waters of the Bosphorus: "You see that fellow there with a white hat on? He's the President of the British Chamber of Commerce; he's an awful nuisance. He's always bothering me about some peddling commercial business!"

Abdul Hamid was exceeding kind to me and invited me to Constantinople, and he descanted (the Boer War then being on) what a risk there was of a big coalition against England. Curiously enough, his colleague the Pope had the same feeling. It is very deplorable, not only in the late War but also in the Boer War especially, how utterly our spies and our Intelligence Departments failed us. I was so impressed with what the Sultan told me that I set to work on my own account; and through the patriotism of several magnificent

Englishmen who occupied high commercial positions on the shores of the Mediterranean, I got a central forwarding station for information fixed up privately in Switzerland; and it so happened, through a most Providential state of circumstances, that I was thus able to obtain all the cypher messages passing from the various Foreign Embassies, Consulates and Legations through a certain central focus, and I also obtained a key to their respective cyphers. The Chief man who did it for me was not in Government employ; and I'm glad to think that he is now in a great position—though not rewarded as he should have been. No one is. But as to any information from an official source reaching me, who was so vastly interested in the matter, in the event of war where the Fleet should strike first—all our Diplomats and Consuls and Intelligence Departments might have been dead and buried. And how striking the case in the late War—the Prime Minister not knowing at the Guildhall Banquet on November 9th, 1918, that the most humiliating armistice ever known would be accepted by the Germans within thirty-six hours, and one of our principal Cabinet Ministers saying the Sunday before that the Allies were at their last gasp. And read now Ludendorff, Tirpitz, Falkenhayn, Liman von Sanders, and others—they knew exactly what the Allies' condition was and what their own was. And if the Dardanelles evidence is ever published, it will be found absolutely ludicrous how the official spokesmen gravely give evidence that the Turks had come to their last round of ammunition and that the roofs of the houses in Constantinople were crowded with people looking for the advent of the approaching British Fleet. Why! it took our Admiral, on the conclusion of the Armistice, with the help of the Turks and all his own Fleet, several weeks to clear a passage through the mines, on which Marshal Liman von Sanders so accurately based his reliance against any likelihood of the Dardanelles being forced.

ADMIRAL OF THE FLEET LORD FISHER, G.C.B., O.M., ETC., 1917.

CHAPTER VII
A JEU D'ESPRIT BOWS AND ARROWS—SNAILS AND TORTOISES—FACILE DUPES AND SERVILE COPYISTS

"Not the wise find salvation."—*St. Paul.*

ONE of the charms of the Christian religion is that the Foolish confound the Wise. The Atheists are all brainy men. Myself, I hate a brainy man. All the brainy men said it was impossible to have aeroplanes. No brainy man ever sees that speed is armour. Directly the brainy men got a chance they clapped masses of armour on the "Hush-Hush" ships. They couldn't understand speed being armour, and said to themselves: "Didn't she draw so little water she could stand having weight put on her? Shove on armour!" and so bang went the speed, and the "Hush-Hush" ships, whose fabulous beauty was their forty shore-going miles an hour, were slowed down by these brainy men. Don't jockeys have to carry weights? Isn't it called handicapping? Isn't it the object to beat the favourite—the real winner? There really is comfort in the 27th verse of the 1st chapter of I Corinthians, where the Foolish are wiser than the Wise.

What!—A battle cruiser called the "Furious" going 40 shore-going miles an hour with 18-inch guns reaching 26 miles! "Take the damn guns out and make it into an aeroplane ship!" (And I'm not sure they could ever get the aeroplanes to land on her, owing to the heat of the funnels causing what they call "Air pockets" above the stern of the ship.)

Yes! and we still have ancient Admirals who believe in bows and arrows. There's a good deal to be said for bows and arrows. Our ancestors insisted on all churchyards being planted with yew trees to make bows. There you are! It's a home product! Not like those damn fools who get their oil from abroad! And I have now the Memorandum with me delivered to me when I was Controller of the Navy by a member of the Board of Admiralty desiring to build 16 sailing ships! Again, didn't the Board of Admiralty issue a solemn Board Minute that wood floated and iron sank? So what a damnable thing to build iron ships! Wasn't there another solemn Board Minute that steam was damnable and fatal to the supremacy of the British Navy? Haven't we had Admirals writing very brainy articles in magazines to prove that there was nothing like a tortoise? You could stand on the tortoise's back; you weren't rushed by the tortoise, whereas these "Hush-Hush" ships, they were flimsy, and speed was worshipped as a god. One mighty man of valour (only "he was a leper" as regards sea fighting) told me at his luncheon table that when one of these "Hush-Hush" ships encountered at her full strength of nearly a hundred thousand horse power a gale of wind in a mountainous sea she was actually strained! It's all really too lovely; but of course the humour of it can't be properly appreciated by the ordinary shore-going person. Yes, the brainy men, as I said before, crabbed the "Hush-Hush" ships; they couldn't understand that speed was armour when associated with big guns because the speed enabled you to put your ship at such a distance that she couldn't be hit by the enemy, so it was the equivalent of impenetrable armour although you had none of it, and you hit the enemy every round for the simple reason that your guns reached him when his could not reach you. Q.E.D. as Euclid says. What these splendid armour bearers say is "Give me a strong ship which no silly ass of a Captain can hurt." Of course this implies that if it's Buggins's turn to be Captain of a ship he gets it; it's his turn, even if he is a silly ass. The phase of mind they have is this: "None of your highly strung racehorses for me, give me a good old cart-horse!" So we build huge costly warships which will last a hundred years, but become obsolete in five.

It all really is very funny—if it wasn't disastrous and ruinous! And they are such a motley crew, these discontented ones who come together in John Bright's cave of Adullam; and the Poor Dear Public read an interview in a newspaper with some Commander Knowall; and then a magazine article by Admiral Retrograde; and some old "cup of tea" writes to *The Times* (wonderful paper *The Times*—"Equal Opportunity for All") and there you are! Lord Fisher is a damned fool; and if he isn't a damned fool he's a maniac. Oh! very well then, if he isn't a maniac, then he's a traitor. Wasn't Sir Julian Corbett very seriously asked if he (Sir John Fisher) hadn't sold his country to Germany? Sir Julian thought the report was exaggerated, and that satisfied the Searcher after Truth. But I ask my listeners, however should we get on without these people? How dull life would be without their dialectical subtleties and "reasoned statements" (I think they call them) and "considered judgments"!

My splendid dear old friend, who could hardly write his name, the Chief Engineer of the first ironclad, the "Warrior," told me, when I was Gunnery Lieutenant of her in 1861, that he had arranged for his monument at death being of "malleable" iron. No cast iron for him, he said! It played you such pranks. So it is with these carbonised cranks who wield the pen, actuated by the wrong kind of grey matter of their brain, and, their tongues acidulated with lies, sway listening Senates and control our wars. It requires a Mr. Disraeli to deal with these victims of their own verbosity, who are the facile dupes of their vacuous imaginations and the servile copyists of the Billingsgatean line of argument!

CHAPTER VIII
NAVAL WAR STAFF AND ADMIRALTY CLERKS

"A wise old owl lived in an oak;

The more he heard, the less he spoke;

The less he spoke, the more he heard;

Why can't we be like that wise old bird?"

LORD HALDANE with his "art of clear thinking" elaborated the Imperial War Staff to its present magnificent dimensions. If any man wants a thing advertised, let him take it over there to the Secret Department. Only Sir Arthur Wilson and myself, when I was First Sea Lord of the Admiralty, knew the Naval plan of war. He was the man, so head-and-shoulders above all his fellows, who in his time was our undoubted, indeed our incomparable, Sea Leader. No one touched him; and I am not sure that even now, though getting on for Dandolo's age, he would not still achieve old Dandolo's great deeds. What splendid lines they are from Byron:

"Oh for one hour of blind old Dandolo,

Th' Octogenarian Chief, Byzantium's Conquering Foe!"

I loved Sir Arthur Wilson's reported reply to the maniacs who think the Navy is the same as the Army. If it is not true it is *ben trovato*. He said the Naval War Staff at the Admiralty consisted of himself—assisted by every soul inside the Admiralty, and he added, "including the charwomen"—they emptied the waste-paper baskets full of the plans of the amateur strategists— Cabinet and otherwise.

No such rubbish has ever been talked as about the Navy War Staff and also, in connexion therewith, the Admiralty clerks who are supposed to have wrecked its first inception in the period long ago when my great friend the late Admiral W. H. Hall was introduced into the Admiralty to form a Department of Naval Intelligence. I give my experience. I have been fifteen or more years in the Admiralty—Director of Ordnance and Torpedoes, Controller of the Navy, Second Sea Lord and First Sea Lord. Inside the Admiralty, for conducting administrative work, the Civil Service clerk is incomparably superior to the Naval Officer. The Naval Officer makes a very bad clerk. He hasn't been brought up to it. He can't write a letter, and, as you can see from my dictation, he is both verbose and diffuse. The Clerk is terse and incisive.

I'll go to instances. My Secretary, W. F. Nicholson, C.B., was really just as capable of being First Sea Lord as I was, when associated with my Naval Assistant. I often used to say that the First Sea Lord was in commission, and that I was the facile dupe of these two; and I was blessed with a succession of Naval Assistants who knew so exactly their limitations as regards Admiralty work as allowed the Admiralty machine to be, as was officially stated, the best, most efficient, and most effective of all the Government Departments of the State. I have a note of this, made by the highest authority in the Civil Service. I would like here to name my Naval Assistants, because they were out and away without precedent the most able men in the Navy: Admirals Sir Reginald Bacon, Sir Charles Madden, Sir Henry Oliver, Sir Horace Hood, Sir Charles de Bartolomé, Captain Richmond and Captain Crease—I'll back that set of names against the world.

I was the originator of the Naval War College at Portsmouth—that's quite a different thing from an Imperial General Staff at the War Office. The vulgar error of Lord Haldane and others, who are always talking about "Clear thinking" and such-like twaddle, is that they do not realise that the Army is so absolutely different from the Navy. Every condition in them both is different. The Navy is always at war, because it is always fighting winds and waves and fog. The Navy is ready for an absolute instant blow; it has nothing to do with strategic railways, lines of communication, or bridging rivers, or crossing mountains, or the time of the year, when the Balkans may be snowed under, and mountain passes may be impassable. No! the ocean is limitless and unobstructed; and the fleet, each ship manned, gunned, provisioned and fuelled, ready to fight within five minutes. The Army not only has to mobilize, but—thank God! this being an island—it has to be carried somewhere by the Navy, no matter where it acts. I observe here that when Lord Kitchener went to Australia to inaugurate the scheme of Defence, he forgot Australia was an island. What Australia wants to make it impregnable is not Conscription—it's Submarines. However, I fancy Kitchener was sent there to get him out of the way. They wanted me to go to Australia, but I didn't.11 Jellicoe has gone there. But then, Jellicoe hasn't always sufficient foresight; *exempli gratia*, he was persuaded to take the deplorable step of giving up command of the Grand Fleet and going as First Sea Lord of the Admiralty. Never was anything so regrettable. I told the War Council that I am very glad Nelson never went to the Admiralty, and that Nelson would have made an awful hash of it. Nelson was a fighter, not an administrator and a snake charmer—that's what a First Sea Lord has to be.

Gross von Schwartzhoff told me on the sands of Scheveningen:—

"Your Navy can strike in thirteen hours; Our Army can't under thirteen days."

Frau von Pohl tells us the Germans did expect us so to strike, but Nelson was in heaven (Dear Reader, look again at what Frau von Pohl said, you'll find it in Chapter III.). On one occasion I got into a most unpleasant atmosphere. I arrived at a country house late at night, and at breakfast in the morning, I not knowing who the guests were, a Cabinet Minister enunciated the proposition that sea and land war were both in principle and practice alike. At once getting up from the breakfast table, in the heat of the moment, and not knowing that distinguished military officers were there, I said, "Any silly ass could be a General." I graphically illustrated my meaning. I gave the contrast between a sea and a land battle. The General is somewhere behind the fighting line, or he ought to be. The Admiral has got to be *in* the fighting line, or he ought to be. The Admiral is indeed like the young Subaltern, he is often the first "Over the top." The General, at a telescopic distance from the battle scene and surrounded by his Kitcheners, and his Ludendorffs, and his Gross von Schwartzhoffs, has plenty of time for the "Clear thinking" *à la* Lord Haldane; and then, acting on the advice of those surrounding him, he takes his measures. So far as I can make out from the Ludendorff extracts in *The Times*, Hindenburg, the Generalissimo, was clearly not in it. He was "the silly ass"! Ludendorff did it all as Chief of the Staff.

Now what's the corresponding case at sea? The smoke of the enemy, not even the tops of his funnels, can be seen on the horizon. (I proved this myself with the great Mediterranean fleet divided into two portions.) Within twenty minutes the action is decided! Realise this—it takes some minutes for the Admiral to get his breeches on, to get on deck and take in the situation; and it takes a good many more minutes to deploy the Fleet from its Cruising Disposition into its Fighting Disposition. In the Cruising Disposition his guns are masked, one ship interfering with the fire of another. The Fleet for Battle has to be so disposed that all the guns, or as many as possible, can concentrate on one or a portion of the enemy's fleet. Each fleet pushes on at its utmost speed *to meet the other*, hoping to catch the other undeployed. Every telescope in the fleet (and there are myriads) is looking at the Admiral as he goes to the topmost and best vantage spot on board his flag ship to see the enemy, and sees him alone outlined against the sky—neither time nor room for a staff around him, and if there were they'd say, "It's not the Admiral who is doing it," and be demoralized accordingly—fatal to victory. In the fleet the Admiral's got to be like Nelson—"the personal touch" so that *"any silly ass can't be an Admiral"*; and the people of the Fleet watch him with unutterable suspense to see what signal goes up to alter the formation of the fleet—a formation on which depends Victory or Defeat. So it was that Togo won that second Trafalgar; he did what is technically known as "crossing the T," which means he got the guns of his fleet all to bear, all free to fire, while those of the enemy were masked by his own ships. One by one Rozhdestvensky's ships went to the bottom, under the concerted action of concentrated fire. What does it? Speed. And what actuates it? One mind, and one mind only. Goschen was right (when First Lord of the Admiralty); he quoted that old Athenian Admiral who, when asked what governed a sea battle, replied, "Providence," and then with emphasis he added: "and a *good Admiral.*" Which reminds me too of Cromwell—a pious man, we all know; when asked a somewhat similar question as to what ruled the world, he replied "The Fear of the Lord," and he added with an emphasis equal to that of the Athenian Admiral—"And a broomstick." No one votes more for the Sermon on the Mount than I do; but I say to a blithering fool "*Begone!*"

A Naval War Staff at the Admiralty is a very excellent organisation for cutting out and arranging foreign newspaper clippings in such an intelligent disposition as will enable the First Sea Lord to take in at a glance who is likely amongst the foreigners to be the biggest fool or the greatest poltroon, who will be opposed to his own trusted and personally selected Nelson who commands the British Fleet. The First Sea Lord and the Chief Admiral afloat have got to be Siamese twins. And when the war comes, the Naval War Staff at the Admiralty, listening every moment to the enemy's wireless messages (if he dare use it), enables the First Sea Lord to let his twin at sea know exactly what is going on. He takes in the wireless, and not necessarily the Admiral afloat, on account of the far greater power of reception in a land installation as compared with that on a ship. When you see that spider's web of lines of wire on the top of the Admiralty, then thank God this is more or less a free country, as it got put up by a cloud of bluejackets before a rat was smelt! An intercepted German Naval letter at the time gave me personally great delight, for it truly divined that wireless was the weapon of the strong Navy. For the development of the wireless has been such that now you can get the direction of one who speaks and go for him; so the German daren't open his mouth. But if he does, of course the message is in cypher; and it's the elucidation of that cypher which is one of the crowning glories of the Admiralty work in the late war. In my time they never failed once in that elucidation. Yes, wireless is the weapon of the strong. So also is the Submarine—that is if they are sufficiently developed and diversified and properly applied, but you must have quantities and multiplicity of species.

What you want to do is to fight the enemy's fleet, make him come out from under the shelter of his forts, where his ships are hiding like rabbits in a hole—put in the ferrets and out come the rabbits, or they kill 'em where they are. Nelson blockading Toulon, as he told the Lord Mayor of London in one of his most characteristic letters, didn't want to keep the French fleet in; he wanted them to come out and fight. But he kept close in for fear they should evade him in darkness or in fog.

But the mischief of a Naval War Staff is peculiar to the Navy. I understand it is quite different in the Army—I don't know. The mischief to the Navy is that the very ablest of our Officers, both young and old, get attracted by the brainy work and by the shore-going appointment. I asked a splendid specimen once whatever made him go in for being a Marine Officer. He said he wanted to be with his wife! Well, it's natural. I know a case of a Sea Officer whose long absence caused his children not to recognise him when he came home from China and, indeed, they were frightened of him. The land is a shocking bad training ground for the sea. I once heard one bluejacket say to another the reason *he* believed in the Bible was that in heaven there is "no more sea." I didn't realise it at the time, but I looked up "Revelations" and found it was so. A shallower spirit observed: "Britannia rules the waves, but the mistake was she didn't rule them straight." A very distinguished soldier who came to see me when I was Port Admiral at Portsmouth said that the Army, as compared with the Navy, was at a great disadvantage. In the Army, or even in the country, he said, anyone who had handled a rifle laid down the law as if he were a General; but the Navy, he said, was "A huge mystery hedged in by sea-sickness."

So far as the Navy is concerned, the tendency of these "Thinking Establishments" on shore is to convert splendid Sea Officers into very indifferent Clerks. The Admiralty is filled with Sea Officers now who ought to be afloat; and the splendid civilian element—incomparable in its talent and in its efficiency—is swamped. Before the war, when I was First Sea Lord, when I left the Admiralty at 8 p.m., prior to some approaching Grand Manœuvres, I left it to my friend Flint, one of the Higher Division Clerks, to mobilize the fleet by a wireless message from the roof of the Admiralty; and the deciding circumstances having arisen, he did it off his own bat at 2 a.m. A weaker vessel, knowing of the telephone at my bedside, might have rung me up; but Flint didn't. Good old Flint! Always one of the Clerks was on watch, all the year round, night and day; and that obtained in the Admiralty long before any other Department adopted it.

Now for such work as I have described you don't want sea art; you want the Craven scholar, and I had him. A Sea Officer can never be an efficient clerk—his life unfits him. He can't be an orator; he's always had to hold his tongue. He can't argue; he's never been allowed. Only a few great spirits like Nelson are gifted with the splendid idiosyncrasy of insubordination; but it's given to a few great souls. I assure you that long study has convinced me that Nelson was nothing if not insubordinate. This is hardly the place to describe his magnificent lapses from discipline, which ever led to Victory. It's only due on my part, who have had more experience than anyone living of the civilian clerks at the Admiralty, to vouch for the fact that Sir Evan Macgregor, the ablest Secretary of the Admiralty since Samuel Pepys, Sir Graham Greene, Sir Oswyn Murray, Sir Charles Walker and my friends V. W. Baddeley, C.B., and J. W. S. Anderson, C.B., W. G. Perrin, J. F.

Phillips, and many others have done work which has never been exceeded as regards its incomparable efficiency. I can't recall a single lapse.

The outcome of this expanded Naval War Staff beyond its real requirements, such as I have indicated, and which were provided for while I was First Sea Lord, was that a Chief of the Staff, in imitation of him at the War Office, was planked into the Admiralty and indirectly supplanted the First Sea Lord. I won't enlarge on this further. It's many years before another war can possibly take place, and it's now a waste of educated labour to discuss it further. All I would ask is for anyone to take up the last issue of the Navy List and see the endless pages of Naval Officers at the Admiralty or holding shore appointments. There has never been anything approaching these numbers in all our Sea History! It is deplorable!

The Naval War College, which I established at Portsmouth, is absolutely a different affair. There it can be arranged that all the Officers go to sea daily and work as if with the fleet, with flotillas of Destroyers that are there available in quantities. These Destroyers would represent all the items of the fleet; and the formations of war and the meetings of hostile fleets could be practised and so constitute the Naval War College a real gem in war efficiency.

AGED 14. MIDSHIPMAN.

H.M.S. "Highflyer," China.

CHAPTER IX
RECAPITULATION OF DEEDS AND IDEAS

"Friends, Romans, Countrymen, lend me your ears!"

We have arranged that in this book you (to whom I am dictating) are to insert a *réchauffé* of my fugitive writings and certain extracts from the three bulky volumes of my letters to Lord Esher, which he has so very kindly sent me.

All, then, that I have to say in this chapter will be a summing up of all that is in my opinion worth saying, and you are going to be responsible for the rest. My judgment is that the British Public will be sick of it all long before you come to the end of your part. One can have too much jam. Nor do you seem inclined to put in all the "bites." For instance, it was told King Edward, who warned me of what was being said, that my moral character was shocking. No woman will ever appear against me at the Day of Judgment. One dear friend of mine attributed all his life's disasters to kissing the wrong girl. I never even did that. However, there is no credit in my morality and early piety. For I ever had to work from 12 years old for my daily bread, and work hard, so the Devil never had a "look in." I love Dr. Watts, he is so practical.

"And Satan finds some mischief still.

For idle hands to do."

Bishop Jeremy Taylor, who wrote that Classic, "Holy Living and Dying," who had a nagging wife who made him flee from home and youthful lusts, said "That no idle rich healthy man could possibly go to Heaven." No doubt it is difficult for such a one. You will remember the Saviour told us that the Camel getting through the eye of a needle is more likely. Usually, earthly judgments on heavenly subjects are wrong. Observe Mary Magdalene, and the most beautiful Collect for her Saint's Day which was in our First Prayer Book of 1540. This was later expunged by the sacerdotal, pharisaic, self-righteous mandarins of that period. The judgments of this world are worse than the judgments of God. When David was offered three forms of punishment—Famine or the Sword or Pestilence—he chose the pestilence, saying, "Let us now fall into the hands of the Lord; for his mercies are great; and let me not fall into the hand of man." At the moment of making this note of which I am speaking I am looking at two very beautiful old engravings I rescued from the room here allotted to the Presbyterian Minister! One of them is the "Woman Taken in Adultery" and the other is "Potiphar's Wife"! My host tells me it was a pure accident that these pictures came to be in the Minister's room; but such events happen to Saints. Wasn't there "The Scarlet Letter"—that wonderful book by Hawthorne?

I observe in passing how wonderfully well these Presbyterians do preach. Our hosts have a beautiful Chapel in the house, and they have got a delightful custom of selecting one from the Divines of Scotland to spend the week-end here. Their sermons so exemplify what I keep on impressing on you—that the printed word is a lifeless corpse. Can you compare the man who reads a sermon to the man who listens to one saturated with holiness and enthusiasm speaking out of the abundance of the heart? No doubt there is tautology, but there's conviction. Two qualities rule the world—*emotion and earnestness*. I have said elsewhere, with them you can move far more than mountains; you can move multitudes. It's the personality of the soul of man that has this immortal influence. Printed and written stuff is but an inanimate picture—a very fine picture sometimes, no doubt, but you get no aroma out of a picture. Fancy seeing the Queen of Sheba herself, instead of only reading of her in Solomon's print! And those Almug trees—"And there came no such Almug trees, nor were seen until this day."

To a friend I was once adoring St. Peter (I love his impetuosity)—I am illustrating how earthly judgments are so inferior to heavenly wisdom. St. John, who was a very much younger man, out-ran Peter. Up comes Peter, and dashes at once into the Sepulchre. Those men in war who get there and then don't do anything—*Cui bono?* A fleet magnificent, five times bigger than the enemy, and takes no risks! A man I heard of—his wife, separated from him, died at Florence. He was on the Stock Exchange. They telegraphed, "Shall we cremate, embalm, or bury?" "Do all three," he replied, "take no risks!" Some of our great warriors want the bird so arranged as to be able to put the salt on its tail. But I was speaking of my praising St. Peter. What did my friend retort (the judgment of this world, mind you!)? "Peter, Sir! he would be turned out of every Club in London!" So he would! Thank God, we have a God, so that when our turn comes we shall be forgiven much because we loved much.

From this Christian homily I return to what I rather vainly hope is my concluding interview.

Before beginning—one of my critics writes to *The Times* saying I am not modest—I never said I was. However, next day, Sir Alfred Yarrow mentions perhaps the most momentous thing I ever did—that is the introduction of the Destroyer; and the day following Sir Marcus Samuel writes that I am the God-father of Oil—and Oil is going to be the fuel of the world. Sir George Beilby is going to turn coal into Oil. He has done it. Thank God! we are going to have a smokeless England in consequence, and no more fortified coaling stations and peripatetic coal mines, or what coal mines were. And then, I was going to give some more instances, but that's enough *"to point the moral and adorn the tale."*

"SEEKEST THOU GREAT THINGS FOR THYSELF? SEEK THEM NOT!" (THE PROPHET JEREMIAH.)

You have given me a list of subjects which you think require elucidation in regard to my past years—a *résumé* especially of the incidents which claim peculiar notice between 1902 and 1910; and you ask me to add thereto such episodes from the past as will enlighten the reader as to how it came about that those big events between 1902 and 1910 were put in motion.

It's a big order, in a life of some sixty years on actual service—with but three weeks only unemployed, from the time of entry into the Navy to the time of Admiral of the Fleet.

I begin by being heartfelt in my thankfulness to a benign Providence for being capable yesterday, September 13th, 1919, of enjoying suet pudding and treacle with a pleasure equal to that which I quite well remember, of having suet pudding and treacle on July 4th, 1854, when I went on board H.M.S. "Victory," 101 guns, the flagship at Trafalgar of Admiral Lord Viscount Nelson. Yes! my thankfulness, I hope, is equal to but hardly as wonderful as that of the almost toothless old woman who, being commiserated with, replied: *"Yes, I only 'as two left; but thank God they meet!"* So I say, to express the same thankfulness with all my heart for the years that remain to me, though I have all my teeth—or nearly all—notwithstanding that I have not had even one single "thank you" for anything that I have done since King Edward died. Nevertheless, I thank that same God as the old woman thanked, Who don't let a sparrow fall without a purpose and without knowledge.

I have no doubt the slight has done me a lot of good!

I thought at the age of nineteen, when I was Acting Captain of H.M.S. "Coromandel," that I never could again be so great. Please look at my picture then. It's a very excellent one—rather pulled down at the corners of the mouth even then. (The child is father to the man.) And though now nearly as old as Dandolo I don't feel any greater than at 19. Dandolo after an escapade at the Dardanelles similar to mine, became conqueror of Byzantium at 80 years of age. And Justinian's two Generals, Belisarius and Narses, were over 70. Dolts don't realise that the brain improves while the body decays— provided of course that the original brain is not that of a congenital idiot, or of an effete poltroon who never will run risks.

"Risks and strife" are the bread of Life to a growing brain.

I beg the reader of this dictation to believe that, whatever he may hear to the contrary (and he probably will), though swaggering as I did just now at suet-puddening at 79 as efficiently as at nineteen, yet I do daily realise what that ancient monk wrote in the year 800, when he studied the words of Job—that "Man that is born of a woman hath but a short time" compared to eternity, and death may be always near the door; and no words are more beautiful in connection therewith than when a parting friend at the moment of departure makes us say: "Teach us who survive in this and other like daily spectacles of mortality to see how frail and uncertain our own condition is."

First of all in this Recapitulation comes back to me a prophecy I ventured at that age of 19 I have just mentioned—that the next great war that we should have at sea would be a war of young men. And how beautifully this is illustrated by the letter received only a few days ago from that boy in Russia (see Chapter IV) where two battleships were sent to the bottom and the British sailors in command were only Lieutenants. And in passing one cannot help paying a tribute to the Subalterns on shore. General Sir Henry Rawlinson said lately: "Those who really won the war were the young Company Leaders and the Subalterns," and pathetic was the usual Gazette notice of those killed:

"Second Lieutenants *unless otherwise mentioned.*"

There was little "otherwise!" So has it been in the Navy, at Zeebrugge and elsewhere.

There is, however, a very splendid exception—when all hands, old and young, went to the bottom; and that is in the magnificent Merchant Navy of the British Nation. Seven million tons sank under these men, and the record of so many I've seen who were saved was: "Three times torpedoed." And remember! for them no Peerage or Westminster Abbey. They didn't even get paid for the clothes they lost, and their pay stopped the day the ship was sunk. Except in the rare cases where the shipowner was the soul of generosity, like my friend Mr. Petersen, who paid his men six months or a year to do nothing after such a catastrophe. But we go with Mr. Havelock Wilson: "We hope to change all that." For who is going to deny, when we all stand up for them, that the Merchant Navy shall be incorporated in the Navy of the Nation and with all the rights and money and rank and uniform and widows' pensions and pensions in old age? All this has to come; and I am Mr. Havelock Wilson's colleague in that matter, as he was mine in that wonderful feeding and clothing of our thousands of British Merchant sailor prisoners, who didn't, for some damned red tape reason, come within the scope of the millions of money in that enormous Prince of Wales's Fund, and the Red Cross.

Somebody will have to be a martyr, perhaps it's me. And I expect I am going to be burnt at the stake for saying these things; but in those immortal words of the past "I shall light the candle!" Isn't it just too lovely—when Bishop Latimer, as the flames shot up around him at the stake in Oxford in A.D. 1555, cried to his brother Bishop, equally burning:

"Play the man, Master Ridley! We shall this day light such a candle by God's Grace in England as I trust shall never be put out."

So may it be in our being burnt for the sake of the great Merchant Navy that saved our country!

*   *   *   *   *

As regards the years 1902 to 1910, the first conceptions of these great changes stole upon me when I perceived in that great Fleet in the Mediterranean how vague were the views as to fighting essentials. For instance, in one of the lectures to the Mediterranean Fleet Officers I set forth a case of so dealing with a hostile fleet that we should ourselves first of all deliberately and in cold blood sacrifice several of our fastest cruisers. Why?

To delay the flying enemy by the wounding of his hindermost ships. Possibly a ruthless German Admiral might leave a "Blücher" to her fate; but not so our then probable and chivalrous foe! The most shocking description I have ever read of the horrors of war was that detailed by one of the crew of the "Blücher" as he describes Beatty's salvoes gradually approaching the "Blücher" and falling near in the water, and then the hell when these salvoes arrived, immediately extinguishing the electric light installation, till all below between decks was pitchy darkness only lighted up by the bursting shells as they penetrated and massacred the crew literally by hundreds, who, huddled up together in the "Blücher's" last moments, were hoping behind the thickest armour to escape destruction.

I saw that the plan of sacrificing vessels in the pursuit of an enemy seemed a new feature to my hearers; and yet it was as old as the hills. And another "eye-opener" I had—in the inability to realise so obvious a fact as, alas! was somewhat the case in the North Sea recently—that you need not be afraid of a mine field; for where the enemy goes you can go, if you keep in his wake, that is. In close regard with this matter, I am an apostle of "End-on Fire," for to my mind broadside fire is peculiarly stupid. To be obliged to delay your pursuit by turning even one atom from your straight course on to a flying enemy is to me being the acme of an ass. And, strange to say, in connection with this I, only yesterday, September 13th, 1919, got a letter from Admiral Weymouth—a most excellent letter, delightfully elaborating with exceptional acuteness this very idea, which came along so long ago as 1900, when the first thought of the "Dreadnought" came into my brain, when I was discussing with my excellent friend, Mr. Gard, Chief Constructor of Malta Dockyard, the vision of the "Dreadnought."

I greatly enjoyed years ago overhearing a lady describe to another lady, when crossing over to Ryde, a passing Ryde passenger steamer (just built and differing very greatly from the one we were on board of) as a Battleship. And she wasn't far out as to what a battleship should be. The enterprise of the Ryde Steam Packet Company had just produced that vessel, which went just as fast astern as she did ahead. In fact, she had no stern. There was a bow at each end and a rudder at each end and screws at each end; so they never had any bother to turn round. Now when you go to Boulogne or Folkestone, I don't know how much time you don't waste fooling around to go in stern first, so as to be able to come out the right way; and having escaped sea-sickness so far, I myself have found that the last straw. Let us hope every ship now built after this Chapter will be a "Double-Ender." But in this world you are a lunatic if you go too fast.

Take now the submarines. They began by diving head first to get below water; and in the beginning some stuck their noses in the mud and never came up again, and in the shallow waters of the North Sea this limited the dimension of the submarine. But now there's no more diving. A lunatic hit by accident on the idea of sinking the ship horizontally; so there is no more bother about the metricentric problems, and all the vagaries of Stabilities. No limit to size!

This sort of consideration brought into one's mind that a great "Education" was wanted; and that we wanted "Machinery Education," both with officers and men; and also that the education should be the education of common sense. My full idea of Osborne was, alas! emasculated by the schoolmasters of the Nation; but it is yet going to spread. As sure as I am now dictating to you, the practical way of teaching is "*Explanation, followed by Execution.*" Have a lecture on Optics in the morning: make a telescope in the afternoon. Tell the boys in the morning about the mariner's compass and the use of the chart; and in the afternoon go out and navigate a Ship.

Similarly, with the selection of boys for the Navy, I didn't want any examination whatsoever, except the boy and his parents being "vetted," and then an interview with the boy to examine his personality (his *soul*, in fact); and not to have an article in the Navy stuffed by patent cramming schoolmasters like a Strasburg goose. A goose's liver is not the desideratum in the candidate. The desideratum was: could we put into him the four attributes of Nelson:—

I. Self reliance.

(If you don't believe in yourself, nobody else will.)

II. Fearlessness of Responsibility.

(If you shiver on the brink you'll catch cold, and possibly not take the plunge.)

III. Fertility of Resource.

(If the traces break, don't give it up, get some string.)

IV. Power of initiative.

(Disobey orders.)

AIRCRAFT.

Somewhere about January 15th, 1915, I submitted my resignation as First Sea Lord to Mr. Churchill because of the supineness manifested by the High Authorities as regards Aircraft; and I then prophesied the raids over London in particular and all over England, that by and by caused several millions sterling of damage and an infinite fright.

I refer to my resignation on the aircraft question with some fear and trembling of denials; however, I have a copy of my letter, so it's all right. I withdrew my resignation at the request of Authority, because Authority said that the War Office and not the Admiralty were responsible and would be held responsible. The aircraft belonged to the War Office; why on earth couldn't I mind my own business? I didn't want the Admiralty building and our wireless on the roof of it to be bombed; so it *was* my business (the War Office was as safe as a church, the Germans would never bomb that establishment!).

Recently I fortuned to meet Mr. Holt Thomas, and he brought to my recollection what was quite a famous meeting at the Admiralty. Soon after I became First Sea Lord on October 31st, 1914, I had called together at the Admiralty a Great Company of all interested in the air; for at that moment I had fully satisfied myself that small airships with a speed of fifty miles an hour would be of inestimable value against submarines and also for scouting purposes near the coast. *So they proved.*

Mr. Holt Thomas was a valued witness before the Royal Commission on Oil and Oil Engines, of which I was Chairman (a sad business for me financially—I only possessed a few hundred pounds and I put it into Oil—I had to sell them out, of course, on becoming Chairman of the Oil Commission, and what I put those few hundreds into caused a disappearance of most of those hundreds, and when I emerged from the Royal Commission the oil shares had more than quintupled in value and gone up to twenty times what they were when I first put in).

Through Mr. Holt Thomas we obtained the very important evidence of the French inventor of the Gnome engine—that wonderful engine that really made aeroplanes what they now are. His evidence was of peculiar value; and so also was that of Mr. Holt Thomas's experience; and the result of the Admiralty meeting on aircraft was that we obtained from Mr. Holt Thomas an airship in a few weeks, when the experience hitherto had been that it took years; and a great number of this type of aircraft were used with immense advantage in the war. I remember so well that the very least time that could be promised with every effort and unstinted money, was three months (but Mr. Holt Thomas gave a shorter time). In three *weeks* an airship was flying over the Admiralty at 50 miles an hour ("there's nothing you can't have if you want it enough"), and now we've reached the Epoch—prodigious in its advent—when positively the Air commands and dominates both Land and Sea; and we shall witness quite shortly a combination in one Structure of the Aeroplane, the Airship, the parachute, the common balloon, and an Aerial Torpedo, which will both astound people by its simplicity and by its extraordinary possibilities, both in War and Commerce (the torpedo will become cargo in Commerce). The aeroplane has now to keep moving to live—but why should it? The aerial gyroscopic locomotive torpedo suspended by a parachute has a tremendous significance.

And let no one think like the ostrich that burying one's head in the sand will make Invention desist. At the first Hague Peace Conference in 1899, when I was one of the British Delegates, huge nonsense was talked about the amenities of war. War has no amenities, although Mr. Norman Angell attacked me in print for saying so. It's like two Innocents playing singlestick; they agree, when they begin, not to hit hard, but it don't last long! Like fighting using only one fist against the other man with two; the other fist damn soon comes out! The Ancient who formulated that "All's fair in love and war" enunciated a great natural principle

"War is the essence of violence."

"Moderation in War is imbecility."

"HIT FIRST. HIT HARD. KEEP ON HITTING."

The following Reports and letter will illustrate this history of my efforts in this direction:—

Lord Fisher returned to the Admiralty on October 30th, 1914.

38 S.S. airships were at once ordered—single engine type. Six improved type.

Before Lord Fisher left the Admiralty, a design of a double-engine type was got out, and subsequently another 32 airships were ordered.

CIRCULAR LETTER issued by Lord Fisher in 1914 when First Sea Lord:—

Lord Fisher desires to express to all concerned his high appreciation of the service rendered by those who carried out the recent daring raid on Lake Constance.

He considers that the flight mentioned, made over 250 miles of enemy country of the worst description, is a fine feat of endurance, courage, and skill, and reflects great credit on all who took part in the raid, and through them on the Air Service to which they belong.

        *   *   *   *   *

The following précis of correspondence is inserted because contributory to Lord Fisher's resignation. He had previously written to Mr. Churchill, resigning on the ground of the disregard of his warnings respecting the Aircraft menace:—

An Official Secret German Dispatch, obtained from a German Source, dated December 26th, 1914:—

The General Staff of the German Army are sending aircraft to attack French fortified places. Full use to be made of favourable weather conditions for attack of Naval Zeppelins against the East Coast of England with the exception of London. The attack on London will follow later combined with the German Army Airships.

        *   *   *   *   *

Précis of History of Rigid Airships of Zeppelin Type.—

Lord Fisher, when First Sea Lord, in December, 1908, instructed Admiral Bacon to press for the construction of rigid airships for naval purposes at the meetings of a Sub-Committee of the Committee of Imperial Defence, which held its first meeting in December, 1908, after many meetings at which Admiral Bacon presented the naval point of view with much lucidity. The Committee recommended on January 28th, 1909, the following:—

(*a*) The Committee are of opinion that the dangers to which we might be exposed by developments in aerial navigation cannot be definitely ascertained until we ourselves possess airships.

(*b*) *There are good grounds for assuming that airships will prove of great value to the Navy for scouting and possibly for destructive purposes.*12 From a military point of view they are also important.

(*c*) A sum of £35,000 should be included in the Naval Estimates for the purpose of building an airship of a rigid type. The sum alluded to should include the cost of all preliminary and incidental expenses.

(*d*) A sum of £10,000 should be included in Army Estimates for continuing experiments with navigable balloons of a non-rigid type, and for the purchase of complete non-rigid airships and their component parts.

January 28th, 1909.

Approved by Committee of Imperial Defence, *February 25th, 1909.*

And nothing more was done till I came back to Admiralty on October 30th, 1914!

Letter from Admiral Sir S. Eardley Wilmot, formerly Superintendent of Ordnance Stores, Admiralty:—

THE OLD MALT HOUSE,
Marlow,
August 13th, 1916.

DEAR LORD FISHER,

Having given us splendid craft to fight on and under the sea, I wish you would take up the provision of an air fleet. There is going to be a great development of air navigation in the future and all nations will be at it. With our resources and wealth we can take and keep the lead if we like.

As a modest programme to start with we might aim at 100 air battleships and 400 air cruisers: all on the "lighter than air" principle.

I met a young fellow who had been in the Jutland action and asked him how the 15-inch guns did. "Splendidly," he said—"They did nearly all the real execution." I hear the Germans have got 17-inch guns which is what I anticipated, but they won't get ahead of us in that time tho' we can't yet snuff out their Zepps, thanks to you know who.

Yours sincerely,

(Signed)   S. EARDLEY WILMOT.

Note.—More than a year before I got this letter I had got a 20-inch gun ready to be built for a new type of Battle Cruiser!

AGED 19. LIEUTENANT.

In temporary command of "Coromandel" in China.

THE SUBMARINE MINE

As quite a young Lieutenant, with extraordinary impudence I told the then First Sea Lord of the Admiralty that the Hertz German Submarine Mine, which I had seen a few days before in Kiel Harbour, would so far revolutionise sea warfare as possibly to prevent one fleet pursuing another, by the Fleet that was flying dropping submarine mines in its wake; and certainly that sudden sea operations of the old Nelsonic type would seriously be interfered with. He very good humouredly sent me away as a young desperado, as he remembered that I had been a lunatic in prophesying the doom of masts and sails, which were still then magnificently supreme, and the despised engineer yet hiding his diminished head had to keep the smell of oily oakum away from the noses of the Lords of the ship.

That same Hertz mine in all its essentials remains still "The King of Mines," and if only in those years immediately preceding the war we had manufactured none else, instead of trying to improve on it, we should have bagged no end of big game. But as it was, our mines were squibs; the enemy's ship always steamed away and got into harbour, while ours always went down plump.

The Policy of the Submarine Mine favoured us, but our authorities couldn't see it. I printed in three kinds of type:

(1) Huge capitals; (2) Italics; (3) big Roman block letters the following words, submitted to the authorities very early in the war—

"Sow the North Sea with Mines on such a huge scale that Naval Operations in it become utterly impossible."

So you nip into the Baltic with the British Fleet.

That British Mining Policy blocked the North Sea entrance to the Kiel Canal—that British Mining Policy dished the neutrals. When the neutrals got blown up you swore it was a German mine—it was the Germans who began laying mines; and a mine, when it blows you up, don't hand you a ticket like a passport, saying what nationality it is. In fact, our mines were so damned bad they couldn't help believing it was a German mine. But I might add I think they would have sunk any Merchant ship, squibs though they were; and I may add in a parenthesis this British policy of submarine mines for the North Sea would have played hell with the German submarines, not so much blowing them up but entangling their screws.

Well, at the last—*longo intervallo*—towards the close of the war, being the fifteenth "Too Late" of Mr. Lloyd George's ever memorable and absolutely true speech, the British Foreign Office did allow this policy, and the United States sent over mines in thousands upon thousands, and we're still trying to pick 'em up, in such vast numbers were they laid down!

We really are a very peculiar people.
Lions led by Asses!

I bought a number of magnificent and fast vessels for laying down these mines in masses—no sooner had I left the Admiralty in May, 1915, they were so choice that they were diverted and perverted to other uses.

But perhaps the most sickening of all the events of the war was the neglect of the Humber as the jumping-off place for our great fast Battle Cruiser force, with all its attendant vessels—light Cruisers, Destroyers, and Submarines, and mine-layers, and mine-sweepers—for offensive action at any desired moment, and as a mighty and absolute deterrent to the humiliating bombardment of our coasts by that same fast German Battle

Cruiser force. The Humber is the nearest spot to Heligoland; and at enormous cost and greatly redounding to the credit of the present Hydrographer of the Navy, Admiral Learmonth (then Director of Fixed Defences), the Humber was made submarine-proof, and batteries were placed in the sea protecting the obstructions, and moorings laid down behind triple lines of defence against all possibility of hostile successful attack.

However, I had to leave the Admiralty before it was completed and the ships sent there; and then the *mot d'ordre* was Passivity; and when the Germans bombarded Scarborough and Yarmouth and so on, we said to them *à la Chinois*, making great grimaces and beating tom-toms; "If you come again, look out!" But the Germans weren't Chinese, and they came; and the soothing words spoken to the Mayors of the bombarded East Coast towns were what Mark Twain specified as being "spoke ironical."

I conclude this Chapter with the following words, printed in the early autumn of 1914:—

"By the half-measures we have adopted hitherto in regard to Open-Sea Mines we are enjoying neither the one advantage nor the other."

That is to say, when the Germans at the very first outbreak of war departed from the rules of the Hague Conference against the type of mine they used, we had two courses open to us: there was the moral advantage of refusing to follow the bad lead, or we could seek a physical advantage by forcing the enemies' crime to its utmost consequences. We were effete. We were pusillanimous, and we were like Jelly-fish.

And we "Waited and See'd."

CHAPTER X
APOLOGIA PRO VITA SUA

WE started out on the compilation of this book on the understanding that it was not to be an Autobiography, nor a Diary, nor Meditations (*à la* Marcus Aurelius), but simply "MEMORIES." And now you drive me to give you a Synopsis of my life (which is an artful periphrasis), and request me to account for my past life being one continuous series of fightings—Love and Hate alternating and Strife the thread running through this mortal coil of mine. (When a coil of rope is made in a Government Dockyard a coloured worsted thread is introduced; it runs through the centre of the rope: if the rope breaks and sends a man to "Kingdom Come," you know the Dockyard that made it and you ask questions; if it's purloined the Detective bowls out the purloiner.) So far my rope of life has not broken and the thread is there—Strife.

Greatly daring, and "storms of obloquy" having been my portion, I produce now an *apologia pro vita mea*, though it may not pulverise as that great Cardinal pulverised with his famous Apologia ("He looked like Heaven and he fought like Hell").

*   *   *   *   *

Here I would insert a note which I discovered this very afternoon sent me by an unknown friend when Admiral von Spee and all his host went to the bottom. Before that event there had been a series of disasters at sea, and a grave uneasy feeling about our Navy was spreading over the land. The three great Cruisers—"Hogue," "Cressy" and "Aboukir"—had been sunk near the German coast. What were they doing there? Did they think they were Nelson blockading Toulon? The "Goeben" and "Breslau" had escaped from our magnificent Battle Cruisers, then in the Mediterranean, which had actually boxed them up in the Harbour of Messina; and they had gone unharmed to Constantinople, and like highwaymen had held a pistol at the head of the Sultan with the threat of bombarding Constantinople and his Palace and thus converted Turkey, our ancient ally, into the most formidable foe we had. For is not England the greatest Mahomedan Power in the world? The escape of the "Goeben" and "Breslau" was an irreparable disaster almost equalled by our effete handling of Bulgaria, the key State of the Balkans; and we didn't give her what she asked. When we offered it and more next year, she told us to go to hell. Then there was the "Pegasus," that could neither fight nor run away, massacred in cold blood at Zanzibar by a German Cruiser as superior to her as our Battle Cruisers were to von Spee. And last of all, as a climax, that sent the hearts of the British people into their boots, poor Cradock and his brave ships were sunk by Admiral von Spee. I became First Sea Lord within 24 hours of that event, and without delay the Dreadnought Battle Cruisers, "Inflexible" and "Invincible," went 7,000 miles without a hitch in their water tube boilers or their turbine machinery, and arrived at the Falkland Islands almost simultaneously with Admiral von Spee and his eleven ships. That night von Spee, like another Casablanca with his son on board, had gone to the bottom and all his ships save one—and that one also soon after—were sunk. I have to reiterate about von Spee, as to this day the veil is upon the faces of our people, and they do not realise the Salvation that came to them.

1. We should have had no munitions—our nitrate came from Chili.

2. We should have lost the Pacific—the Falkland Islands would have been another Heligoland and a submarine base.

3. Von Spee had German reservists, picked up on the Pacific Coast, on board, to man the fortifications to be erected on the Falkland Islands.

4. He would have proceeded to the Cape of Good Hope and massacred our Squadron there, as he had massacred Cradock and his Squadron.

5. General Botha and his vast fleet of transports proceeding to the conquest of German South-West Africa would have been destroyed.

6. Africa under Hertzog would have become German.

7. Von Spee, distributing his Squadron on every Ocean, would have exterminated British Trade.

That's not a bad *résumé*!

Now I give the note, for it really is first-rate. Who wrote it I don't know, and I don't know the paper that it came from:—

"It is amusing to read the eulogies now showered on Lord Fisher. He is the same man with the same methods, the same ideas, and the same theories and practice which he had in 1905 when he was generally abused as an unscrupulous rascal for whom the gallows were too good. Lord Fisher's silence under storms of obloquy while he was building up Sea Power was a striking evidence of his title to fame."

The writer of the paragraph quotes the above words from some other paper; then he goes on with the following remark:—

"We cordially endorse these observations. At the same time, not all of those who raised the 'storms of obloquy' in 1905 and for some years subsequently are now indulging in eulogy. Many of them just maintain a more or less discreet silence, varied by an occasional insinuation either in public or in private that everything is not quite as it should be at the Admiralty, or that Lord Fisher is too old for his job, etc., etc., etc. As we have often remarked, many of the vituperators of Lord Fisher hated him for this one simple reason, that he had weighed them up and found them wanting. They had imposed on the public, but they couldn't impose on him. Some of these vituperators are now discreetly silent, but we know for a fact that their sentiments towards the First Sea Lord are not in the slightest degree changed."

To proceed with this synopsis:—

I entered the Navy, July 12th, 1854, on board Her Majesty's Ship "Victory," after being medically examined by the Doctor on board of her, and writing out from dictation The Lord's Prayer; and I rather think I did a Rule of Three sum. Before that time, for seven years I had a hard life. My paternal grandfather—a splendid old parson of the fox-hunting type—with whom I was to live, had died just before I reached England; and no one else but my maternal grandfather was in a position to give me a home. He was a simple-minded man and had been fleeced out of a fortune by a foreign scoundrel— I remember him well, as also I remember the Chartist Riots of 1848 when I saw a policeman even to my little mind behaving, as I thought, brutally to passing individuals. I remember seeing a tottering old man having his two sticks taken away from him and broken across their knees by the police. On the other hand, I have to bear witness to a little phalanx of 40 splendid police (who then wore tall hats and tail coats) charging a multitude of what seemed to me to be thousands and sending them flying for their lives. They only had their truncheons—but they knew how to use them certainly. They seized the band and smashed the instruments and tore up their flags.

I share Lord Rosebery's delightful distaste; and wild horses won't make me say more about those early years. These are Lord Rosebery's delicious words:—

"There is one initial part of a biography which is skipped by every judicious reader; that in which the pedigree of the hero is set forth, often with warm fancy and sometimes at intolerable length."

How can it possibly interest anyone to know that my simple-minded maternal grandfather was driven through the artifices of a rogue to take in lodgers, who of their charity gave me bread thickly spread with butter—butter was a thing I otherwise never saw—and my staple food was boiled rice with brown sugar—very brown?

Other vicissitudes of my early years—until I became Gunnery Lieutenant of the first English Ironclad, the "Warrior," at an extraordinarily early age—may be told some day; and all that your desired synopsis demands is a filling in of dates and a few details, till I became the Captain of the "Inflexible"—the "Dreadnought" of her day. I was promoted from Commander to Captain largely through a Lord of the Admiralty by chance hearing me hold forth in a Lecture to a bevy of Admirals.

H.M.S. "VIGILANT," PORTSMOUTH.
October 3rd, 1873.

Mr. Goschen and Milne left at 10 a.m. I stayed and went on board "Vernon," Torpedo School Ship, at 11. Had a most interesting lecture from Commander Fisher, a promising young officer, and witnessed several experiments. The result of my observations was that in my opinion the Torpedo has a great future before it *and that mechanical training will in the near future be essential for officers.* Made a note to speak to Goschen about young Fisher.

That was in 1873. More than thirty years after, "Young Fisher" was instrumental in making this principle the basis of the new system of education of all naval cadets at Osborne.

I remember so well taking a "rise" out of my exalted company of Admirals and others. The voltaic element, which all lecturers then produced with gusto as the elementary galvanic cell, was known as the "Daniell Cell." A bit of zinc, and a bit of copper stuck in sawdust saturated with diluted sulphuric acid, and there you were! A bit of wire from the zinc to one side of a galvanometer and a bit of wire from the copper to the other side and round went the needle as if pursued by the devil.

There were endless varieties of this "Daniell Cell," which it was always considered right and proper to describe. "Now," I said, "Sirs, I will give you without any doubt whatsoever the original Daniell Cell"—at that moment disclosing to their rapt and enquiring gaze a huge drawing (occupying the whole side of the lecture room and previously shrouded by a table cloth)—the Lions with their mouths firmly shut and Daniel apparently biting his nails waiting for daylight! Anyhow, that's how Rubens represents him.

I very nearly got into trouble over that "Sell." Admirals don't like being "sold."

I should have mentioned that antecedent to this I had been Commander of the China Flagship. I wished very much for the Mediterranean Flagship; but my life-long and good friend Lord Walter Kerr was justly preferred before me. The Pacific Flagship was also vacant; and I think the Admiral wanted me there, but I had a wonderful good friend at the Admiralty, Sir Beauchamp Seymour, afterwards Lord Alcester, who was determined I should go to China. So to China I went; and, as it happened, it turned out trumps, for the Admiral got softening of the brain, and I was told that when he got home and attended at the Admiralty I was the only thing in his mind; the only thing he could say was "Fisher!" And this luckily helped me in my promotion to Post Captain.

After starting the "Vernon" as Torpedo School of the Navy and partaking in a mission to Fiume to arrange for the purchase of the Whitehead Torpedo, I was sent at an hour's notice overland to Malta, where on entering the harbour I noticed an old tramp picking up her anchor, and on enquiry found she was going to Constantinople, where the ship I was to command was with the Fleet under Sir Geoffrey Hornby. I went alongside, got up a rope ladder that was hanging over the side and pulled up my luggage with a rope's end, when the Captain of the Tramp came up to me and said: "Hullo!" I said "Hullo!" He said "What is it you want?" He didn't know who I was, and I was in plain clothes, just as I had travelled over the Continent, and I replied: "I'm going with you to Constantinople to join my ship"; and he said "There ain't room; there's only one bunk, and when I ain't in it the mate is." I said "All right, I don't want a bunk." And he said "Well, we ain't got no cook." And I said "That don't matter either." That man and I till he died were like Jonathan and David. He was a magnificent specimen of those splendid men who command our merchant ships—I worshipped the ground he trod on. His mate was just as good. They kept watch and watch, and it was a hard life. I said to him one day "Captain, I never see you take sights." "Well," he said, "Why should I? When I leaves one lamp-post I steers for the other" (meaning lighthouses); "and," he says, "I trusts my engineer. He gives me the revolutions what the engine has made, and I know exactly where I am. And," he says, "when you have been going twenty years on the same road and no other road, you gets to know exactly how to do it." "Well," I said, "what do you do about your compass? are you sure it's correct? In the Navy, you know, we're constantly looking at the sun when it sets, and that's an easy way of seeing that the compass is right." "Well," he said, "what I does is this. I throws a cask overboard, and when it's as far off as ever I can see it, I turns the ship round on her axis. I takes the bearing of the cask at every point of the compass, I adds 'em all up, divides the total by the number of bearings, which gives me the average, and then I subtracts each point of the compass from it, and that's what the compass is wrong on each point. But," he says,

"I seldom does it, because provided I make the lamp-post all right I think the compass is all right."

I found Admiral Hornby's fleet at Ismid near Constantinople, and Admiral Hornby sent a vessel to meet me at Constantinople. He had heard from Malta that I was on board the tramp. That great man was the finest Admiral afloat since Nelson. At the Admiralty he was a failure. So would Nelson have been! With both of them their Perfection was on the Sea, not at an office desk. Admiral Hornby I simply adored. I had known him many years; and while my cabins on board my ship were being painted, he asked me to come and live with him aboard his Flagship, which I did, and I was next ship to him always when at sea. He was astounding. He would tell you what you were going to do wrong before you did it; and you couldn't say you weren't going to do it because you had put your helm over and the ship had begun to move the wrong way. Many years afterwards, when he was the Port Admiral at Portsmouth, I was head of the Gunnery School at Portsmouth, and, some war scare arising, he was ordered to take command of the whole Fleet at home collected at Portland. He took me with him as a sort of Captain of the Fleet, and we went to Bantry Bay, where we had exercises of inestimable value. He couldn't bear a fool, so of course he had many enemies. There never lived a more noble character or a greater seaman. He was incomparable.

*   *   *   *   *

After commanding the "Pallas" in the Mediterranean under Sir Geoffrey Hornby, I was selected by Admiral Sir Cooper Key as his Flag Captain in North America in command of the "Bellerophon"; and I again followed Sir Cooper Key as his Flag Captain in the "Hercules" when he also was put in command of a large fleet on another war scare arising. It was in that year I began the agitation for the introduction of Lord Kelvin's compass into the Navy, and I continued that agitation with the utmost vehemence till the compass was adopted. After that I was chosen by Admiral Sir Leopold McClintock, the great Arctic Explorer, to be his Flag Captain on the North American Station, in the "Northampton," then a brand new ship. He again was a splendid man and his kindness to me is unforgettable. He had gone through great hardships in the Arctic—once he hadn't washed for 179 days. He was like a rare old bit of mahogany; and I was told by an admirer of his that when the thermometer was 70 degrees below zero he found the ship so stuffy that he slept outside on the ice in his sleeping bag.

1885. AGED 41. POST CAPTAIN.

In command of Gunnery School at Portsmouth.

I was suddenly recalled to England and left him with very deep regret in the West Indies to become Captain of the "Inflexible." I had the most trying parting from that ship's company of the "Northampton"; and not being able to stand the good-bye, I crept unseen into a shore boat and got on board the mail steamer before the crew found out that the Captain had left the ship. And the fine old Captain of the Mail Steamer—Robert Woolward by name—caught the microbe and steamed me round and round my late ship. He was a great character. Every Captain of a merchant ship I meet I seem to think better than the last (I hope I shan't forget later on to describe Commodore Haddock of the White Star Line, for if ever there was a Nelson of the Merchant Service he was). But I return to Woolward. He had been all his life in the same line of steamers, and he showed me some of his correspondence, which was lovely. He was invariably in the right and his Board of Directors were invariably in the wrong. I saw a lovely letter he had written that very day that I went on board, to his Board of Directors. He signed himself in the letter as follows:—

"Gentlemen, I am your obedient humble servant" (he was neither), "ROBERT WOOLWARD—Forty years in your employ and never did right yet."

I must, while I have the chance, say a few words about my friend Haddock. It was a splendid Captain in the White Star steamer in which I crossed to America in 1910, and I remarked this to my Cabin Steward, as a matter of conversation. "Ah!" he said, "you should see 'addick." Then he added "We knows him as 'addick of the 'Oceanic.' Yes," he said, "and Mr. Ismay (the Head of the White Star Line) knows him too!" The "Oceanic" was Mr. Ismay's last feat in narrowness and length and consequent speed for crossing the Atlantic. I have heard that when he was dying he went to see her. This conversation never left my mind, although it was only the cabin steward that told me; but he was an uncommon good steward. So when I came back to the Admiralty as First Sea Lord on October 31st, 1914, I at once got hold of Haddock, made him into a Commodore, and he commanded the finest fleet of dummy wooden "Dreadnoughts" and Battle Cruisers the world had ever looked on, and they agitated the Atlantic, and the "Queen Elizabeth" in wood got blown up by the Germans at the Dardanelles instead of the real one. The Germans left the other battleships alone chasing the "Elizabeth." If this should meet the eye of Haddock, I want to tell him that, had I remained, he would have been Sir Herbert Haddock, K.C.B., or I'd have died in the attempt.

*   *   *   *   *

Now you have got perhaps not all you want, but sufficient for the Notes to follow here.

THE "WARRIOR"

I was appointed Gunnery Lieutenant of the "Warrior" our First Ironclad in 1863, when I was a little over 22 years old. I had just won the Beaufort Testimonial (Senior Wrangler), and that, with a transcendental Certificate from Commodore Oliver Jones, who was at that time the demon of the Navy, gave me a "leg up."

The "Warrior" was then, like the "Inflexible" in 1882 and the "Dreadnought" in 1905, the cynosure of all eyes. She had a very famous Captain, the son of that great seaman Lord Dundonald, and a still more famous Commander, Sir George Tryon, who afterwards went down in the "Victoria." She had a picked crew of officers and men, so I was wonderfully fortunate to be the Gunnery Lieutenant, and at so young an age I got on very well, except for sky-larking in the ward-room, for which I got into trouble. There was a dear old grey-headed Paymaster, and a mature Doctor, and a still more mature Chaplain, quite a dear old Saint. These, with other willing spirits, of a younger phase, I organised into a peripatetic band. The Parson used to play the coal scuttle, the Doctor the tongs and shovel, the dear old Paymaster used to do the cymbals with an old tin kettle. The other instruments we made ourselves out of brown paper, and we perambulated, doing our best. The Captain came out of his cabin door and asked the sentry what that noise was? We were all struck dumb by his voice, the skylight being open, and we were silent. The Sentry said: "It's only Mr. Fisher, Sir!" so he shut the door! The Commander, Sir George Tryon, wasn't so nice! He sent down a message to say the Gunnery Lieutenant was "to stop that fooling!" (However, this only drove us into another kind of sport!) We were all very happy messmates; they kindly spoilt me as if I was the Baby. I never went ashore by any chance, so all the other Lieutenants liked me because I took their duty for them. One of them was like Nelson's signal—he expected every man to do his duty! I was his bosom friend, which reminds me of another messmate I had who, the witty First Lieutenant said, always reminded him of Nelson! Not seeing the faintest resemblance, I asked him why. "Well," he said, "the last thing Nelson did was to die for his country, and that is the last thing this fellow would do!" It may be an old joke, but I'd never heard it before, and it was true.

I got on very well with the sailors, and our gunnery was supposed to be A 1. They certainly did rush the guns about, so I was sent in charge of the bluejackets to a banquet given them ashore. I imagined that on our return they might have had a good lot of beer, so I appealed to their honour and affection, when we marched back to the ship in fours, to take each other's arms. They nobly did it! And I got highly complimented for the magnificent way they marched back through the streets!! And this is the episode! The galleries at the banquet were a mass of ladies, and very nice-looking ones. When the banquet was over, the Captain of the Maintop of the "Warrior," John Kiernan by name, unsolicited, stood up in his chair and said: "On behalf of his top-mates he wished to thank the Mayor and Corporation for a jolly good dinner and the best beer he'd ever tasted." He stopped there and said: "Bill, hand me up that beer again." Bill said there was no more! A pledge had been given by the Mayor that they should have only two bottles of beer each. But this episode was too much for the Mayor, and instantly in came beer by the dozen, and my beloved friend, the Captain of the Maintop, had another glass. This is how he went on (and it was a very eloquent speech in my opinion. I remember every word of it to this day) He said: "This is joy," and he looked round the galleries crowded with the lovely ladies, and said: "Here we are, British Sailors entirely surrounded by females!!" They waved their handkerchiefs and kissed their hands, and that urged the Captain of the Maintop into a fresh flight of eloquence. "Now," he said, "Shipmates, what was it like now coming into this 'ere harbour of Liverpool" (we had come in under sail); "why," he said, "this is what it was like, sailing into a haven of joy before a gale of pleasure." I then told him to shut up, because he would spoil it by anything more, and Abraham Johnson, Chief Gunner's Mate, my First Lieutenant, gave him more beer! and so we returned.

Abraham Johnson was a wonder! When the Admiral inspected the "Warrior," Abraham Johnson came to me and said he knew his Admiral, and would I let him have a free hand? I said: "All right!" When the ship was prepared for battle, the Admiral suddenly said: "I'll go down in the Magazine," and began going down the steps of the Magazine with his sword on! Abraham was just underneath down below, and called up to the Admiral: "Beg pardon, Sir! you can't come down here!" "D—n the fellow! what does he mean?" Abraham reiterated: "You can't come down here." The Admiral said: "Why not?" "Because no iron instrument is allowed in the Magazine," said Abraham. "Ah!" said the Admiral, unbuckling his sword, "that fellow knows his duty. This is a properly organised ship!"

It is seldom appreciated—it certainly was not then appreciated on board the "Warrior" when I was her Gunnery Lieutenant—that this, our first armour-clad ship-of-war, the "Warrior," would cause a fundamental change in what had been in vogue for something like a thousand years! For the Navy that had been founded by Alfred the Great had lasted till then without any fundamental change till came this first Ironclad Battleship. There is absolutely nothing in common between the fleets of Nelson and the Jutland Battle! Sails have given way to steam. Oak to steel. Lofty four-decked ships with 144 guns like the "Santissima Trinidad," to low-lying hulls like that of the first "Dreadnought." Guns of one hundred tons instead of one ton! And Torpedoes, Mines, Submarines, Aircraft. And then even coal being obsolete! And, unlike Nelson's day, no human valour can now compensate for mechanical inferiority.

I rescue these few words by a survivor of the German Battle Cruiser "Blücher," sunk on January 24th, 1915, by the British Battle Cruisers "Lion" and "Tiger." The German Officer says:

"The British ships started to fire at us at 15 kilometres distant" (as a matter of fact it was about 11 to 12 miles). "The deadly water spouts came nearer and nearer! The men on deck watched them with a strange fascination!

"Soon one pitched close to the ship, and a vast watery billow, a hundred yards high, fell lashing on the deck!

"The range had been found!

"The shells came thick and fast. The electric plant was destroyed, and the ship plunged into a darkness that could be felt! You could not see your hand before your nose! Below decks were horror and confusion, mingled with gasping shouts and moans! At first the shells came dropping from the sky, and they bored their way even to the stokeholds!

"The coal in the bunkers was set on fire, and as the bunkers were half empty the fire burnt fiercely. In the engine-room a shell licked up the oil and sprayed it around in flames of blue and green, scarring its victims and blazing where it fell. Men huddled together in dark compartments, but the shells sought them out, and there Death had a rich harvest."

I forgot to say we had a surprise visit from Garibaldi on board the "Warrior"—Garibaldi, then at the zenith of his glory. The whole crew marched past him singing the Garibaldi Hymn. He was greatly affected. It was very fine indeed; for we had a picked stalwart crew, and their sword bayonets glistening in the sun, and in their white hats and gaiters they looked, as they were, real fighting men! And then, in a moment, they stripped themselves of their accoutrements and swarmed up aloft and spread every sail on the ship, including studding sails, in a few minutes. It was a dead calm, and so was feasible.

From the "Warrior" I went to the gunnery school ship, the "Excellent"; and it was during these years that some of my "manias" began to display themselves, the result being that three times I lost my promotion through them.

It had fortuned that in 1868, when starting the Science of Under-Water Warfare as applied to the Ocean, I met a humble-minded armourer whose name was Isaac Tall, and for many years we worked together. He devised, amongst other inventions, an electrically-steered steam vessel that could tow barges laden with 500 lb. mines which were dropped automatically at such a distance apart as absolutely to destroy all hostile mines in a sufficient area to give a passage for Battleships. Small buoys were automatically dropped as the countermines were dropped to mark the cleared passage. That invention, simplicity itself, still holds the field for clearing a passage, say, into the Baltic. Not one single man was on board the steam vessel of the Barges carrying the counter mines.

Before leaving the Admiralty, in January, 1910, I introduced the use of Trawlers, and we employed them in experimental trials, clearing away hostile mines. Our mines in those days were very inferior to the Hertz German Mine, which really remains still the efficient German Mine we have to contend with. In 1868 I took out a provisional patent for a Sympathetic Exploder, and, strange to say, it is now coming into play in a peculiar form as a most effective weapon for our use.

I have remarked elsewhere how the First Lord of that date did not believe in mines or torpedoes, and I left for China as Commander of the China flagship.

Archbishop Magee, that wonderful Prelate who asked some layman to interpret his feelings when the footman spilt the onion sauce over him, said of "Exaggerations" that they were needful! He said you wanted a big brush to produce scenic effects! A camel's-hair brush was, no doubt, the inestimable weapon of Memling in those masterpieces of his minute detail that were at Bruges when I was a young Post Captain, and that so entranced me there. Ah! that wonderful Madame Polsonare where we lodged! How she did so well care for us! The peas I used to watch her shelling! The three repositories:

First—the old ones to be stewed.

Second—those for the Polsonare Family.

Thirdly—the youngest and sweetest of the peas for us—her lodgers!

And how most delicious they were! And how delightful was old "Papa" Polsonare! and the daughters so plump and opulent in their charm!

And their only son the "brave Belge!" He was a soldier! What has become of them now? They cared for us as their very own, and charged us the very minimum for our board and lodging! And having nothing but my pay then I was grateful! And the Kindergarten so delightful! The little children all tied together by a rope when they went out walking. Pamela was my youngest daughter. "The last straw" was her nickname! And it was written up over the mantelpiece that it was "défendu" to kiss Pamela! She was about three years old, I think, and went to school with a bun and her books strapped to her back, and when the Burgomaster gave away the prizes she was put on a Throne to hand them out (dressed as a Ballet Dancer!). But alas! when the moment came she was found to be fast asleep!

I am always so surprised that so little notice is taken of Satan's dramatic appearance before the Almighty with reference to the Patriarch Job. It's so seldom that Satan in person comes before us. He usually uses someone else, and in this case of Job it's quite the most subtle innuendo I ever came across! It so accentuates what occurs in common life!

"*Doth Job fear God for nought?*" Well may one be thankful and prayerful when prosperity is showered on one! Can you be so in adversity and affliction— undeserved and unexplainable? However, Job got through all right! But Prayer is as much misunderstood as Charity. A splendid Parson in Norfolk replied to his congregation who asked him to pray for rain that really it was useless while the wind was east! Also it appears to me that one farmer, wanting rain for his turnips, doesn't have any feeling for the other man who is against rain because of carrying his crop of something else. Indeed the pith and marrow of prayer is that it must be absolutely unselfish, and so Dr. Chalmers accordingly acutely said the finest prayer he knew was: "Almighty God, the Fountain of all Wisdom, who knowest our necessities," etc. (*see* Collects at end of Communion Service).

Coming home from the China Station in 1872, I was Commander of the old Battleship "Ocean." She was an old wooden Line of Battleship that had armour bolted on her sides. When we got into heavy weather, the timbers of the ship would open when she heeled over one way, and shut together when she heeled the other, and squirted the water inboard! And always we had many fountains playing in the bottom of the ship from leaks, some quite high. At Singapore the Chaplain left us; he couldn't face it, as we were going home round the Cape of Good Hope at the stormy season. So I did chaplain! When we put into Zanzibar on the East Coast of Africa, I heard there was a sick Bishop ashore from Central Africa who had been carried down on a shutter with fever. I went to see him, to ask whether he could take on next day, Sunday, and give the crew a change! He turned out to be a splendid specimen, and had given up a fat living in Lincolnshire to be a Missionary. I found him eating boiled rice and a hard boiled egg on a broken plate—we gave him a good feed when he came on board—but I am telling the story because his Sermon was on Prayer. He gave us no text, but began by saying he had been wondering for the last half-hour what on earth that thing was overhead between the beams on the main deck where we were assembled! Of course we knew it was one of the long pump handles for pumping the ship out with the chain pumps (a thing of past ages)—all the crew had to take continually to the pumps, she was leaking so badly—and "There!" he said, "I'm a Bishop, and instead of saying my prayers I've been letting my thoughts wander," and he gave us a beautiful extempore sermon on wandering thoughts on Prayer that hit everyone in the eye!

I believe he died there in Central Africa, a polished English gentleman, with refined tastes and delighting in the delicacies of a cultured life! A missionary had come preaching at his Country Church and had made him ashamed of his life of ease, so he told me!

We got into a fierce gale off the Cape, and I began to envy the Chaplain we had left behind at Singapore, especially when the Captain said he thought there was nothing for it but for me, the Commander, to go aloft about the close reefed fore topsail as the men would follow no one of lower rank. My monkey jacket was literally "blown into ribbons!" I had heard the expression before, but never had realised it could be exact!

Sir Thomas Troubridge foundered with all hands in the exact place in an old two-decker—I think it was the "Blenheim." He was Nelson's favourite, and got ashore in the "Culloden" at the Nile; but that's another story as Mr. Kipling says!

How I became Captain of the "Inflexible"

The "Inflexible" in 1882 was a wonder. She had the thickest armour, the biggest guns, and the largest of everything beyond any ship in the world. A man could crawl up inside the bore of one of her guns. Controversy had raged round her. The greatest Naval Architects of the time quarrelled with each other. Endless inventions were on board her, accumulated there by cranks in the long years she took building. A German put a new type of gas into the engine room, which was lovely, and no smell, so bright, so simple! But when it chanced to escape from a leaky joint, it descended and did not rise, so it got into all the double bottoms and nearly polished off a goodly number of the crew. There were whistles in my cabin that yelled when the boiler was going to burst, or the ship was not properly steered, and so on. So to be Captain of the "Inflexible" was much sought after. As each name was discussed by the Board of Admiralty it got "butted," that is to say, it would be remarked: "Yes, he's a splendid officer and quite fit for it, but——" and then some reason was adduced why he should not be selected (he had murdered his father, or he had kissed the wrong girl!). Lord Northbrook, who was First Lord, got sick of these interminable discussions as to who should be Captain of the "Inflexible," so he unexpectedly said one morning: "Do any of you know a young Captain called Fisher?" And they all—having no notion of what was in Lord Northbrook's mind, and I being well known to each of them—had no "buts"! So he got up and said: "Well, that settles it. I'll appoint him Captain of the "Inflexible." I was about the Junior Captain in the biggest ship!

However, the "Inflexible" brought me to death's door, as I was suddenly struck down by dysentery when ashore in charge of Alexandria after the bombardment. I had arranged an armoured train, with which we used to reconnoitre the enemy, who were in great strength and only a few miles off. The Officer who took my place in the armoured train the day after I was disabled by dysentery was knocked over by one of the enemy shells, and so it was telegraphed home that I was killed, and Queen Victoria telegraphed back for details, and very interesting leading articles appeared as to what I might have been had I lived. Lord Northbrook telegraphed for me to be sent home immediately, kindly adding that the Admiralty could build another "Inflexible" but not another Fisher.

As I was being carried on board, in a brief moment's consciousness I heard the Doctor say: "He'll never reach Gibraltar!" and then and there I determined I would live. When I got home, Lord Northbrook appointed me Head of the Gunnery School of the Navy. Queen Victoria asked me to stay at Osborne, and did so every year till she died; and this in spite of the fact that she hated the Admiralty, and didn't much care for the Navy.

I kept on being ill from the effects of the dysentery for a long time, but Lord Northbrook never let go my hand. When all the doctors failed to cure me, I accidentally came across a lovely partner I used to waltz with, who begged me to go to Marienbad, in Bohemia. I did so, and in three weeks I was in robust health. It was the Pool of Bethesda, and this waltzing angel put me into it, for it really was a miracle, and I never again had a recurrence of my illness.

CHAPTER XI
NELSON

LORD ROSEBERY may have forgotten it, but in one of our perigrinations round and round Berkeley Square (I lived next door to him) he made a remark to me which made a deep and ineffaceable impression on me—that he felt sure one of the great reasons of Nelson being so in the hearts of his countrymen was the conviction that he had been slighted by Authority and even so after his death. Unquestionably his brother Admirals were envious. He was kept kicking his heels at Merton on half pay in momentous times, and so poor as to necessitate his getting advances from his Banker. He was cavalierly treated when he was told to haul down his flag and come home after the Battle of the Nile. I know all about the Queen of Naples and Lady Hamilton; but what was that in comparison with his astounding genius for war and his hold on the Fleet? And I want to draw attention to this delightful trait in his glorious character. Supposing (what I don't admit) that there was any irregularity in his attachment to Lady Hamilton, he never disguised his feeling for her, or his gratitude to her for all she did for his grievously wounded and frail body after the Nile and her splendid conduct in getting his Fleet revictualled and stored by the Neapolitans through her influence with the King and Queen, when all the Authorities were against it. He used to ask his Captains to drink her health, and said (in my opinion quite truly), that if there were more Emmas there would be more Nelsons.

Then look at the Battle of the Nile! It was an incomparable battle—but it only made Nelson into a Common or Garden Lord; when the Battle of Cape St. Vincent, which was practically won by Nelson, made Sir John Jervis into an Earl. History is so written that no end of literary gentlemen will endeavour to confute all I am saying by extracts (or, as they will call them, facts) from Contemporary Documents and Newspapers. Well now, to-day, read the *Morning Post* and *Daily News* on the same incident! (For myself I prefer the *Daily News*.) Again, Nelson died poor. That appeals. What Prize Money might he not have accumulated, had he chased dollars as he chased the enemy! Then with his dying breath, mortally wounded in the hour of the greatest of sea victories, he asks his country to provide for his friend as he could do nothing for her himself; and, whatever may have been her faults, she had nursed and tended him, not only when sorely wounded after the Nile, but afterwards when his frail body was almost continuously racked with pain. She died in penury and found a pauper's grave in a foreign land. A passing Englishman paid her funeral expenses. It makes one rise up and say "Damn!"

That vivid immortal spirit, whose life was his country's, who never flogged a man; whose heart was tender and "worn on his sleeve for daws to peck at," has to suffer even now for miscreants who published his letters to this friend of his that only her eye was meant to see. Also, Prudes nowadays forget how very different was the standard of morals at that time. Does not history tell us that Dukes were the honoured results of illicit relationships? And we don't think any the worse of Abraham because he was the husband of more than one wife. But let that pass. I heard yesterday that a distinguished Bishop said he loved my sentiments but not my words. But fancy! Nelson left on half-pay in War! It's unbelievable, but yet it so happened. It was envy; and he was no sycophant, so he couldn't be a courtier. It was so with him as with our great Exemplar: "The Common People heard him gladly." And what a "Send-off" it was on Southsea beach at Portsmouth when he embarked for Trafalgar! What a scene it was, with these Common People surging round him—none else were there, and neither the King nor the Admiralty sent a dummy, as is customary, to represent them. But isn't it always the way? General Booth and Doctor Barnardo weren't buried in Westminster Abbey; but they had a more glorious funeral—millions of the "Common People" followed them to their graves, unmarshalled and unsolicited. Give me the Common People, and a fig for your State ceremonial!

1904. AGED 63. ADMIRAL.

Commander-in-Chief at Portsmouth.

Perhaps in this cursory view of Nelson one may be permitted to seize on what appears to me the central incident of his life, which so peculiarly illustrates his extraordinary genius for War. His audacity! His imagination! His considered rashness! I think myself the Battle of the Nile is that incident—for this reason: that it has been recorded in writing what actually occurred to Lord Nelson and to the French Admiral at the very same instant of time—each having at his side the very same officer in each Fleet. It was sunset. Nelson was walking the deck with the Navigating Officer of the Fleet—the "Master of the Fleet" was his technical title. The look-out man at the mast-head reports seeing on the horizon the mast-heads of a mass of ships at anchor—it was the French Fleet in Aboukir Bay. Nelson instantly stops in his walk and orders the signal to the Fleet to make all possible sail and steer for the enemy. He is remonstrated with, both by his own officers on board and by his favourite Captain of the Fleet at going in to fight the French Fleet without any charts. If he waited till the sun rose, they would be able to see from aloft the shoal water and so steer with safety alongside the enemy. Nelson answers his favourite Captain that if that Captain's ship does get on shore, as he fears, then she'll be a buoy to show him where anyhow one shoal is. Troubridge *did* get on shore, and he *was* a buoy. Nelson went in. The French Admiral blew up at midnight in his flagship the "Orient" and Casabianca, his Captain, and his son are the theme of a great poem: "The boy stood on the burning deck."

The French Admiral was walking up and down the deck with *his* Master of the Fleet, when *his* look-out man at the mast-head reported on the horizon the topmast sails of a number of ships. The French Admiral stopped in his walk as abruptly as Nelson and at the very same instant that Nelson stopped in his walk; but he said "It's the English Fleet, but they won't come in to-night. They have no charts!" So he did not recall his men from the shore—and in the result his fleet was destroyed, and the one or two ships that did escape under Admiral Dumanoir were captured. And Napoleon wrote, "But for Nelson at the Nile I would have been Conqueror of the World"—or words to that effect. And yet Nelson was only made a common or garden Lord for this great battle, and spent two years on the Continent kicking his heels about to pass the time before returning to England. Imagine! he wasn't wanted! I think Lord Rosebery was right—Nelson being slighted has led to his greater appreciation.

Again—even a greater slight, a slight he feels more—when he looks down from his monument in Trafalgar Square, does he see anywhere those splendid Captains of his? But let alone those Captains of his—does he see anywhere a single Admiral? *Not one.* And yet who made England what she is? Those splendid Sea Heroes are in very deed "*England's forgotten worthies*"! Yes!

Nelson looks down from his isolated column, and looks in vain for Hawke, Dundonald, Howe, Hood, Rodney, Cornwallis, Benbow, "*and a great multitude which no man can number*"—all Seamen of Deathless Fame, fighting single frigate actions, cutting out the enemy's ships from under the guns of forts, sending in fire ships and burning the enemy's vessels thought to be safe in harbour under the guns of their forts—Doers of Imperishable Deeds![13] Death found them fighting. We have heaps of statues to everybody else. Indeed such a lot of them that they reach down as far off as Knightsbridge. But who knows about Quiberon—one of the greatest of sea fights? And if you mention Hawke, your friend probably thinks only of his worthy descendant—the cricketer.

An old woman eating a penny bun asked a friend of mine called Buggins, when she was passing through Trafalgar Square, "*What are them lions a-guarding of?*" Buggins told her that her penny bun would have cost her threepence if it hadn't been for the man them lions were a-guarding of.

When I see the Duke of York's Column still allowed to rear its futile head, and scores of other fifth-rate nonentities glorified by statues, I thank God I'm a sailor—we don't want to be in that galley!

I began my sea life with the last of Nelson's Captains, through Nelson's own niece; and I fitly, I think, among my last words may ask the Nation to do justice to Nelson's Trade! This country owes all she has to the sea, it was the sea that won the late war, and if we'd stuck to the sea we should not now be thinking of bankruptcy and some of us imagining Carthage! We were led away by Militarist folly to be a conscript Nation and it will take us all we know to recover from it. We shall recover, *for England never succumbs!*

———————————————————

CHAPTER XII
LETTERS TO LORD ESHER

LORD ESHER has kindly sent me three bulky volumes of letters I wrote him from 1903 onwards—I have others also. Many of them are unquotable, so blasting are they in their truth to existing reputations. It's not my business to blast reputations—so the real gems are missing.

Somebody felt in 1903 that the War Office was wrong, and so a Committee was set up with Lord Esher as President, Sir George Clarke and myself the other two members; and that very able and not sufficiently recognised man, now General Sir C. Ellison, was Secretary. How I got there is still a mystery; but it was a great enjoyment as Generals came to stay with me at Admiralty House, Portsmouth—I was the Port Admiral. I always explained to them I was Lord Esher's facile dupe and Sir George Clarke's servile copyist, and thereby avoided odium personally (I was getting all the odium I wanted from the Admirals!).

As usual, when we reported, the Government didn't appreciate those inestimable words *"Totus Porcus"* (No Government—anyhow no English Government—ever yet went "the whole hog"—"Compromise" is the British God!).14

1903 [*Sir John Fisher, Commander-in-Chief at Portsmouth*].

... My humble idea is that *"men are everything and material nothing"* whether it's working the War Office or fighting a fleet! So some day I am going to try and entice you to read my lectures to the Officers of the Mediterranean Fleet because the spirit intended to be diffused by them is what I think is the one great want in the British Army, and without it 50,000 Lord Eshers would be no good in producing "Angel Gabriel" organisations! The Military system is rotten to the very core! You want to begin *ab ovo*! The best of the Generals are even worse than the subalterns because they are more hardened sinners! I fear I shocked Ellison, but he is simply first class and I most heartily congratulate you on your selection.... I really begin to feel I never ought to have joined you as I have some very big jobs on now which require incessant personal attention and this must be my excuse for not coming up to see Girouard this week. I have the new Civil Lord staying with me and I have got to prevent him joining with a lot of asses at the Admiralty, who want to throw half a million of money in the gutter.

*   *   *   *   *

Nov. 19th, 1903.

On my return I found the first proofs of your three papers. I have studied them with close care and interest. There are some points of detail which puzzle me, but it seems you are absolutely convincing on the main lines. What I venture to emphasise is this:—We cannot reform the Army Administration until it is laid down what it is the Administration is going to Administer! For instance, the Citizen Army for Home Defence! Are we going to have it? If so, then you will certainly want a Member of the Board or Council to superintend it! Again, I say, the *Regular Army* (as distinguished from the Home Army and the *Indian Army*) should be regarded as a projectile to be fired by the Navy! The Navy embarks it and lands it where it can do most mischief!—Thus, the Germans are ready to land a large Military Force on the Cotentin Peninsula in case of War with France and my German Military Colleague at the Hague Conference told me this comparatively small Military Force would have the effect of demobilising half a million of men who would thus be taken away from the German Frontier—they never know where the devil the brutes are going to land! Consequently instead of our Military Manœuvres being on Salisbury Plain and its vicinity (ineffectually aping the vast Continental Armies!) we should be employing ourselves in joint Naval and Military Manœuvres embarking 50,000 men at Portsmouth and landing them at Milford Haven or Bantry Bay!—This would make the Foreigners sit up! Fancy! in the Mediterranean Fleet we disembarked 12,000 men with guns in *19 minutes*! What do you think of that! and we should hurry up the soldiers! No doubt there would be good-natured chaff! Once we embarked 7,000 soldiers at Malta and took them round and landed them elsewhere for practice, and I remember having a complaint that the Bluejackets said "Come on, you bloody lobsters! Wake up!" However all the above *en passant*. I expect the Prime Minister must have pretty good ideas now crystallised as to how the Army should be constituted—let us ask him for this at once—if he hasn't got it, let us tell him we must have it, because as I said at starting, you can't organise an administration without clearly knowing what you are going to administer. This is a hasty bit of writing but not a hasty thought.

*   *   *   *   *

1903.
Nov. 25th.

I send you two books—a more portly volume I hesitate to send!—Also I fear without some verbal explanation you may not see the application to Military matters of these purely Naval Notes, but they do apply in the spirit if not in the letter! For instance I had an overwhelming confidence that every Officer and man in the Mediterranean Fleet had also an overwhelming confidence that we thoroughly knew all we had to do in case of war in every conceivable eventuality! Well! that is the confidence you also want in an Army! Have you got it!

*   *   *   *   *

Dec. 2nd.

Here is a letter just come from Prince Louis of Battenberg illustrating what I was saying to you this morning as to a Member of the Board of Admiralty however junior in rank being accepted as a superior controlling authority by all in rank above him. An Officer actually at the moment serving under Prince Louis in the Admiralty itself being put over Prince Louis in the Admiralty itself, and sending for him and giving him orders! I don't know that it would be possible to have a stronger case to quote when by and by we have to defend or rather have to lay down and define the status of the Members of the New War Office Board. Inglefield, the new Naval Lord, being a Junior Captain, will be sending for *Admiral* Boys, Director of Transports, who is specially under him and who I rather think entered the service before Inglefield was born.

*   *   *   *   *

Dec. 4th.

... You are right about the Submarines!

"We strain at the gnat of perfection and swallow the camel of unreadiness," and that permeates every branch of Naval and Military Administration, forgetting the homely proverb that "half a loaf is better than no bread!" but please God! *"the dauntless three"* [Sir Geo. Clarke, Lord Esher and Sir John Fisher] (as I see we are now called) will change all that! "We'll stagger humanity" as old Kruger said!

*   *   *   *   *

Dec. 7th.

Arnold-Forster [Secretary for War] has been here three days and he is most cordially with us. I wish you had been here with him. He places implicit trust in us. He has shown me an outline of an excellent memorandum proposing an immediate reduction of 300,000 men and he will let me have a copy as soon as printed, also a memorandum of his difficulties in the War Office.... This is another proof of the value of the advice of my Military Nicodemus (he is one of the Sanhedrin!) that there must be an active "clear-out" of the present military gang, root and branch, lock, stock, and gunbarrel! Sir John French and General Smith-Dorrien (lately Adjutant-General in India) are names I have suggested to Arnold-Forster as members of his new Board.

∗   ∗   ∗   ∗   ∗

Dec. 11th.

... Don't forget your phrase *"the biennial fortnightly picnic"! it's splendid!* That will fetch the mothers of families and reconcile them to the Swiss system! I hope you won't lose any time in talking to the Prime Minister and showing him the immense advantages that will accrue from his turning over further matters to us instead of dear Arnold-Forster "raising Cain" as he surely will do! It would be so easy to associate Sir John French, Hildyard and Smith-Dorrien (very curious that all these three Generals were first in the Navy and got their early education there) with us for the further matters.

∗   ∗   ∗   ∗   ∗

Dec. 17th.

Another Military Nicodemus came to see me yesterday. I had never met him before! He occupies a high official position. He highly approved of you and me, "but he had never heard of the third member of the Committee. What a pity they had not put a soldier on the Committee!" (How these Christians hate one another!) But the point of his remarks was the present system of Army Promotions, which he said was as iniquitous and baleful in its influence as could be possibly conceived, and then he illustrated by cases of certain officers made Generals. My only object in writing this to you is Selborne having spoken of the Admiralty method where the first Lord has the Naval Members of the Board in consultation, but he and his Private Secretary (who is always a Naval Officer of note) have the real responsibility.

∗   ∗   ∗   ∗   ∗

Dec. 20th.

—— is and always has been drastic in his ideas of military reform, and I cordially agree with him and Stead agrees with me that the British Public loves a root and branch reform. One remnant left of the old gang or the organisations and you taint the whole new scheme!

Don't fear about Arnold-Forster. He will come with us all right—you are absolutely sound on the Patronage question, but I would have the soldiers precisely on the same footing as Tyrwhitt at the Admiralty [Private Secretary. He was my Flag Captain] for detailed reasons I will give you when we meet. It is an ideal arrangement (the Private Secretary at Admiralty). He has the power, he pulls the strings, he has no position, he causes no jealousy, he talks to all the Lords as their servant, and he manipulates them all and oils the machine for his special master, the First Lord, to perpetrate a job when necessary! Make him a big-wig like an Official Military Secretary, and all this goes—he becomes too big for his boots!

*　　*　　*　　*　　*

Dec. 21st.

... I've been bombarded by Stead. I tried to boom him off but the scoundrel said if I didn't see him, he would have to invent! I pointed out to him my *métier* was that of the mole! Trace me by upheavals! When you see the Admirals rise it's that d—d fellow Jack Fisher taking the rise out of them! So I implored Stead to keep me out of the *Magazine Rifle* [this was my name for *The Review of Reviews*] or he will interfere with my professional career of crime. So please use your influence with him in the same direction. You and Clarke are the two legitimate members of the Committee to be trotted out, as you are both so well known. No sailor is ever known. The King was awfully good about this. He said "Sailors went all round the world but never went in it"! Stead is a very keen observer, as you know. He said our Committee could do anything, and that neither the Press nor Parliament nor the Public would tolerate any Military opposition to us because the whole Military hierarchy was utterly discredited from top to bottom; but he doubted *The Times—I don't*. Further he expressed his firm belief there would be a change of Government possibly at Easter but certainly soon—if so we ought on that ground alone to "dig out" with our Report.

*　　*　　*　　*　　*

1903.
(No date.)

Knollys was very much impressed by the possibilities of the Submarine when he was down here. He saw them to better advantage than you did as it was blowing half a gale of wind with a good sea on when he saw the evolutionising! and it was very striking. I am working subterraneously about the Submarines and there are already "upheavals" in consequence.

*　　*　　*　　*　　*

1904.
Jan. 5th.

... I yesterday sent all my plans to French for embarking the whole of his First Army Corps on Monday, June 27th (Full Moon) at Portsmouth, and he is coming here with his Chief Staff Officer, Sir F. Stopford, next week, and we'll land him like Hoche's Army in Bantry Bay! [Sir John French commanded at Aldershot. *The War Office stopped this.*]

*　　*　　*　　*　　*

1904.
Jan. 17th.

... For the reason I have given you at length in another letter I am convinced that French should be 1st Military Member and under him there should be 3 *Directors* (not Hieroglyphics such as A.Q.M.G., D.A.Q.M.G., A.Q.M.G. 2, etc., etc.).

Sir   F.   Stopford—Director   of   Intelligence   and   Mobilisation.
Gen.   Grierson—Director   of   Training.
Gen. Maxwell—Director of Home Defence.

Also I still maintain that Smith-Dorrien and Plumer should be the 2nd and 3rd Military Members, and perhaps one young distinguished Indian Officer as 4th Military Lord. Haig, Inspector-General of Cavalry in India, should be brought home as the principal Director under *2nd Military Lord*. We must have youth and enthusiasm, because it is only by the agency of young and enthusiastic believers in the immense revolution which must be carried out, that our scheme can bear fruit. The first thing of all is that every one of the "old gang" must be cleared out! "lock, stock, and gunbarrel, bob and sinker!" The next is that every one of the new men *must be successful men*, and must be young and enthusiastic and cordial supporters of the new policy—over every fellow's door at the War Office under the new régime has got to be written in large letters:—

"No looking back. Remember Lot's wife!"

*   *   *   *   *

1904.
(No date.)

The next pressing and important matter we have to deal with is *to get the right men as Members of the new Army Council.* Either you or Clarke have made a splendid observation that a rotten system may be run effectively by good men but duffers would spoil the work of the Angel Gabriel!... *If we don't get in men who will enthusiastically adopt our scheme and work with us,* LET US THROW UP AT ONCE! as we shall only have an awful fiasco and I (for one) don't want to go down with my grey hairs to the grave sorrowing and discredited! Therefore I suggest to you that we should agree on our men and *run them at once!* Like fighting the French Fleet! it's half the battle gained to take the offensive, propose our men, give their advantages and ask them (our enemies) what they have to say against them and suggest every beastly thing we can against any likely competitors—Selection by Disparagement! I put forward names in enclosed paper simply as a basis.

1st Military Member—*Sir John French*, because he never failed in Africa (the grave of Military Reputations). He is *young* and *energetic*, has commanded the 1st Army Corps so far with conspicuous success and has the *splendid gift* of choosing the right men to work with him (*vide* his Staff in S. Africa, the best Staff out there) and as 1st Military Lord it would be his special function to prepare the Army in the Field for fighting, and who therefore better to command it when war breaks out, as his functions then at the War Office would disappear and be transferred to the Commander-in-Chief at the seat of war—Further, he is an enthusiastic and out-and-out believer in joint Naval and Military operations as the proper species of manœuvres for this Nation. In this belief he is almost solitary amongst all the Generals, who all want to play at the German Army. *"Plump for French and Efficiency!" Any vote given against French is a vote given for Kelly-Kenny instead!*

2nd Military Member.—SMITH-DORRIEN. Has been with great success in every campaign for the last 20 years, has been *Adjutant-General* in India (a much bigger billet than *Adjutant-General* in London!). He is *young and energetic* and is an extremely conciliatory and accomplished gentleman and would work the personnel of the Army (which would be his chief function as the Second Military Member) far better than some "safe" old man because he is in touch with the young generation. He took a Marine Officer of the Mediterranean Fleet as his A.D.C. when appointed a Brigadier in South Africa, because he considered him the ablest young officer in the Malta Garrison! Utterly shocking all the Military Mandarins. *"Vote for Smith-Dorrien and Progress!"*

"Every vote given against Smith-Dorrien is a vote for ——" [*A lady who then "ran" the War Office!*]

3rd Military Member. Supplies and Transport.—*General Plumer.* The only man besides French that *never failed in anything he undertook in Africa!* They say he has "the luck of the Devil," but the fact is that "the luck of the Devil" is wholly attributable to a minute attention to anything that will ensure the success of his (Satanic Majesty's) designs, and he leaves nothing to chance! Such is Plumer! He also is young, energetic and enthusiastic.

"Vote for Plumer and a full belly!"

"Every vote given against Plumer is a vote given for paper boots and no ammunition!"

4th Military Member—*General F. G. Slade*, now Inspector General of Garrison Artillery—has served in six campaigns and always come out top: has been in the Horse, Field and Garrison Artillery and commanded at Gibraltar. He is *young and energetic and enthusiastic* and will blow the trumpet of the Board (*as well as his own!*).

"Vote for Slade and hitting the Target!"

"Every vote given against Slade will be a vote given in favour of some d—d old woman."...

*   *   *   *   *

1904.
Jan. 31st.

Post Office Telegraphs. Government Despatch No.... "Await Arrival."

Lord Esher Windsor Castle.

In reply to your telegram just received our committee manœuvres commenced at Portsmouth on December 30 beating Moses by nine days as he took 40 days before he got down from the Mount with his report but if you refer to submarine manœuvres I have last night put them off to February twenty third to last three weeks from that date stop I see we are accused of not giving credit to the good motives that have always actuated the War Office stop Why is the War Office like hell answer because it is paved with good intentions Sir John Fisher Portsmouth.

[Not bad for an official telegram!]

*   *   *   *   *

1904.
Feb. 1st.

... I really think it is of extreme importance that you should be on the spot daily just now as without doubt "wire-pulling" of the "Eve" order will be going on. When the other day I met those three ladies on the back stairs of the War Office all in picture hats and smelling of White Rose or some other beastly thing, I thought to myself "How about Capua?" for really they were very nice looking indeed. You know the story about them having the entrée to the War Office!

*   *   *   *   *

1904.
Feb. 28th.

Best of Chairmen! Snatch a moment to look through enclosed ... as I am dead gone on starting the idea of a general list of officers, and general uniform and early entry and they will all go to sea, but I don't want to mention that yet awhile; it will come of itself when ⅗ths of every man-of-war's crew are soldiers; that's not many years hence and will bring the income tax down to 3 pence in the pound! Mark my words! this will come, but it's no use giving people premature shocks, so let me keep it quiet now. My idea is to acclimatise the chosen few to it first of all and then gradually spread it about, and when Kitchener comes home he will see it through. (He shares my view, I know.)

∗   ∗   ∗   ∗   ∗

1904.
(?) March.

... Campbell-Bannerman told me last night he intended to make a special point of the Secretary of State's responsibility and power being unduly lessened, and he would not admit that the new order of things makes him the same as the First Lord of the Admiralty!... To avoid the slightest misconception that may arise as to the lessening of the parliamentary responsibility of the Secretary of State for War by the formation of the Army Council or of his supreme authority as the Cabinet Minister responsible for the Army, it's only necessary to reiterate and emphasise the statement that he is absolutely in the same position as the First Lord of the Admiralty, the patent constituting the Army Council being absolutely similar to the Admiralty Patent and no question has ever been raised nor is there any doubt whatever of the reform and present responsibility of the First Lord of the Admiralty as the Cabinet Minister responsible for the Navy.

∗   ∗   ∗   ∗   ∗

1904.
March 10th.

Just back from the English Channel with the Submarines and am very enthusiastic!... We really must arrange to get the British Army to Sea somehow or other! Yesterday all the mice died in their cages and two of the crew fainted, but the young Lieutenant of the Submarine didn't seem to care a d—n whether they all died so long as he bagged the Battleship he was after, and he practically got her and then he came up in his Submarine to breathe! Depend on it we shall have more "Niles" and "Trafalgars" so long as we continue to propagate such "young bloods" as this! But see how splendid if we could shove the same "ginger" into the young Military aspirants, and they all came from the same schools! but the whole secret is to catch them very young and mould them while they are then so plastic and receptive to be just what you want them. Another submarine had an explosion which made the interior "*Hell*" for some seconds (as the Submarine was bottled up and diving to evade a Destroyer who had caught her with a hook) but the Submarine Lieutenant saw them all d—d first before he would rise up and be caught. Another young fire-eater had his periscope smashed but bagged a battleship nevertheless by coming up stealthily to blow just like a beaver, and look round. *It really is all lovely!* but what I am writing about is—*you must embark an Army Corps every year and give them sea training.*

["THE ARMY AND NAVY CO-OPERATIVE SOCIETY."

I must here interpose a few words to explain that I had submitted an elaborate method of increasing the military efficiency of officers—first by very early entry as in the Navy—having free or State education for them—hence "Equal opportunity for all": Officers' pay of all ranks to be sufficient for them to live on—and the regimental system abolished—and the same system as in the Navy by which military officers would serve in all arms—Engineers, Artillery, Cavalry and Infantry, instead of being familiar with but one part of their profession. When the Sea Lords sit round the Board of Admiralty they can talk about anything, because they've been in every type of vessel and every branch of their Profession. Again, in a good regiment the promotion is slow because the officers stick to it. In a bad regiment the promotion is rapid because everyone wants to leave it. Then, finally, I submitted the idea of the Army and Navy being incorporated in one great Service. There is no going aloft now—a ship can be manned by soldiers with equal efficiency as by sailors. You want nucleus crews thoroughly used to the ship and always in her, knowing all her foibles. Brains—the Beef needn't be equally clever! The military officers in the Peninsular War only 16 years old were splendid and they were numerous.]

1904.
March 20th. Telegram.

Suggest if Prime Minister takes no immediate action he may be asked that the Committee in self-defence be allowed to make correspondence public as already I am hearing from influential friends that we are discredited by having made exaggerated and unjustifiable statements and that besides the scandalous and disparaging words of the Secretary of State in the House of Commons that the Prime Minister has more or less disavowed us by the tenour of his remarks.... I venture to suggest to you that it is a great mistake for our Committee to be made a catspaw to suit Cabinet susceptibilities or parliamentary wirepulling and that we press for a full and complete publication.

*   *   *   *   *

1904.
May 26th.

... Arnold-Forster spent several hours here with me yesterday and he is coming again to-day discussing his difficulties. I tell him he can't expect his

Council all at once to possess the attributes of the Board of Admiralty (which he so intensely admires) which began in 1619! They want to be educated. The individual Members are far too subservient now and do not realise they are administrative members and *not* Army Officers. They must go about in plain clothes and a tall hat, and order Field Marshals about like schoolboys!...

*   *   *   *   *

1904.
June 17th.

... It would have been simply disastrous to have had an increased Army Vote. Has Clarke ever come to close quarters with you as to his project for getting the Army Estimates down to 23 millions? for that is really the figure which represents the proportionate part of the total sum which I make out to be available for the fighting services, and unless some such figure can be arrived at for the Army, I do not think the British Public will face the reduction in the Navy Estimates *which I see to be possible with the increased efficiency*; because they will rightly argue that the Navy is the 1st, 2nd, 3rd, 4th *ad infinitum* line of defence, and it is simply monstrous therefore that the bloated Army should starve the essential Navy.... It is this Army Vote that absolutely blocks me, because I am perfectly certain it will wreck us unless it can be brought down to some such figure as 23 millions at the outside. That N.-W. Frontier of India is the bug-bear which has possessed the whole lot of our present rulers! and there is no "advocate of the devil" to plead the other side. So I hope you will put that mind of yours to work to make the Prime Minister see his mission to cut down the Army Vote to 23 millions and *then* we can go ahead and get that threepenny income tax we all so long for *and which we can get if we like*!

*   *   *   *   *

1904.

I was with the Prime Minister from 12.30 to 4 p.m. He was most pleasant and delightful but evidently didn't see his way to making the reduction in the Army Vote which is imperative.... He and all the rest appear stupefied by the Indian Frontier Bogey and the 100,000 men wanted. I gave him figures to show the Army had been increased 60,000 odd men in 10 years. If he would reduce them at once he would get nearly threepence off the income tax and get rid of his recruiting difficulties. The Auxiliary Forces 4½ millions— absurd—the Volunteers 2 millions—still more absurd!

*   *   *   *   *

1904.
July 16th.

A.-F.'s scheme rotten! You have hit the nail on the head about expense. He had the remedy in the palm of his hand! He simply had to reduce what the Army had *unnecessarily* increased in 10 years—the 60,000 officers and men—and he got 6 millions sterling (including the accessories) and solved the recruiting question!... 3,700 Royal Engineers put on in 10 years and only ⅓ of them went to the war in S.A.! the rest enjoying themselves in civilian work! and was there ever such ineptitude as trying to make them into railway men, electric engineers and sailors for submarine mines when you have the real thing in abundance in the railway and telegraph workmen of the country and fishermen for any water work? This is only one sample. Every blessed item of the military organisation is similarly rotten! Why? Because the military system of entry and education is rotten.

* * * * *

1904.
July 28th.

... We have a new scheme for a reorganisation of the whole Admiralty and have got the Order in Council for it! *The new scheme gives the First Sea Lord nothing to do*, except think and send for Idlers! It also resuscitates the old titles of *Sea Lords* dating from A.D. 1613, but which some silly ass 100 years ago altered to *Naval Lords.*

* * * * *

1904.
August 17th.

... I have got 60 sheets of foolscap written with all the new Naval proposals and am pretty well prepared for the fray on October 21st.

[Sir John Fisher became First Sea Lord of the Admiralty on October 21st (Trafalgar Day), 1904; and the correspondence is scanty between that date and the autumn of 1907.]

1907.
Sept 12th.

... I really can't understand Mr. Buckle giving —— his head in this way in the columns of *The Times*! but I suppose it "catches on" and makes the flesh creep of the "*old women of both sexes*" (as Lord St. Vincent called the "Invasion lot" in his day!) and his memorable saying so infinitely more true now than then. When asked his opinion of the possibility of an invasion, he replied "that if considered as a purely military operation he was loth to offer an opinion but he certainly could positively state it could never take place by sea!"

*   *   *   *   *

1907.
Oct. 7th. MOLVENO.

... My unalterable conviction is that the Committee of Imperial Defence is tending rapidly to become a sort of Aulic Council and the man who talks glibly, utterly irresponsible, will usurp the functions of the *two* men who *must* be the "Masters of the War"—the First Sea Lord and the Chief of the General Staff. Make no mistake—I don't mean those two men are to be Dictators, but the Government says: "Do so and so!" *These are the two executive Officers*.... In regard to the "Invasion Bogey" about which I am now writing to you, how curious it is that from the German Emperor downwards their hearts were stricken with fear that *we* were going to attack *them*.... Here is an interview between Beit and the German Emperor given me at first hand, immediately on Beit's return from Berlin.

Beit: "Your Majesty is very greatly mistaken in supposing that any feeling exists in England for war with Germany. I know both Mr. Balfour and Sir Henry Campbell-Bannerman are absolutely averse to any such action. I know this of my own personal knowledge."

The Emperor: "Yes, yes, but it doesn't matter whether either of them is Prime Minister or what party is in power. *Fisher remains! that's the vital fact!* I admire Fisher. I say nothing against him. If I were in his place I should do all that he has done (in concentrating the British Navy against Germany) and I should do all that *I know* he has it in his mind to do. Isvolsky, the Russian Minister of Foreign Affairs, holds the same opinion."

And yet Mr. Leo Maxse gibbets Sir John Fisher every month in the *National Review* as a traitor to his country and a panderer to Germany, who "ought to be hung at his own yard arm!"

*   *   *   *   *

1907.
Nov. 28th.

Can you manage to be at my room at Admiralty at 11.30 sharp to-day (Saturday) to see arrangements for swallowing the German Mercantile Marine, and other War Apparatus? [*i.e.* "The Spider's Web"].

*   *   *   *   *

1907.
Dec. 12th.

... I hope the Admiralty memorandum is to your satisfaction—of course it is only the first instalment. What fascinates me is that the Committee as a whole don't seem to take the point that the whole case of Roberts rests on an absolute Naval surprise, which is really a sheer impossibility in view of our organised information.

*   *   *   *   *

1908.
Jan. 1st.

... I had a *tête-à-tête* lunch with Winston Churchill; he unexpectedly came to the Admiralty and I was whirled off with him to the Ritz. I had two hours with him. He is very keen to fight on my behalf and is simply kicking with fury at —— & Co., but I've told him the watchword is "Silence." He is an enthusiastic friend certainly! He told me he would get six men on both sides to join in *con amore*, F. E. Smith, &c., &c. I forget the other names. It was rather sweet: he said his penchant for me was that I painted with a big brush! and was violent!—I reminded him that even "The Kingdom of Heaven suffereth violence, and the violent take it by force"—*vide* yesterday's Second Lesson.

*   *   *   *   *

1908.
Jan. 17th.

Secret.... I rather want to keep clear of Defence Committee till Morocco is settled, as I don't want to disclose my plan of campaign to *anyone*, not even C.-B. himself. The only man who knows is Sir Arthur Wilson, and he's as close as wax! The whole success will depend upon *suddenness and unexpectedness*, and the moment I tell anyone there's an end of both!!! So just please keep me clear of any Conference and personally I would sooner the Defence Committee kept *still*. I'm seeing about the Transports. I started it about 7 weeks ago and got 3 of my best satellites on it.... So you'll think me a villain of the deepest dye!

*   *   *   *   *

1908.
(?) Feb. 9th.

... We want both a *re-distribution* as well as a *re-organisation* of the Army—and the (comparatively) small Regular Army should be based on the system of "Nucleus Crews"—that is to say the *whole body of Officers* are provided and

⅖ths (or the expert) part of the crew, and the other ⅗ths of the Army you get from the outside Army by whatever name you like to call it—National Army, or Citizen Army, or Lord Lieutenant's Army.

*   *   *   *   *

1908.
Feb. 21st.

... *Secret.* Tirpitz asked a mutual civilian friend living in Berlin to enquire very privately of me whether I would agree to limiting size of guns and size of ships, as this is *vital* to the Germans, who *can't* go bigger than the Dreadnought in guns or size. I wrote back by return of post yesterday morning "Tell him I'll see him d—d first!" (*Them's the very words!*) I wonder what Wilhelm will say to that if Tirpitz shows him the letter!

*   *   *   *   *

1908.
APR. 19TH.

... I got a note to say the King wanted to see me this afternoon at 3 p.m. ... *Private.* I got 3 letters from the King at Biarritz, all extremely cordial and communicative and unsought by me. I mention this to prove to you his kindly feelings and support.... When I met the King on arrival he said I was to be sure and see him as he had something serious to say to me. I suppose I was with him more than an hour, and he was as cordial and friendly as ever; and this was the serious thing—"that I was Jekyll and Hyde! *Jekyll* in being successful at my work at the Admiralty—but *Hyde* as a failure in Society! That I talked too freely and was reported to say (which of course is a lie) that the King would see me through anything! That it was bad for me and bad for him as being a Constitutional Monarch; if the Prime Minister gave me my congé, he couldn't resist it, &c., &c."... I told the King that if I had never mentioned His Majesty's name in my life, precisely the same thing would be said out of sheer envy of His Majesty being kindly disposed, and it could not be hid that the King had backed up the First Sea Lord against all kinds of opposition—As a matter of fact I *never* do go into Society, and only dine out when I'm worried to meet the King, and I'm not such a born idiot as to have said any such thing as has been reported to the King (it is quite likely *someone else has said it!*). Well he left that (having unburdened his mind) and smoked a cigar as big as a capstan bar for really a good hour afterwards, talking of everything from China to Peru, not excluding *The Times* article on himself.... Oh! he said something of how I worked the Press, but I didn't follow that up. No one knows, except perhaps yourself, that unless I had arranged to get the whole force of public opinion to back up the Naval Revolution it would have been simply impossible to have carried it through successfully, for the vested interests against me were enormous and the whole force of Naval opinion was *dead* against me. But I did venture one humble remark to the King: "Has anyone ever been able to mention to Your Majesty one single little item that has failed in the whole multitude of reforms introduced in the last 3½ years?" No! he said. No one had! So I left it there.... If the Angel Gabriel were in my place he would be falsely accused. I'm only surprised that the King hasn't been told worse things—perhaps he has! "*Let him that thinketh he standeth take heed lest he fall.*" I always have that thought, and hope the King will have a cottage somewhere in Windsor Forest or elsewhere which he will kindly give me when it happens, so that I can come over and have a yarn with you!

*   *   *   *   *

1908.
May 5th.

4.15 a.m. The *Early* Bird!!... Yesterday, with all Sea Lords present, McKenna formally agreed to 4 Dreadnoughts *and if necessary* 6 Dreadnoughts next year (perhaps the greatest triumph ever known!)... He tells me Harcourt for certain will resign on it ... and he is paring down the money with a view to Supplementary Estimates.... This is what I suggest to you to impress on Lloyd George: *Let there he no mistake about the two Keels to one in Dreadnoughts!* Let Lloyd George reassure McKenna and tell him to have no fear—it doesn't affect next year, as McKenna consents to 4 or even 6; but it does affect the year after, and the Admiralty Finance should be arranged accordingly and not deplete next year at expense of year after. I wonder if this is all clear to you—that McKenna is going to give us the *numbers* for next year all right. Shove in again the great fact—The Navy and Army Estimates not far different in magnitude, and yet the Army not big enough to fight Bulgaria, and the Navy can take on all the Navies of the world put together.—"*Ut veniant omnes!!!*"—"Let 'em all come!" You might tell Lloyd George he can rely on my parsimony.

*   *   *   *   *

1908.
Sept. 8th.

... "The heart untravelled fondly turns to home."—We have no poets nowadays like Pope, Goldsmith and Gay—only damned mystical idiots like Browning and Tennyson that want a dictionary and the Differential-Calculus sort of mind to understand what they are driving at!

... I sat several times [on a recent visit abroad] between Stolypin, the Russian Prime Minister, and Isvolsky, the Foreign Secretary. I didn't begin it, but Stolypin said to me "What do you think we want most?" He fancied I should answer "So many battleships, so many cruisers, &c., &c.," but instead I said: "Your Western Frontier is denuded of troops and your magazines are depleted. *Fill them up*, and then talk of Fleets!" Please see enclosure from Kuropatkin's secret report: "*The foundation of Russia's safety is her Western boundary!!!*"... Have you seen Monsieur Rousseau (I think is his name) in *Le Temps*? I had an extract of it, and put it aside to send you, but alas! it has gone. "Procrastination is the thief of good intentions"—which is not so good as "Punctuality is the curse of comfort." But the good Frenchman (like Monsieur Hanotaux before him) is lost in admiration of what moved Mahan to his pungent saying that Garvin seized on with the inspiration of genius— "that 88 per cent. of the English guns were trained on Germany!"... By the way, I've got Sir Philip Watts into a new *Indomitable* that will make your mouth water when you see it! (and the Germans gnash their teeth!)

* * * * *

1908.
Dec.

The King has sent me a dear letter, and adds "*Don't print this!*" Isn't he a sweet? *What wonderful friends I have!* It's a marvel! All I do is to kick their shins.

* * * * *

1908.
(No date.)

... I am going to ask you to reconsider your supplementary paper herewith. I can't find that the Admiralty have admitted that 24,000 men would ever start off together as two raids of 12,000 each. I personally have expressed my decided opinion (I think at the 7th meeting) [of the Committee of Imperial Defence] to the contrary. Indeed, I am emphatically of opinion that no raid of any kind [that is, *landing of troops*] is feasible with all our late developments, which are developing further every day (*e.g.* we have our wireless on top of Admiralty Building and are communicating with the Scilly Islands now and shortly I hope Gibraltar and so certainly to every point of the German coast where we shall have Wireless Cruisers all over the place. (*Not a dog will wag its tail without being reported.*) So don't let us get a scare over 24,000 men coming unobserved. *One lot of 12,000* can be put in as the limit; but my suggestion is—*leave out numbers*, and simply say as a precautionary measure for the confidence of the country, *it's a good safe arbitrary standard to lay down that two Divisions of Regular Troops* are always to be left in the Country just in the same way as laid down at the Admiralty that the Home Fleet is not for Service abroad.

*　　　*　　　*　　　*　　　*

1909.
Jan. 26th.

... The Admiralty hear (by wireless every moment) what all the Admirals and Captains are saying to each other anywhere in Europe and even over to the coasts of America.

*　　　*　　　*　　　*　　　*

1909.
March 15th.

Private & Secret & *Personal.* I have just finished in these early hours a careful re-study of your paper E. 5 (which I love) and the criticisms thereon by French and the General Staff. I dismiss French's criticism as being that of a pure correct Cavalry expert and not dealing with the big questions. The General Staff criticism is on the other hand *the thin end of the insidious wedge of our taking part in Continental War as apart absolutely from Coastal Military Expeditions in pure concert with the Navy*—expeditions involving hell to the enemy because backed by an invincible Navy (the citadel of the Military force). I don't desire to mention these expeditions and never will, as our military organisation is so damnably leaky! but it so happens for two solid hours this morning I have been studying one of these of inestimable value only involving 5,000 men, and some guns, and horses about 500—a mere fleabite! but a collection of these fleabites would make Wilhelm scratch himself with fury! However, the point of my letter is this—Ain't we d—d fools to go on wasting our very precious moments in these abstruse disquisitions on this line and that or the passage of the Dutch German Frontier River and whether the bloody fight is to be at Rheims or Amiens, until the Cabinet have decided the great big question raised in your E. 5: *Are we or are we not going to send a British Army to fight on the Continent as quite distinct and apart from Coastal Raids and seizures of Islands, etcetera, which the Navy dominate?* Had not the Prime Minister better get this fixed up before we have any more discussions such as foreshadowed to-morrow?

*　　　*　　　*　　　*　　　*

9.
March 21st.

... It won't do to resign on a *hypothesis* but on a fact! All is in train for the *8* Dreadnoughts! and as Grey says when the day is reached to sign the contracts and *then* a veto—*then* is the day to go in a great company and not one alone!...

I am vehemently urged to squash my "malignant stabbers-in-the-back" by making a speech somewhere and saying as follows—but I won't—it would be an effectual cold douche to the 8 Dreadnoughts a year! I might say

"The unswerving intention of 4 years has *now* culminated in *two* complete Fleets in Home Waters, *each of which* is incomparably superior to the whole German Fleet mobilised for war. Don't take my word! Count them, see them for yourselves! You *will* see them next June. This can't alter for years, even were we supinely passive in our building; but it won't alter because we will have 8 Dreadnoughts a year. *So sleep quiet in your beds!*"

And I might also add:—

"The Germans are not building in this feverish haste to fight you! *No!* it's the daily dread they have of a second Copenhagen, which they know a Pitt or a Bismarck would execute on them!

"Cease building or I strike!"

$$* \qquad * \qquad * \qquad * \qquad *$$

1909.
March 30th.

... Grey rubbed in two great points yesterday:—

(i) Lack of information as to German acceleration will be acted on as if acceleration were a fact.

(ii) The *8* this year won't affect next year.

$$* \qquad * \qquad * \qquad * \qquad *$$

1909.
June 15th.

... Yes, we made a good job of Saturday; but the two most noticeable things of all were never noticed:—

(i) The swarm of Destroyers going 20 knots past the Dreadnought found themselves suddenly confronted by a lot of passenger steamers and yachts, which at the last moment got right in their way—the accidents might have been intense—but the young Destroyer commanders kept their nerve and their speed and scootled through the eye of the needle just grazing them all. It was splendid to see and made my heart warm! (N.B.—A Press delegate—

the *Toronto Globe*, I think, seized me by the arm and said, "*Sir, I see the glint of battle in your eye!*")

(ii) I saw the Speaker of the House of Commons being bundled into a "char-à-banc" holding 24 other promiscuous persons by a bluejacket. Truly a democratic sight!

*   *   *   *   *

1909.
July 3rd.

... The latest development is that somebody has a pile of my private letters to various people—not printed or typewritten but *the original letters*, so he says, which he is going to produce unless I agree to resign in October! Some of the letters stolen and some given (so I am told!). However "hot" they may be I don't regret a word I ever wrote, and I believe my countrymen will forgive me. *Anyhow I won't be blackmailed!* There was murder in the King's eye when I told him (but I didn't tell him all!)... *I am going to fight to the finish! Heaven bless you for your help.*

*   *   *   *   *

1909.
August 3rd.

... The Mouse was able to help the Lion yesterday as the King got on to you in regard to vile attempts of jealousy as to your being on the Defence Committee. The King is certainly A 1 in sticking to his friends! but you have always said this yourself to me when I have been down on my luck! All has gone most splendidly in all ways and the King is enormously gratified at the magnificent show of the Fleet to put before the Emperor of Russia. I told the Emperor it was a fine avenue!—18 miles of ships—the most powerful in the world and none of them more than 10 years old!

*   *   *   *   *

1909.
August 27th.

[A letter on the Beresford Report speaks of two "base innuendoes," of which the second is]

(ii) The "*suggestio falsi*" that the Admiralty had been wanting in Strategical Thought—whereas we had effected the immense advance of establishing the Naval War College and gave evidence of practical strategy in effecting the concentration of our Fleets instead of the previous state of dispersion. No such redistribution of strategical force since the days of Noah!

But worse still—Not one word of commendation for the Admiralty for its unparalleled work in gaining fighting efficiency and instant readiness for war by the institution of the Nucleus Crew system—the introduction of Battle practice—the unexampled advance in Gunnery (the "Invincible" with her 12-inch guns hitting the target 1/14th her own size *15 times out of 18 at 5 miles*, she herself going 20 knots and the target also moving at an unknown speed and unknown course) and getting rid of 160 vessels that could neither fight nor run away—*Not one word of appreciation of all this by the Committee!* and yet they had the practical result before them in the manœuvres of 374 vessels manœuvring in fogs and shoals without a single mishap or a single defect and 96 Submarines and Torpedo Craft on the East Coast making Invasion ridiculous! No—it has been a bitter disappointment—more bitter because each of the five members of the Committee so expressive to me and to others of the complete victory of the Admiralty. *Cowards all!* It is the one redeeming feature that *The Times* came down decidedly on the right side of the fence! the one and only paper that got at the kernel of the matter. *Discipline!* where art thou now after this Report?

THE FUNERAL OF KING EDWARD VII.

Lord Fisher as Principal Aide-de-Camp.

*　　*　　*　　*　　*

1909.
Sept. 13th.

... What pleases me most is the King having sent for you, and your 1½ hours' breakfast and afterwards driving with him, because as no doubt you know, —— (and some others) started a propaganda against you which fell absolutely flat and it's a rattling good thing the King making much of you in this way as it gets *about and without any question the King now largely moulds the public will!* As to your letter in regard to myself, it of course gives me great joy that the King gives me his blessing and also dear Knollys's wonderful fidelity to me is a miracle! (I always think of an incident long ago when he calmly ignored a furious effusion of mine to the King and put the letter in the fire without saying a word to me till long afterwards! I all the time joyful— thinking I had done splendidly!)

[After a forecast of a coming change in the Government the letter goes on]

You will at once say: What is the First Sea Lord going to do? Answer— Nothing! It is the ONLY course to follow! I have thought it all out most carefully and decided to keep absolutely dumb. When a new Admiralty patent appears in the *London Gazette* without my name in it, I pack up and walk out and settle down in the Tyrol. Temperature 70° in the shade and figs ten a penny and wear out all my white tunics and white trowsers! McKenna, to whom I am absolutely devoted, may force my hand to help him. In view of all he has risked for me (he was practically out of the Cabinet for 24 hours at one time! This is a fact) I am ready to go to the stake for him; but if he is well advised he also will be dumb.... I am so surprised how utterly both the Cabinet and the Press have failed to see the "inwardness" of the new "Pacific Fleet"! I had a few momentous words in private with Sir Joseph Ward (the Prime Minister of New Zealand). *He saw it!* It means *eventually* Canada, Australia, New Zealand, the Cape (that is South Africa) and India *running a complete Navy!* We manage the job in Europe. They'll manage the job ... as occasion requires out there! The very wonderful thing is that only dear old Lord Kelvin and the First Sea Lord at the first wanted the Battle Cruiser type alone and *not "Dreadnoughts"*; but we had a compromise, as you know, and got 3 *Indomitables* with the Dreadnoughts; and all the world now has got "Indomitables" on the brain! Hip! Hip! Hurrah!

*　　*　　*　　*　　*

1909.
Dec. 25th.

... Wilson and I have talked a lot about our War plan for the Navy. You know he told the Defence Committee that only he and I knew of the War Plan, which is quite true and it was the same when his fleet was joined with mine when South African War was in progress. He would sooner die than disclose it. (God bless Sir Arthur Wilson!)

        *   *   *   *   *

1910.
Jan. 23rd.

Of course no question as to strategic merits of a Canal, and it ought originally to have been the scheme instead of Rosyth, but now is it possible to make the *volte-face*? *I fear not!* I got Rosyth delayed 4 years as NOT being the right thing or the right place and hoping for our Kiel Canal; but though I succeeded in the delay, alas! I did not in the substitution. However, I will see Hankey as you suggest. Yes, I'm quite happy, and my cry is NOT "à Berlin!"... I've got some war charts that would make your mouth water!

[Sir John Fisher left the Admiralty on his birthday, Jan. 25th, 1910, and was raised to the Peerage.]

        *   *   *   *   *

1910.   KILVERSTONE   HALL,
February 2nd. THETFORD.

... I've just got here from Cheshire, where for days running I've had Paradise. 3 lovely girls in the house, a *splendid* ball room and music always on hand! 3 young Guardsmen there, but I held my own!

Dancing till 4 a.m. took it out of me a bit, but it revivified me and I renewed my strength like the Eagle!... I hope the King talked politics with McKenna, who is very acute and would sacrifice himself for the King. Didn't you think McKenna excellent, the night he dined with me, as to the course the King should pursue? You see he knows so exactly how the Cabinet will be actuated....

There are great risks. Both political sides unscrupulous....

P.S.—Wasn't it the Emperor Diocletian who doffed the Imperial Purple to plant cabbages? and d—d fine cabbages, no doubt! So don't blackguard me for leaving the Admiralty of my own free will, to plant roses!

1910.
Feb. 18th.

... Things look ugly.... However, I'm a pure outsider! There will be desperate efforts to supplant Wilson, so I hear from trustworthy quarters. But McKenna will be the real loss to the Navy. The sacred fire of efficiency burns brightly in him! and he's a born fighter and a good hater, which I love (as Dr. Johnson did) with all my heart. You really *must* come here when the weather is nicer—it's lovely! I've never known till now what joy there is in Nature. Even beauteous woman fades in the comparison! I've just seen the wild swans flying over the Lake! "The world forgetting—By the world forgot!" is appropriate to me now!... I've just thought of a lovely Preamble for my approaching "Midshipman's Vade-Mecum" ... I rather think it's Blackie, though perhaps not his words:

"Four Things for a Big Life
  I. A great Inspiration
 II. A great Cause
III. A great Battle
IV. A great Victory

Having got those 4 things then you can preach the Gospel of Rest and Build an Altar to Repose."

*   *   *   *   *

1910.
March 14th.

... I lunched with Asquith, he was *more than cordial!* How funny it is that I did *infinitely more* for the Conservatives than for the *Radicals*, and yet the Radicals have given me all I have got and the Conservatives have only given me abuse and calumny!

The Radicals gave me my Pension and a Peerage, and yet I increased the Radical estimates nearly ten millions! I decreased the estimates 9 millions and reduced prospective charges by nineteen millions sterling for the Conservatives, and they never lifted even a little finger to help me, *but on the contrary* have heaped dunghill abuse on me! *How do you explain this?*

McKenna, whose life has been a burden on my account, gives me a thing that would do for an Ascot Gold Cup with the inscription I enclose—luckily it's in Latin or I dare not let it be seen! (The Craven Scholar writes to me it's the best Latin he ever read in his life!) I wouldn't write all this to anyone else, but *is it not all of it phenomenally curious?* Well, *longo intervallo* I took your advice and seized an opportunity which called for my communicating with Winston, and he sent me *by return of post* a most affectionate letter and says I am the one man in the world he really loves! (Well! I really love him because he's a great Fighter.) What a joke if you, I and George Clarke were put on to reform the House of Lords!

*　　*　　*　　*　　*

1910.
March 24th.

I sent you a telegram from Ely on my way down (I caught my train by ½ a minute!) as my cogitations impelled me to suggest to you that Asquith obviously does not see the fallacy of ——'s reasoning, which as you very acutely observed would kill the Defence Committee as a whole in its *guiding*, but not its administrative or executive power, which are non-existent and inimical to its existence. But its "*guiding*" power is England's all-in-all, if only its sufficiency and efficiency could be digested.

I had an immense talk with McKenna.... He was "dead on" for your Committee. Of course the Ideal was your being President, but I suppose the "Shifting Man" as President, according to the subject and the Department concerned, has its merits and advantages.

*　　*　　*　　*　　*

1910.
APRIL 8TH.

Old Stead's letter in *Standard* on 2 keels to 1 is unsurpassable! *It ought to be circulated in millions as a leaflet!*... What d—d fools the Tories are not to swallow it whole—the 2 keels to 1!... I told "the Islanders" secretly I could do more as the "mole," so not to put my name down—(The Mole is my *métier*! only to be traced by upheavals!) Get Stead's letter sent all over the Nation as a leaflet.

I am to meet you on April 19th, Suez Canal.

I don't know Wilson's views. These are mine:—

General principle: The Admiralty should *never* engage itself to lock up a single vessel even—not even a torpedo-boat, or submarine—anywhere *on any consideration whatever. The whole principle of Sea fighting is to be free to go anywhere with every d—d thing the Navy possesses.* The Admiralty should engage to do their best but to reserve entire freedom of action. The responsibility of the Suez Canal therefore cannot be theirs. If this clashes with your views you had better cancel me on Committee, for I'll fight like Hell for the above vital War Principle!

*   *   *   *   *

1910.
April 25th.

I congratulate you on the latest by "Historicus"; but do you sufficiently intensify the intolerable tyranny of the permanent Tory majority in the Lords that has meant a real single chamber government for so many years? The Radicals are on the win and no one can stop it. We exaggerate the consequences. The silly thing is to have a General Election. Who gains? Everybody loses! Certainly the Tories won't win. Tariff Reform dead. Winston's last speeches have been very high class, especially where he shows how far greater issues are settled by the Government than anything appertaining to legislation without the House of Lords having a voice and we have always taken those risks in the past without a thought!

What is this about Kitchener hoisting out French as Inspector General? Anything to get Kitchener out of England!

[King Edward VII. died on May 6th, 1910.]

1910.
May.
(Saturday.)

What an *inexpressible* sorrow!. How we both know the loss! What a great National Calamity! And *personally* what can I say? *What a splendid and steadfast friend!* No use saying any more to each other—is it? *I really feel heart broken!*

*   *   *   *   *

1910.
May 24th. KILVERSTONE HALL.

... I really can't get over the irreparable loss. *I think of nothing else!* Treves gave me a wonderful account of the King's last day. I rather think the King was coming to see me here, had he remained at Sandringham. The Queen [Queen Alexandra] has been very sweet to me. She stopped to notice me going up the steps of St. George's Chapel and so did her Sister [the Empress Marie]. I appreciated it very much—but most of all my interview with her.... She told me she would come here to see me and how the King had told her about me being disappointed at her not having been to Kilverstone before. You'll think me morbid writing like this.

I dined with Asquith, McKenna and George Murray last week in London. If the Tories weren't such d—d stupid idiots I should rejoice at things being certain to go well.... My day is past. I have no illusions. You will enjoy the roses I've planted when you come here. How one's life does change!

*　　　*　　　*　　　*　　　*

1910.
May 27th.

... The Commonwealth Government [of Australia] have just sent a confidential telegram to Sir George Reid to ask me to go as their Guest to advise on the Navy. I've declined. I'd go as Dictator but not as Adviser. Also they have commenced all wrong and it would involve me in a campaign I intend to keep clear of with the soldiers. By the wording of the telegram I expect further pressure. Besides what a d—d fine thing to get me planted in the Antipodes! [Kitchener and the Australians, in drawing up their scheme of defence, forgot that Australia was an island. So do we here in England.]

*　　　*　　　*　　　*　　　*

1910.
June 7th.

... I can't shake off my sense of loss in the King's death. Though personally it practically makes no difference of course—yet I feel so curious a sense of isolation—which I can't get over—and no longer seem to care a d—n for anything!...

As you told me, it was miraculous I left the Admiralty when I did! It was the nick of time! A. K. Wilson is doing splendidly and is unassailable. I had much pressure to emerge the other day, but I won't, nor have I the heart now.

*　　　*　　　*　　　*　　　*

1910.
August 5th. KILVERSTONE HALL.

McKenna has just been here on his second visit (so he liked the first, I suppose! I mention this as an inducement to you to come!) He has shewn me various secret papers. HE IS A REAL FIGHTER, and the Navy Haters will pass over his dead body! If our late Blessed Master was alive I should know what to do; but I feel my hands tied now. Perhaps a kindly Providence put us both on the Beach at the right moment! Who knows?

"The lights begin to twinkle on the rocks"! I've told —— and others that the 2 keels to 1 policy is of inestimable value because it eliminates the United States

- 135 -

Navy, *which never ought to be mentioned—criminal folly to do so*—Also it gives us such an ample margin as to allow for discount!

The insidious game is to have an enquiry into Ship Designs, which means delay and no money!

Two immense episodes are doing Damocles over the Navy just now. I had settled to shove my colleagues over the precipice about both of them, but as you know I left hurriedly to get in Wilson—so incomparably good! We pushed them over the precipice about Water Tube Boilers, the Turbine, the Dreadnought, the Scrapping [of ships that could neither fight nor run away], the Nucleus Crews—the Redistribution of the Fleet, &c., &c. In each and all it was *Athanasius contra mundum*, but each and all a magnificent success; so also these two waiting portents full of immense developments.

1. Oil Engines and internal combustion, about which I so dilated at our dinner and bored you. Since that night (July 11th) Bloom & Voss in Germany have received an order to build a Motor Liner for the Atlantic Trade. *No engineers, no stokers, and no funnels, no boilers! Only a d—d chauffeur! The economy prodigious!* as the Germans say "*Kolossal billig*"! But what will it be for War? *Why! all the past pales before the prospect!!!* I say to McKenna: "Shove 'em over the precipice! *Shove!*" But he's all alone, poor devil!

The Second is that this Democratic Country won't stand 99 per cent. *at least* of her Naval Officers being drawn from the "Upper Ten." It's amazing to me that anyone should persuade himself that an aristocratic Service can be maintained in a Democratic State. The true democratic principle is Napoleon's: "*La carrière ouverte aux talents!*" The Democracy will shortly realise this, and there will be a dangerous and mischievous agitation. The secret of successful administration is the intelligent anticipation of agitation. Again I say to McKenna "*Shove!!! Shove them over the precipice.*" I have the plan all cut and dried.

The pressure won't come from inside the Navy but from outside—an avalanche like A.D. 1788 (the French Revolution)—and will sweep away a lot more than desirable! It is essentially a political question rather than a Naval question proper. *It is all so easy*, only the d—d Tory prejudices stand in the way! But I gave you a paper about all this printed at Portsmouth, so won't bore you with more. I am greatly inclined to leave the Defence Committee and move out in the open on these two vital questions on the Navy. The one affects its fighting efficiency as much as the other. I am doing the mole, and certain upheavals will appear shortly, but it wants a Leader in the open!

*　　　*　　　*　　　*　　　*

1911.
May 1st.

... I want you to think over getting the Prime Minister to originate an enquiry for a great British Governmental Wireless Monopoly, or rather I would say "English Speaking" Monopoly! No one at the Admiralty or elsewhere has as yet any *the least idea* of the *immense* revolution both for Peace and War purposes which will be brought about by the future development of wireless!... The point is that this scheme wants to be engineered by the Biggest Boss, i.e. the Prime Minister.... *Believe me* the wireless in the future is the soul and spirit of Peace and War, and therefore must be in the hands of the Committee of Defence! *You can't cut the air!* You can cut a telegraph cable!

*   *   *   *   *

1911.
June 25th. BAD NAUHEIM.

... You will see in the *Standard* of May 29th the London Correspondent of the *Irish Times* lets out about Lord Fisher and war arrangements, but as the *Standard* in the very same issue makes this announcement in big type: "We (Great Britain) are in the satisfactory position of having *twice as many Dreadnoughts* in commission as *Germany and a number greater by one unit than the whole of the rest of the world put together!*" I don't think there is the very faintest fear of war! How wonderfully Providence guides England! Just when there is a quite natural tendency to ease down our Naval endeavours comes AGADIR!

"Time and the Ocean and some Guiding Star

In High Cabal have made us what we are!"

"The Greatest Power on 'Airth,'" as Mr. Champ Clarke would say! (You ought to meet Champ Clarke.) He is likely to succeed Taft as President, *but I put my money on Woodrow Wilson.* He is Bismarck and Moltke rolled into one!... I need not say that I remain in the closest bonds with the Admiralty. I never did a wiser thing than coming abroad and remaining abroad and working like a mole. *I shall not return till July, 1912.* Most damnable efforts against me continue in full swing: nevertheless like Gideon—"Faint yet pursuing" is my motto.... And yet because in 1909 at the Guildhall when our Naval supremacy had been arranged for in the Navy Estimates of the year I said to my countrymen "Sleep quiet in your beds!" I was vehemently vilified with malignant truculence, and only yesterday I got a letter from an Aristocrat of the Aristocrats, saying he had heard it stated by a Man of Eminence the day before that I was in the pay of Germany! It is curious that I can't get over the personal great blank I feel in the death of our late blessed Friend King

Edward! There was something in the charm of his heart that still chains one to his memory—some magnetic touch!

*　　　*　　　*　　　*　　　*

1911.

Sept. 20th. LUCERNE.

Through dancing with a sweet American (and indeed they are truly delightful, especially if you have the same partner all the evening!) I hear via a Bremen multi-millionaire that though the most optimistic official assurances of peace emanate from Berlin yet there is the most extreme nervousness amongst the German business men because of the revelation to them of the French power both financially and fightingly, so unexpected by them. I suppose if a Pitt or a Palmerston had now been guiding our destinies we should have war. They would say any Peace would be a bad Peace because of the latent damnable feeling in Germany against England. It won't be France any more, it will be England that will be the red rag for the German Bull! And as we *never* were so strong as at present, then Pitt & Co. would say the present is the time to fight. Personally I am confident of Peace. I happen to know in a curious way (but quite certainly) that the Germans are in a blue funk of the British Navy and are quite assured that 942 German merchant steamers would be "gobbled up" in the first 48 hours of war, and also the d—d uncertainty of *when* and *where* a hundred thousand troops embarked in transports and kept "in the air" might land! N.B.—There's a lovely spot only 90 miles from Berlin! Anyhow they would demobilize about a million German soldiers! But I am getting "off the line" now! I really sat down to write and tell you of a two days' visit paid to me here by the new American Ambassador to Berlin. *He is a faithful friend.* He is *very, very* PRO-English (he has such a lovely daughter whom I have been dancing with, A PERFECT GEM! if she don't turn Wilhelm's head I'll eat my hat!). My friend was American Ambassador at Constantinople when I was Commander-in-Chief of the Mediterranean Fleet—you know it was a ticklish time then, at the worst of the Boer War and the British Navy kept the Peace! That old Sultan [Abdul Hamid] told me so, and gave me a 500-guinea diamond star, bless him! and he called Lord Salisbury a d—d fool for having left him in the lurch and for having said that "England had put her money on the wrong horse" in backing Turkey. The Turks being the *one* people in the whole world to be England's fast (and if put to it) *only* friend! Well, my dear Friend! Leishman saw this *then* in 1899, and sees it *now*, and hence we were locked up for hours in a secret room here! It all bears immensely on the present Franco-German Crisis! That *"greater-than-Bismarck"* who is now German Ambassador at Constantinople (Marschall von Bieberstein), and who is the real director of German policy (Waechter is only his factotum! as I will prove to you presently!) sees his rear and flanks quite safe by having the Turks in the palm of his hand (as Leishman describes it!) and so has been led to bluff at Agadir—but those choice words of Lloyd George upset the German apple-cart in a way it was never upset before! (I suppose they were "written out" words and Cabinet words, and they were d—d fine words!) Before I go on with the next bit of my letter I must explain to you that Leishman is a very great friend and admirer of Marschall von Bieberstein and also of Kiderlen-Waechter, the present German Foreign Minister. When Marschall went on his annual 4 months' leave from Constantinople he always had Waechter to take his place while away, who was then the German Minister at Bucharest! Leishman is also an ardent admirer of the German Emperor, and he is also the most intimate friend possessed by Mr. Philander Knox, the American Secretary of State, who has forced Leishman to Berlin when he was in Paradise at Rome (at all events his family were!) Well! dear Friend, it's a good thing that Leishman loves England. I couldn't possibly write to Sir E. Grey what I am writing to you (I shouldn't write to you except that this letter goes through France only!) and it would be simply fatal to Leishman if it ever leaked out about his conversations with me, but his heart is with us. I knew this when I spent many weeks at Constantinople (and we had no friends then, 1899 and 1900!). He says *our Turkish policy is the laughing stock of Diplomacy*! "Every schoolboy knows" that we have a Mahomedan Existence and the Turks love us, but all we do is to kick their ——! As Leishman truly says, the Germans were in the dust by the deposition of Abdul Hamid and England was "all" to the New Turks, but slowly Marschall has worked his way up again, and the Germans again possess the Turks, instead of England. The Turkish Army, the very finest fighting army in the world, was ours for the asking, and *"Peace—perfect Peace"* in India, Egypt and Persia; but we've chucked it all away because we have had d—d fools as our Ambassadors! But how can it be otherwise unless you put in men from outside, like for instance Bryce at Washington? Our strength is Mahomedan, but we are too d—d Christian to see it! and fool about Armenian atrocities and Bulgarian horrors! Tories and Radicals are both the same. Isn't it wonderful how we get along! I repeat again to you my copyright lines:—

"Time and the Ocean and some Guiding Star

In High Cabal have made us what we are!"

Look at Delagoa Bay, that might have been ours—indeed *was* ours only we "fooled" it away! Look at Lord Granville and the Cameroons! Well! I haven't given Leishman away, I don't think! The real German *bonne bouche* was the complete belt across Africa, but this only if the right of pre-emption as regards the Belgian Congo could have been acquired. I simply tremble at the consequences if the British Redcoats are to be planted on the Vosges

Frontier [meaning the dread of Conscription and a huge Army for Continental Warfare].

*   *   *   *   *

1911.
October 10th. LUCERNE.

... I yesterday had a long letter from McKenna begging me to return and "put the gloves on again," and in view of his arguments I am going to do so when A. K. Wilson vanishes early next year! It is, however, distasteful to me. I've had a lovely time here.

*   *   *   *   *

1911.
October 29th. REIGATE PRIORY, SURREY.

... I am here 3 days with Winston and many of the Cabinet. I got a very urgent letter to come here, and I think my advice has been fully and completely digested, but don't say a word, please, to a soul! I am returning direct to Lucerne on Wednesday, after Tuesday at Kilverstone.

*   *   *   *   *

1911.
November 9th. LUCERNE.

These are very ticklish times indeed! I have got to be extremely careful. I must not get between Winston and A. K. W. in any way—it would not only be very wrong but fatal to any smooth working. So I begged Winston not to write to me. With extreme reluctance I went to Reigate as I did, but McKenna urged me on the grounds of the good of the Navy, and from what Winston has since said to a friend of mine I think I did right in going.

*   *   *   *   *

1911.
December. LUCERNE.

... I shouldn't have written again so soon except for just now seeing in a Paris paper that Sir John French, accompanied by four Officers, had landed at Calais *en route* to the French Head Quarters, and expatiating on the evident intention of joint military action! Do you remember the classic interview we had with the late King in his Cabin? If this is on the tapis again then we have another deep regret for the loss of that sagacious intuition! King Edward may not have been clever, but he never failed in his judgment on whose opinion to rely.... Of course there may be nothing in it! Nor do I think there is the least likelihood of war. ENGLAND IS FAR TOO STRONG! Yet I daily get letters anticipating my early return....

I enclose you a letter from ——, received a little time ago. He is a very eminent Civil Engineer. There is a "dead set" being made to get the Midshipmen under the new scheme to rebel against "engineering"! ——, —— — & Co. are persistently at it through their friends in the Fleet, and calling those Midshipmen who go in for engineering—"Greasers." The inevitable result of the present young officers of the Navy disparaging and slighting this chief necessary qualification of engineering in these engineering days will be to force the throwing open of entry as officers in the Navy *to all classes of the population* and adopting State paid Education and support till the pay is sufficient to support!

*　　　*　　　*　　　*　　　*

1911.
December 24th.

... I have had a hectic time with four hurricanes crossing the Channel and balancing on the tight-rope with one end held by Winston and the other by McKenna, but they both held tight and I am all right. Without doubt McKenna is a patriot to have encouraged ME to help Winston as he has done! I have not heard what the War Staff is doing. It does not trouble me. My sole object was to ensure Jellicoe being Commander-in-Chief of the Home Fleet on December 19th, 1913, and that is being done by his being appointed Second-in-Command of the Home Fleet, and he will automatically be C.-in-C. in two years from that date. All the recent changes revolved round Jellicoe, and NO ONE sees it!

*　　　*　　　*　　　*　　　*

1912.
Jan. 3rd. NAPLES.

... I fully agree with you about the Navy want of first-class Intellects. Concentration and Discipline combine to cramp the Sea Officer.... Great views don't get grasped. Winston urges me to come back, but he forgets the greatest of all the great Napoleonic sayings: "*J'ordonne, ou je me tais.*" Besides, you see, I was the First Violin. However, Winston is splendidly receptive. I can't possibly write what has happened, *but he is a brave man.* And as 16 Admirals have been scrapped I am more popular than ever!!! A lovely woman two days ago sent me this riddle: "Why are you like Holland?" "Because you lie low and are dammed all round." But there it is. Jellicoe will be Admiralissimo when Armageddon comes along, and *everything that was done revolved round that*, and *no one has seen it.* He has all the attributes of Nelson, and his age.

[*By kind permission of "The Daily Express."*

THE ANNIVERSARY OF TRAFALGAR.

NELSON (*in Trafalgar Square*):—"I was on my way down to lend them a hand myself, but if Jacky Fisher's taking on the job there's no need for me to be nervous, I'll get back on my pedestal."

Nelson looking up Sir John Fisher on his first day as First Sea Lord,
Trafalgar Day, 1904.

*　　　*　　　*　　　*　　　*

1912.
March 7th. NAPLES.

You nearly saw me to-day, as a King's Messenger roused me out the day before yesterday with papers I really thought I could not cope with by letter; but as obviously the object was to avoid the gossip my appearance in London would cause I did my best with my pen. But I see clearly I am in the middle of the whirlpool again and must force what I feel a great disinclination for and participate once more in the fight. I have had strangely intimate opportunities of learning the very inside of German feeling towards England. *It is bitterly intense and widespread.* Without any doubt whatever the Germans thought they were going to squeeze France out of Morocco. You can take that as a fact, no matter what lies are told by the German Foreign Minister; and Clemenceau's unpublished speech would have proved it, but he said enough. And how treacherous to England was M. Caillaux.—What a dirty business! Anyhow, as a German Admiral of *high repute* wrote confidentially and privately a few days since: "German public opinion is roused in a way I had not before thought possible." And as far as I can make out, the very worst possible thing was Haldane's visit—a British Cabinet Minister crawling up the back stairs of the German Foreign Office in carpet slippers! and judging from all that is told me, it has made the Germans worse than ever, and for a variety of quite opposite reasons, all producing the same result. Any more Heligolands would mean certain war. It's very peculiar how we have left our impregnable position we occupied before Haldane's visit, to take up a most humiliating, weak and dangerous one.

*   *   *   *   *

1912.
April 2nd.

... As you say, Winston has done splendidly. He and I last November discussed every brick of his speech in Devonport Dockyard while visiting the 33-knot *Lion*-Dreadnought by night alone together, and don't accuse me of too much egotism, but he stopped dramatically on the Dockyard stones and said to me "You're a Great Man!"... We are lagging behind in out-Dreadnoughting the Dreadnought! A plunge of course—a huge plunge—but so was the Dreadnought—so was the Turbine—so was the water-tube boiler, and last of all so was the $13\frac{1}{2}$-inch gun which now holds the field, and the whole Board of Admiralty (bar Jellicoe) and all the experts dead against it—but we plunged! So it is now—we want more speed—less armour—a 15-inch gun—more sub-division—oil only—and chauffeurs instead of Engineers and Stokers, and a Dreadnought that will go round the world without requiring to replenish fuel! The *Non-Pareil!* Winston says he'll call her the "Fisher!" *I owe more than I can say to McKenna.* I owe nearly as much to Winston for scrapping a dozen Admirals on December 5th last so as to get Jellicoe 2nd in Command of the Home Fleet. If war comes before 1914, then Jellicoe will be Nelson at the Battle of St. Vincent: if it comes in 1914 then he'll be Nelson at Trafalgar!...

Again, I've had quite affectionate letters from three important Admirals. Why should I come home and filch their credit? All this is to explain to you why I keep abroad, as you ask me what are my future plans. Your letter in *The Times* on the German Book quite excellent. Bernstorff's book is even more popular in Germany: "The War Between England and Germany"— with the picture of the "Dreadnought" with all her guns trained for action! Every little petty German newspaper is dead-on for war with England! *that I can assure you of!* So *anything* would kindle a war!... The banner unfurled on October 21st, 1904, by the d——d scoundrel who on that day became First Sea Lord had inscribed on it:

"The fighting efficiency of the Fleet"
and
"Its instant readiness for War."

and, as Winston bravely said, that is now the case and no credit to himself, but he ought to have gone further back than McKenna for the credit. *It was Balfour!* He saw me through—no one else would allow 160 ships to be scrapped, &c., &c., &c. But you've had enough!

*   *   *   *   *

1912.
April 25th.

... When I was a Delegate at the Hague Conference of 1899—the first Conference—I had very animated conversations, which, however, to my lasting regret it was deemed inexpedient to place on record (on account of their violence, I believe!), regarding "Trading with the Enemy." I stated the primordial fact that *"The Essence of War is Violence; Moderation in War is Imbecility."* And then in my remarks I went on to observe, as is stated by Mr. Norman Angell in the "Great Illusion," where he holds me up as a Terror! and as misguided—perhaps I went a little too far when I said I would boil the prisoners in oil and murder the innocent in cold blood, &c., &c., &c. ... but it's quite silly not to make War damnable to the whole mass of your enemy's population, which of course is the secret of maintaining the right of Capture of Private Property at Sea. As you say, it must be proclaimed in the most public and most authoritative manner that direct and indirect trade between Great Britain, *including every part of the British Empire*, and Germany must cease in time of war.... When war does come *"Might is Right!" and the Admiralty will know what to do!* Nevertheless, it is a most serious drawback not making public to the world beforehand what we mean by War! It is astounding how even very great men don't understand War! You must go to the Foreigner to appreciate our Surpassing Predominance as a Nation. I was closeted for two hours lately—in a locked room—with a great Foreign Ambassador, who quoted great names to me as being in agreement with him that never in the History of the World was the British Nation (as at the present moment) surpassed in power! And therefore we could do what we liked!... I fully agree with you that the schemes of the General Staff of the British Army are grotesque. Their projects last August, had we gone to war, were wild in the extreme. You will remember a famous interview we two had with King Edward in his Cabin on board the Royal Yacht—how he stamped on the idea (that then enthused the War Office mind) of England once more engaged in a great Continental War! "Marlboroughs Cheap To-day!" was the kettle of fish advertised by the Militarists!

I walked the sands of Scheveningen with General Gross von Schwartzhoff in June, 1899. The German Emperor said he (Schwartzhoff) was a greater than Moltke. He was the Military German Delegate at the Hague Conference; he was designated as Chief of the General Staff at Berlin, but he was burnt to death in China instead. I had done him a very good turn indeed, so he opened his heart to me. There was no German Navy then. We were doing Fashoda; and he expatiated on the *rôle* of the British Army—how the absolute supremacy of the British Navy gave it such inordinate power far beyond its numerical strength, because 200,000 men embarked in transports, and God only knowing where they might be put ashore, was a weapon of enormous influence, and capable of deadly blows—occupying perhaps Antwerp, Flushing, &c. (but, of course, he only was thinking of the Cotentin Peninsula), or landing 90 miles from Berlin on that 14 miles of sandy beach [in Pomerania], impossible of defence against a battle fleet sweeping with devastating shells the flat country for miles, like a mower's scythe—no fortifications able to withstand projectiles of 1,450 lb.

Yes! you are *so* right! the average man is incapable of a *wide* survey! he looks through a pinhole and only sees just a little bit much magnified! Napoleon and Cromwell! Where are they?

*　　　*　　　*　　　*　　　*

1912.
April 29th. NAPLES.

... You say to me—"Come home!"—you remind me of *"personal influence."* I KNOW IT! Three days ago I was invited to name one of three week-ends in June to meet two very great men at a country house—no one else. Day before yesterday Winston Churchill asks me. Hardly a week passes without such similar pressure from most influential quarters—*"Why don't I come home and smash and pulverize?"* Of course, they one and all exaggerate—that in ten minutes I could *"sweep the board"* and so on! I know exactly what I can do. I've been fighting 50 years! *But I don't want a personal victory!*

... I am going to take my body and what little money I have ... to the United States in the near future. It would be no use my coming home. *The mischief is done!*... From patriotic motives I've given Winston of my very best in the replies going to him this day from Brindisi by King's Messenger, as regards designs and policy and fighting measures.

*   *   *   *   *

1912.
May 15th.

... Well! as you say, every blessed thing at Weymouth [the Fleet Inspection] *absolutely* dates from 1909, except the aviation, and even that I pressed to its present condition dead against great opposition, but I wrote so strongly that —— took the bit between his teeth on that subject! And you ask me the question "How goes it for the future!"

Well! Lloyd George is the real man, and so far judging from his most intimate conversation with me, *all is well!*... A propos of all this I've been specially invited to meet four people of importance at a week-end meeting—*no others.* I was asked twice before—and again now repeated; but I think it best to abstain. I think you will approve of my not going. I have declined to go with W. C. in the Admiralty Yacht.

*   *   *   *   *

1912.
May 19th. NAPLES.

I have a letter from W. C. this morning that he and the Prime Minister have decided to come direct here to Naples to spend a few days, and a telegram has just come saying they arrive on May 23rd.... I suppose the coming Supplementary Estimates and also types of new ships about which I am in deadly antagonism with every living soul at the Admiralty, and one of the consequences has been that a great Admiralty official has got the boot!!! So Winston is right when he writes to me this morning that in all vital points I have had my way! He adds: "The Future of the Navy rests in the hands of men in whom your confidence is as strong as mine ... and no change of Government would carry with it any change of policy in this respect."

*   *   *   *   *

1912.   KILVERSTONE   HALL,
June 30th. THETFORD.

My plot is working exactly as forecast. By and by you'll say it's the best thing I ever did. The Prime Minister and Winston would not listen at Naples to my urgent cry "Increase your margin!" They have got to recruit without stint and build 8 "Mastodons" instead of 4. Wait and see!

The recruiting HAS begun. The 8 will follow.

We want 8

We won't wait.

No other course but that now in progress would have done it. I don't mind personal obloquy, but it's a bit hard to undergo my friends' doubts of me; but the clouds will roll by.... I've got all my "working bees" round me here of the Royal Commission [on Oil and the Internal Combustion engine]. We shall stagger humanity!

1912.
July 6th. KILVERSTONE HALL.

... Really all my thoughts are with my Royal Commission. I expect you will see that the course of action will inevitably result in what I ventured to indicate *if only* the Admiralty will keep their backs to the wall of the irreducible margin required in Home Waters. The only pity was that dear old ———— said we were sufficiently strong for two years or more, which of course is quite true, but his saying so may prevent Lloyd George being hustled (*as he otherwise would have been*). Luckily I prevented ———— saying even more of our present great preponderance—but let us hope "All's well that ends well." Ian Hamilton came in most effectively with his witnessing the armoured Cruiser "Suffolk" laden with a Battalion of the Malta Garrison being twice torpedoed by a submarine.

*   *   *   *   *

1912.
July 15th.

... This instant the news has come to me that there are 750 eligible and selected candidates for 60 vacancies for Boy-Artificers in the Navy at the approaching examination! When I introduced this scheme 8 years ago every man's hand was against me, and the whole weight of Trades Unionism inside the House of Commons and out of it was organised against me.... We were dominated by the Engineers! We had to accept Engine Room artificers for the Navy who had been brought up on making bicycles! *Now,* these boys are suckled on the marine engine! and they have knocked out the old lot completely. Our very best Engine Room artificers now in the Navy are these boys! Not one of my colleagues or anyone else supported me! *Do you wonder that I don't care a d—n what anyone says?* The man you are going to see on Wednesday—how has he recognised that we are at this moment stronger than the Triple Alliance? The leaders of both political parties—how have they recognised that 19 millions sterling of public money *actually allocated* was saved and the re-arrangement of British Sea Power so stealthily carried out that not a sign appeared of any remark by either our own or by any Foreign

Diplomatists, until an obscure article in the *Scientific American* by Admiral Mahan stated that of a sudden he (Mahan) had discovered that 88 per cent. of the Sea Power of England was concentrated on Germany? But the most ludicrous thing of all is that up to this very moment no one has really recognised that the Dreadnought caused such a deepening and dredging of German harbours and their approaches, and a new Kiel Canal, as to cripple Germany up to A.D. 1915, and make their coasts accessible, which were previously denied to our ships because of their heavy draught for service in all the world!

*   *   *   *   *

1912.
August 2nd.

At the Defence Committee yesterday ... we had a regular set-to with Lloyd George (supported by Harcourt and Morley chiefly) against the provision of defence for Cromarty as a shelter anchorage for the Fleet, and the Prime Minister adjourned the discussion to the Cabinet as the temperature got hot! As you know, I've always been "dead on" for Cromarty and hated Rosyth, which is an unsafe anchorage—the whole Fleet in jeopardy the other day— and there's that beastly bridge which, if blown up, makes the egress very risky without examination.... Also Cromarty is strategically better than Rosyth.... Also Lloyd George had a row about the airships—Seely's Sub-Committee. We *must* have airships.

*   *   *   *   *

1912.
August 7th.

I still hate Rosyth and fortifications and East Coast Docks and said so the other day! but what we devise at Cromarty is for another purpose—to fend off German Cruisers possibly by an accident of fog or stupidity getting loose on our small craft taking their ease or re-fuelling in Cromarty (Oil will change all this in time, but as yet we have for years coal-fed vessels to deal with).... I've got enthusiastic colleagues on the oil business! They're all bitten! Internal Combustion Engine Rabies!

*   *   *   *   *

1912.
September.

... What an ass I was to come home! but it was next door to impossible to resist the pressure put on me, and then can you think it was wise of me to plunge once more into so vast a business as future motor Battleships?

- 148 -

Changing the face of the Navy, and, as Lloyd George said to me last Friday, getting the Coal of England as my mortal enemy!

*   *   *   *   *

1912.
Sept. 14th.

This Royal Commission [on oil] is a wonder! We have our first meeting on September 24th, and practically it is finished though it will go on for years and years and never submit a Report! You will love the *modus operandi* when some day I expound it to you!... In the second week of December we have an illustration on the scale of 12 inches to a foot of producing oil from coal. Twenty-five tons a day will be produced as an example. All that is required is to treble the retorting plant of all gas works in the United Kingdom where there is a Mayor and Corporation, and to treble their "through put" of coal! We get two million tons of oil that way! We only want one million.

I addressed the Directors of the S.E. & Chatham Railway last Tuesday, and hope I persuaded them to build a motor vessel of 24 knots between Calais and Dover, and proved to them they could save an hour between Paris and London—the whole side of the vessel falls down and makes a gangway on to a huge pontoon at Calais and Dover and all the passengers march straight out ("Every man straight before him," like the Israelites did at Jericho, and the walls fell down before them!) No more climbing up Mont Blanc up a narrow precipitous gangway from the steamer to the jetty in the rain, and an old woman blocking you with her parcels and umbrella jammed by the stanchions, and they ask her for her ticket and she don't know which pocket it's in! and the rain going down your neck all the time! A glass roof goes over the motor vessel—she has no funnels, and her telescopic wireless masts wind down by a 2 h.p. motor so as not to go through the glass roof. But all this is nothing to H.M.S. "Incomparable"—a 25 knot battleship that will go round the whole earth without refuelling!... The plans of her will be finished next Monday, and I wrote last night to say I proposed in my capacity as a private British Citizen to go over in three weeks' time in the White Star "Adriatic" to get Borden [the Canadian Prime Minister] to build her at Quebec. The Building Yard put up there by Vickers is under a guarantee to build a Dreadnought in Canada in May and the great Dreadnought Dock left Barrow for Quebec on August 31st. No English Government would ever make this plunge, which is why I propose going to Canada—to that great man, Borden—and take the Vickers people to make their bargain for building.

*   *   *   *   *

1912.
Sept. 20th.

... My idea now is to raise a syndicate to build the "Non-Pareil"! A few millionaires would suffice, and I know sufficient of them to do it. All the drawings and designs quite ready. The one *all pervading, all absorbing* thought is to get in first with motor ships before the Germans! Owing to our apathy during the last two years they are ahead with internal combustion engines! *They have killed 15 men in experiments with oil engines and we have not killed one!* And a d—d fool of an English politician told me the other day that he thinks this creditable to us!

Without any doubt (I have it from an eye-witness of part of the machinery for her at Nuremberg) a big German oil engine Cruiser is under weigh! We must press forward.... These d—d politics are barring the way.... "*What!*" (say these trembling idiots) "ANOTHER *Dreadnought Revolution!*" and these boneless fools chatter with fear like apes when they see an elephant! The imagination cannot picture that "*a greater than the Dreadnought is here!*" Imagine a silhouette presenting a target 33 per cent. less than any living or projected Battleship! No funnels—no masts—no smoke—she carries over 5,000 tons of oil, enough to take her round the world without refuelling! Imagine what that means! Ten motor boats carried on board in an armoured pit in the middle of her, where the funnels and the boilers used to be. Two of these motor boats are over 60 feet long and go 45 knots! and carry 21-inch Torpedoes that go five miles! Imagine these let loose in a sea fight!15 Imagine projectiles far over a ton weight! going over a mile or more further than even the 13½-inch gun can carry, and that gun has rightly staggered humanity!— Yes! that 13½-inch gun that all my colleagues (bar one! and he is our future Nelson! [Jellicoe]) thought me mad to force through against unanimous disapproval! *and see where we are now in consequence!* We shall have 16 British Dreadnoughts with the 13½-inch gun before the Germans *have one!!!* So it will be with the "Non-Pareil"! WE HAVE GOT TO HAVE HER ... *I've worked harder over this job than in all my life before!*16

*　　　*　　　*　　　*　　　*

1912.
DEC. 29TH.

... I'm getting sick of England and want to get back to Naples and the sun! and the "*dolce far niente!*" What fools we all are to work like we do! Till we drop!

CHAPTER XIII
AMERICANS

MY very best friends are Americans. I was the Admiral in North America, and saw "American Beauties" at Bermuda. (Those American roses and the American women are equal!) And without question they are the very best dancers in the world! (I suppose it's from so much skating!) My only son married an American lady (which rejoiced me), and an American gentleman on the steamer complimented me that she had come over and vanquished him instead of his going, as the usual way is, to America to capture her! I had such a time in America when I went over to the wedding! I never can forget the hospitality so boundless and sincere! I really might have spent three years in America (so I calculated) in paying visits earnestly desired. The Reporters (25 of them) asked me when I left what I thought of their country (I tried to dodge them, but found them all in my cabin when I went on board!) I summed it up in the one word I greatly admire—"HUSTLE!" and I got an adhesive label in America which I also loved! Great Black Block letters on a crimson ground—

RUSH

You stick it on a letter or the back of a slow fool. Mr. McCrea, the President of the Pennsylvania Railway, had his private car to take me to Philadelphia from New York. We went 90 miles in 90 minutes, and such a dinner! Two black gentlemen did it all. And I found my luggage in my room when I arrived labelled:

"MR. LORD FISHER"

(How it got there so quick I can't imagine.) I was bombed by a photographer as we arrived late at night, and an excellent photograph he took, but it gave me a shock! I had never been done like that! I had the great pleasure of dining with Mr. Woodrow Wilson. I predicted to the reporters he would be the next President for sure! I was told I was about the first to say so—anyhow, the 25 reporters put it down as my news!

I met several great Americans during my visit; but the loveliest meeting I ever had was when, long before, a charming company of American gentlemen came on July 4th to Admiralty House at Bermuda to celebrate "Independence Day!" I got my speech in before theirs! I said George Washington was the greatest Englishman who ever lived! England had never been so prosperous, thanks *solely* to him, as since *his time and now!* because he taught us how to associate with our fellow countrymen when they went abroad and set up house for themselves! And that George Washington was the precursor of that magnificent conception of John Bright in his speech of the ages when he foretold a great Commonwealth—yes a great Federation—of all those speaking the same tongue—that tongue which is the *"business"* tongue of the world—as it expresses in fewer words than any other language what one desires to convey! And I suppose now we have got Palestine that this Federal House of Commons of the future will meet at Jerusalem, the capital of the lost Ten Tribes of Israel, whom we are without doubt, for how otherwise could ever we have so prospered when we have had such idiots to guide us and rule us as those who gave up Heligoland, Tangier, Curaçoa, Corfu, Delagoa Bay, Java, Sumatra, Minorca, etc., etc.? I have been at all the places named, so am able to state from personal knowledge that only congenital idiots could have been guilty of such inconceivable folly as the surrender of them, and again I say: "Let us thank God that we are the lost ten tribes of Israel!" Mr. Lloyd George, in a famous speech long ago in the War, showed how we had been 14 times "too late!" How many more "too lates" since he made that memorable speech? Especially what about our shipbuilding and the German submarine menace and Rationing? (The only favoured trades seem to be Brewing and Racing! Both so flourishing!)

The American barber on board the "Baltic" told me a good story. He was a quaint man, clean shaved and wore black alpaca throughout. Halfway across the Atlantic I was waiting to have my hair cut, when a gentleman bounced in on him, kicking up a devil of a fuss about wanting something at once! The barber, without moving a muscle, calmed him by saying: "Are you leaving to-day, Sir?" But this was his story. He was barber in the train from Chicago to New York that never stops "even for a death" (so he told me) when the train suddenly stopped at a small village and a lady got out. Mr. Thompson, the President of the Railway, was in the train, and asked why? The conductor showed an order signed by a great man of the Railway to stop there. When Mr. Thompson got to New York he asked this great man "What excuse?" and added: "I wouldn't have done it for my wife!" and the answer he got was: "No more would I!"

But the sequel of the story is that I told this tale at an international cosmopolitan lunch party at Lucerne and said: "The curious thing is I knew the man!" when Mr. Chauncey Depew wiped me out by saying that "he knew the woman!"

This American Barber quaintly praised the Engine Driver of this Chicago train by telling me that *"he was always looking for what he didn't want!"* and so had avoided the train going into a River by noticing something wrong with the points!

By kind Permission of "London Opinion."

AMERICA AND THE BLOCKADE.

"Why Mr. Wilson should expect this country to refrain from exercising a right in return for Germany's refraining from committing wrongs is not very clear to the ordinary intelligence."—*Daily Paper.*

DAME WILSON (*to P. C. Fisher*):—"Oh, Constable! Don't hurt him. I'm sure he won't murder anyone else!"

Admiral Sampson brought his Squadron of the United States Navy to visit me at Bermuda. I was then the Admiral in North America. At the banquet I gave in his honour I proposed his health, and that of the United States. He never said a word. Presently one of his Officers went up and whispered something in his ear. I sent the wine round, and the Admiral then got up, and made the best speech I ever heard. All he said was: "It was a d—d fine old hen that hatched the American Eagle!" His chaplain, after dinner, complimented me on the Officers of my Flagship, the "Renown." He said: "He had not heard a single 'swear' from 'Soup to Pea-nuts'"!

Lord Fisher on John Bright

(FROM "BRIGHT'S HOUSE JOURNAL")

At a dinner held in London the other day to Mr. Josephus Daniels, Secretary to the United States Navy, Lord Fisher made the following speech in which he referred to a speech by Mr. John Bright:—

"Admiral of the Fleet Lord Fisher, who was called upon also to respond, was received with cheers, the whole company standing up and drinking his health. He said he had no doubt it would be pleasing to them if he spoke about America. He was there one week. Mr. Daniels had been here about one week. He was in America one week because his only son was married there to the only daughter of a great Philadelphian.

*   *   *   *   *

"'King Edward who was a kind friend to me—in fact he was my only friend at one time'—remarked Lord Fisher,' said to me, "You are the best hated man in the British Empire," and I replied, "Yes, perhaps I am." The King then said, "Do you know I am the only friend you have?" I said, "Perhaps your Majesty is right, but you have backed the winner." Afterwards I came out on top when I said, "Do you remember you backed the winner and now everyone is saying what a sagacious King you are? The betting was a thousand to one."'

*   *   *   *   *

"But he was going to tell them about America, and some of them would hear things they had never before heard about their own country. When he was at Bermuda a deputation of American citizens waited upon him on July 4th. To tell the honest truth he had forgotten about it. He told the deputation he knew what they had come there for. 'You know,' he said to them, 'the greatest Englishman that ever lived was George Washington. He taught us how to rule our Colonies. He told us that freedom was the thing to give them. Why, if it had not been for George Washington America might have been Ireland.' 'I shook hands with them,' continued Lord Fisher, 'and they went away and said nothing they had come to say....

"'Now I will talk about the League of Nations. In A.D. 1910 an American citizen wished to see me; and he said to me, taking a paper out of his pocket, "Have you read that?" I looked at it and saw it was a speech by John Bright, mostly in words of one syllable—simplicity is, of course, the great thing. That speech is really very little known on this side of the Atlantic or on the other, but it so impressed me at the time that I have been thinking of it ever since. John Bright said he looked forward to the time when there would be a compulsory peace—when those who spoke with the same tongue would form a great federation of free nations joined together.'"

The following is an extract from the speech by Mr. John Bright. It was delivered at Edinburgh in 1868:—

"I do not know whether it is a dream or a vision, or the foresight of a future reality that sometimes passes across my mind—I like to dwell upon it—but I frequently think the time may come when the maritime nations of Europe—this renowned country of which we are citizens, France, Prussia, resuscitated Spain, Italy, and the United States of America—may see that vast fleets are of no use; that they are merely menaces offered from one country to another; and that they may come to this wise conclusion—that they will combine at their joint expense, and under some joint management, to supply the sea with a sufficient sailing and armed police which may be necessary to keep the peace on all parts of the watery surface of the globe, and that those great instruments of war and oppression shall no longer be upheld. This, of course, by many will be thought to be a dream or a vision, not the foresight of what they call a statesman."

SIR HIRAM MAXIM

When Sir Hiram Maxim—that great American—was very little known, he came to see me when I was Captain of the Gunnery ship at Portsmouth, bringing with him his ever-famous Maxim gun, to be tried by me. So we went to Whale Island to practise with the gun; and when he was ready to fire I adopted the usual practice in trying all new guns and ordered the experimental party to get under cover; and at that order they were supposed to go into a sort of dug-out. Evidently old Maxim considered this an insult to his gun, and he roared out at the top of his voice: "Britishers under cover, Yankees out in the open!" The gun didn't burst and it was all right; but it might have, all the same.

Admiral Hornby the bravest of the brave, was one of the Britishers; and he came to lunch with me, being extremely fascinated with Hiram's quaintness. Hiram was a delightful man in my opinion, and I remember his telling me that if I wanted to live long and see good days the thing was to eat Pork and Beans. I never had the chance, till 1910, of eating them cooked à l'Américaine; and I then agreed with Hiram Maxim—no more delicious dish in the world, but you can't get it in England! After lunch there were some oranges on the table; and to my dying day I shall never forget the extraordinary look on Sir Geoffrey Hornby's beautiful, refined face as Hiram reached out and grasped an orange from the centre of the table—tore it apart, and buried his face sucking out the contents, emerging all orange. He told us that was the way to enjoy an orange. We neither of us were up to it!

CHAPTER XIV
SOME SPECIAL MISSIONS

I WAS sent as a very young Lieutenant to a little fishing village called Heppens in Oldenburg. It is now Wilhelmshaven, chief Naval Port of Germany. Its river, the Jahde, was then a shallow stream. The occasion for my visit was the cession to King William of Prussia, as he was then, of this place, Heppens, by the Grand Duke of Oldenburg; and there I met King William, to whom I sat next but one at lunch, and Bismarck and von Moltke and von Roon were there. We had a very long-winded speech from the Burgomaster, and Bismarck, whom I was standing next to, said to me in the middle of it: "I didn't know this was going to happen, or I would have cut him short." The King asked me at lunch why I had been sent, and if there was no one else who knew about torpedoes. Well, I don't think there was. It was an imposing and never-to-be-forgotten sight, that lunch. They all wore their helmets and great-coats at lunch—so mediæval—and telegrams kept coming to Bismarck, who would get up and draw the King aside, and then they would sit down again. Von Roon I thought very *débonnaire*, and Moltke was like an old image, taciturn and inscrutable, but he talked English as well as I did.

Years after this, Prince Adalbert's Naval Aide-de-camp, who was a great friend of mine, told me that on the day of mobilization in the war with France he was sent to von Moltke with a message from Prince Adalbert, who was King William's brother and Head of the Navy, to ask him whether he could see Prince Adalbert for a few moments. To his astonishment, my friend found Moltke lying on a sofa reading "Lady Audley's Secret," by Miss Braddon, and he told him he could see the Prince for as long as he liked and whenever he liked. The word "Mobilize" had finished all his work for the present.

On the occasion of my visit I imagined and reported what Heppens would become, and so it did. I never can make out why I didn't get a German decoration. I think perhaps they thought me too young. However, I had the honour of an empty sentry-box placed outside the little inn where I was staying; and if I had been of higher rank there would have been a sentry in it. The little inn was very unpretentious, and when the landlord had carved for us he came and sat down at table with us. Some days after, at a very exclusive Military Club in Berlin, I met the King's two illegitimate brothers. They were exactly like him; also I breakfasted with the Head of the German Mining School. I remember it, because we only had raw herring and black bread for breakfast. He was very poor, although he was exceeding clever, and had as his right-hand man a wonderful chemist. So far as I know, the present German mine is nearly what it was then, and the sea-gulls rested on the protuberances as they do now, for I went to Kiel Bay to see them. There was a lovely hotel at Kiel, where they treated me royally. I recommended the adoption of these German mines, and it's a pity we didn't. They hold the field to this very day. However, the First Sea Lord of that date didn't believe in mines or torpedoes or submarines, and I was packed off to China in the old two-decker "Donegal," as Commander of the China Flagship. Long afterwards Sir Hastings Yelverton, who became First Sea Lord, unburied my Memorandum headed "Ocean Warfare," and supported the views in it. It enunciated the principle of "Hit first, hit hard, and keep on hitting," and discoursed on Submarines and Mines.

REVAL

You are remarking to me of a charming letter written to me by the late Emperor of Russia's youngest sister—the Grand Duchess Olga. She is a peculiarly sweet creature. Her nickname amongst the Russians was "Sunshine." Stolypin, the Prime Minister, told me that, and he also said to me that she was a kind of life-buoy because if you walked about with her you would not get bombed by an anarchist. All loved her.

I made her acquaintance first at Carlsbad. On my arrival at the hotel I found King Edward's Equerry waiting in the hall. I had written to tell the King, who was at Marienbad, in answer to his enquiry, as to the day I should arrive and what time; and he came over to Marienbad from Carlsbad. I went then and there and found him just finishing lunch with a peculiarly charming looking young lady, who turned out to be the Grand Duchess Olga, and her husband, the Grand Duke of Oldenburg, from whom happily she is now divorced (I didn't like the look of him at all). The King, having satisfied himself that I had had lunch, and he then smoking a cigar as big as a capstan bar, after talking of various things which interested him, told me that his niece, the Grand Duchess Olga, did not know anyone in Carlsbad, and he relied on me to make her time there pleasant, so I promptly asked her if she could waltz. She said she loved it, but she somehow never got the step properly, whereupon I asked the King if he had any objection to getting into the corner of the room while I moved the table and took the rugs up to give her Imperial Highness a lesson. He made some little difficulty at first, but eventually went into the corner; and when the lesson began he was quite pleased and clapped his hands and called out "Bravo!" The best waltz tune in the world is one of Moody and Sankey's hymns. I don't know whether Sankey originated the saying that he didn't see why the Devil should have all the good music. I don't by that implicate that the waltz was the devil's; but, without any doubt, there is a good deal of temptation in it, and when you get a good partner you cleave to her all the evening.

This dancing lesson was an unalloyed success, so I asked her to a dance the next night at the Savoy Hotel; and after some more words with the King I left, and walking down the stairs to go to my hotel, I thought to myself: "How on earth are you going to get up a dance when you don't know a soul in the place?" when who should I meet but a friend of mine—a Spanish Grandee, the Marquis de Villa Vieja, and he arranged what really turned out to be a ball, as he knew everybody, and I having some dear American friends at Marienbad I telegraphed them to come over and dine with the Grand Duchess and stay the night for the ball, and they did. When the dance had begun, and the Grand Duchess was proving quite equal to her lesson of the day before, suddenly an apparition of extraordinary grace and loveliness appeared at the door. Villa Vieja took on the Grand Duchess and I welcomed the beautiful Polish Countess and danced with her many waltzes running in spite of a hint I received that her husband was very jealous and a renowned duellist. Next day, by telegram from the King, I was told by His Majesty that Isvolsky, the Russian Minister of Foreign Affairs, was to be asked by me to lunch on his arrival that day from St. Petersburg. I invited him; and just as we sat down to lunch the Polish angel of the night before came through the door and petrified Isvolsky, and the more so as she kissed her hand to me. He never took his eyes off her, and as she walked to her table I heard him breathe a sigh, and say *sotto voce*, "Alas, in heaven no woman!" I said to him: "Monsieur Isvolsky, pray pardon me; perhaps you did not intend it to be heard, but if it be true what you say, it takes away much of the charm which I had anticipated finding there." He turned to me and said—quoting chapter and verse in the Revelations, "There was silence in heaven."

So when I met the Grand Duchess Olga again, when I accompanied King Edward on that memorable visit to Reval—when, as Prince Orloff, the Emperor's principal aide-de-camp, said to me, King Edward changed the atmosphere of Russian feelings towards England from suspicion to cordial trust—there was quite an affectionate meeting, and we danced the "Merry Widow" waltz—a then famous stage performance—with such effect as to make the Empress of Russia laugh. They told me she had not laughed for two years. At the banquet preceding the dance the Grand Duchess and I, I regret to say, made such a disturbance in our mutual jokes that King Edward called out to me that I must try to remember that it was not the Midshipmen's Mess; and my dear Grand Duchess thought I should be sent to Siberia or somewhere. We sailed at daylight, and I got a letter from her when I arrived in England saying she had made a point of seeing Uncle Bertie and that it was all right, I was not going to be punished. Then she went on to describe that she had had a very happy day (being her birthday) picnicking in the woods; the only drawback was, she told me, that the gnats would bite her ankles. Being, at that period, both a courtier and a sycophant, I telegraphed to her at some Palace she was at in Russia to say "I wished to God I had been one of the gnats." It was weeks before she got the telegram, as the Russian Secret Department believed it was from some anarchist, and was a cypher for bombing the Emperor or something of the sort, and there was a lot of bother to trace out who had sent it.

I find among my papers another charming letter which I received from the Grand Duchess Olga. It runs:

PETERHOF.
11/25 July, 1909.

DEAR ADMIRAL,

I have been going to write to you for ever so long and now is a chance to send you a few lines.

How are you getting on? We speak of you very often. I suppose you'll be going to Carlsbad this automn—and I am very sorry that we are not going—so as to meet you there!

I have a great favour to ask you—but as I believe and think you *can* grant it—I shall ask: Lieutenant —— of your Royal Navy—whom we got to like very much two years ago at Sorrento—is willing to come this automn and spend a month with us at our country place—*if* he gets leaves of course; I write all this to you as I don't know who else can help and give him leave.

We should like to have him about the middle of your September (the very beginning of ours). If you think he can get leave just then would you kindly telegraph to me—then I could write and ask him (I suppose he will be at Cowes?). Today is my namesday, and having received any amounts of presents—we are going to Church—as one always does—on such occasions and then there will be a rather big lunch and the band will play—All this glorious occasion is not only for me—but also for my niece Olga.

My sister Xenia—who does not know you—says she is sorry not to have that honour and pleasure!

My husband sends his best love (or whatever one says). Goodbye dear Admiral. I wish I was going to see you soon it would be awfully amusing. Write to me later on when you will be free please!

Much love and good wishes.

OLGA.

P.S. Mrs. Francklin sends lots of kind messages and love. Mama sends her best love too.

That visit of King Edward to Russia was really quite remarkable for the really eloquent speech the King made, without a note of any sort. I said to him at breakfast the next morning, when they brought in a copy of what they thought he had said, that I wondered on such a momentous occasion he didn't have it written out. "Well!" he said to me, "I did try that once, when the French President Loubet came to visit me, and I learnt the speech off by heart in the garden of Buckingham Palace. When I got up to say it, I could not remember it, and had to keep on beginning again at the beginning. So I said to myself, 'Never again'!" And I must say I share his conviction that there is no such eloquence as when out of the abundance of the heart the mouth speaketh. Emotion and earnestness will do much more than move mountains; they will move multitudes—and that was what King Edward was able to do.

I have spoken elsewhere of what I deemed was a suitable epitaph for him— those great words of Pascal: "le cœur a ses raisons que la raison ne connaît point." The heart has reasons that the mind knows nothing about.

God bless him!

Stolypin, when we met him at Reval on King Edward's visit to the Czar, was described to us as the greatest, the bravest and most single-minded Prime Minister that Russia had ever possessed. He spoke English fluently, and certainly was very pro-English. He was beyond deception. His only daughter, he told me, had been killed by a bomb while he was walking with her in the garden, and one of his hands was greatly mutilated by the same explosion. He was murdered at the theatre at Moscow not very long afterwards. We had many conversations together. He said it was criminal folly having the capital of Russia elsewhere than inland, as at Moscow, for that Petersburg was open to German attack by sea. He seemed to have a prophetic view of England's imbecility as regards using her enormous sea supremacy to prevent the Baltic becoming a German lake, as it became in the war, though we were five times stronger than the German Fleet. So it passed by as an idle dream, any idea of England's interference, and alas! he remembered our betrayal of Denmark when the Germans took Kiel and Schleswig-Holstein.

Stolypin repeatedly said to me the German frontier was his one and only thought, and he was devoting all his life to make that frontier impregnable against Germany, both in men and munitions, and strategic arrangements. But he did not live long enough to carry out his scheme.

CARTAGENA

I also went with King Edward to Cartagena, when he returned the King of Spain's visit. King Alfonso, whom I had previously met in England, was very cordial to me because we had seven "Dreadnoughts" ready before the Germans had one. In fact, when I told him this piece of news, as we were walking up and down the deck, with King Edward and Queen Alexandra watching us from two deck-chairs, King Alfonso was so delighted that he threw his arms round my neck, cried "You darling!" and kissed me. Then he put his hand in his waistcoat pocket, took out a chocolate and popped it into my mouth. He gave me the highest Spanish Order he could. But when the box came on board containing it, it turned out to be the Order of Isabella the Catholic, which is only given to Roman Catholics; but the interesting thing is that when I was a little Midshipman I had been reading "Ferdinand and Isabella," and I remember saying to my messmates that I intended some day to have the Order of Isabella the Catholic. And when, some years after, as a Lieutenant it was the fashion to wear medal ribbons in a rosette, upon some supercilious officer asking me what "that thing" was in my button-hole, I quite remember saying, by way of pulling his leg, that it was the Spanish Order of Isabella the Catholic. However, I got the proper Order in time to wear at the banquet.

The banquet was a very fine sight, as King Alfonso had brought down the tapestries, pictures and other ornaments from the Escurial. The Spanish Admirals were a grand sight. They wore the ancient uniform, and each had a great Malacca cane with a big gold top. They all came on board to call on King Edward in an old-fashioned pulling barge, and the sailors wore crimson and gold sashes. That rowing barge and the splendid uniforms lay at the root of one occasion when King Edward was really angry with me. I had been arranging for him the details of the great Naval Review and was summoned to Buckingham Palace to discuss them with him. I found no Equerries in attendance, no one about, and the King white with anger. "So!" he cried out to me, "I'm to go by such and such a train, am I? And I'm to embark at such and such a time, am I? And I'm to use your barge because it's a better barge than mine, is it? Look here, *am I the King or are you?*" The upshot of the interview was that he threw the papers on the floor, with "Have it your own way!" But the secret cause of his anger was that he had made up his mind to go off in a rowing-boat like the Spanish Admirals, forgetting that there is no tide at Cartagena, whereas the tide at Cowes runs many knots, and it would have taken a rowing-boat hours to do what the barge could do in a few minutes.

KIAMIL PASHA

One of the most pleasurable incidents of my holding the appointment of Commander-in-Chief of the Mediterranean Fleet was going to Smyrna to do honour to that splendid old Turk, Kiamil Pasha. He was then Vali, or Governor, of the Province of Smyrna. He was most hale and vigorous. He so delighted me with his conversations and experiences that it's a sincere joy to me now to recall, even in this humble way, what a magnificent old man he was, and how he had so often placed his life in jeopardy for the sake of right and for the good of his country, which last, he said (he spoke most fluent English), had been "imperishably bound up with England's righteous work in the East." He had been many times Grand Vizier, and he knew all the secret incidents following and preceding the Crimean War. And he said fervidly that England was the only nation that never asked and never schemed to get anything out of Turkey. And he said it was only the insensate folly of the English Authorities that could ever have dislodged England from her wonderful supremacy over the minds of the whole Turkish people. I told him, in return, that the English treatment of Turkey was only on a par with the English folly of giving up Heligoland, Corfu, Tangier, Minorca, Java, Sumatra, Curaçoa (the key of the Panama Canal), Delagoa Bay (the only harbour in Africa), and so on, and so on, and explained, to his delighted amusement, that we were a nation of Lions led by Asses. He pretty well foretold all that has happened since 1902.

With respect to Tangier, which was the dowry of Henrietta Maria, I diverge a moment to mention that a great Spaniard in high office once said to me that it was a curious fact that whenever Spain had left the side of England she had inevitably come to grief.

Following on Kiamil's wonderful prescience, I found on my visit to the Sultan, who had invited me to Constantinople, that all I had heard from him about Bulgaria was confirmed at Constantinople. One and all said that Bulgaria was the fighting nation, and that Bulgaria was the Key of the East. I was so saturated with the importance of this fact that I spoke to Kitchener about it when the War commenced, but we did not give Bulgaria what she wanted, and when, a year afterwards, she was offered the same terms it was too late.

A great Bank always, I believe, has a travelling inspector who visits all the branches. We want such a personage to visit all our representatives in foreign lands, and see what they have done for England in the previous year.

CHAPTER XV
SOME PERSONALITIES

AMONGST the 13 First Lords of the Admiralty I have had to deal with (and with nine of them I was very intimately associated) I should like to record that in my opinion Lord George Hamilton and Lord Spencer had the toughest jobs, because of the constitution of their respective Boards of Admiralty; and yet neither of them received the credit each of them deserved for his most successful administration. With both of them their tact was unsurpassable. They had to deal with extremely able colleagues, and my experience is that it is not a good thing to have a lot of able men associated together. If you take a little of the best Port Wine, the best Champagne, the best Claret, and the best Hock and mix them together, the result is disastrous. So often is it with a Board of Admiralty. That's why I have suffered fools gladly! But Lord George Hamilton and Lord Spencer had an awful time of it. To both of these (I consider) great men I am very specially beholden. Lord George Hamilton more particularly endured much on my behalf when I was Director of Naval Ordnance, fighting the War Office. It was his own decision that sent me to Portsmouth as Admiral Superintendent of the Dockyard, and thus enabled me practically to prove the wisdom and the economy of concentrating workmen on one ship like a hive of bees and adopting piece-work to the utmost limit. Cannot anyone realise that if you have your men spread over many ships building, your capital is producing no dividend as compared with getting a ship rushed and sent to sea ready to fight? I was held up as a dramatic *poseur* because the "Dreadnought" was built in a year and a day. Yes! She was ready to fight in a year and a day. She did fire her guns. The "Inflexible," her famous prototype in former years, which I commanded, was four or five years building. I took up the battleship "Royal Sovereign" when I went as Superintendent of Portsmouth Dockyard and got her completed within two years, and thereby saw my way to doing it in a year. And so would I have done the famous "Hush Hush" ships, as I said I would; only circumstances brought about my departure from the Admiralty, and apathy came back, and those "Hush Hush" ships consequently took more than a year to build. And some armchair quill-drivers still sling ink at 'em. And when I heard from an eye-witness how the whole lot of German cruisers did flee when they appeared and ought to have been gobbled up I rubbed my hands with malignant glee at the devastation of my pen-and-ink enemies. As usual in the war, on that occasion the business wasn't pushed home.

To revert to my theme—I owe also a great debt to Lord George Hamilton, when at a previous stage of my career he dissuaded me from accepting an offer from Lord Rothschild, really beyond the dreams of avarice, of becoming the head of a great armament and shipbuilding combine, which accordingly fell through on my refusal. Had I gone, I'd have been a millionaire instead of a pauper as I am now; but I wouldn't have been First Sea Lord from 1904 to 1910 and then "Sacking the Lot!" Lord George also selected me to be Controller of the Navy.

Lord Spencer called a horse after me—almost as great an honour. Lord Spencer was really a very magnificent man, and he had the attributes of his great ancestor, who selected Nelson over a great many of his seniors to go and win the Battle of the Nile. There was no one else who would have done it; and when Sir John Orde, one of the aggrieved Admirals, told the King that the selected Nelson was mad, he replied, "I wish to God he would bite you all!" My Lord Spencer had the same gift of selection—it's the biggest gift that a man in such a position can have, and the life, the fate of his country may depend upon him. Only war finds out poltroons. Lord Spencer turned out his master, to whom he was faithfully devoted, when he saw the Navy was in danger and that Mr. Gladstone would not agree to strengthen it. His manners were superb. He satisfied that great description of what constitutes a gentleman: "He never hurt any man's feelings."

There's another First Lord I have too faintly alluded to—Lord Northbrook. He also was a great man, but he was not considered so by the populace. He was a victim to his political associates—they let him in. His finance at the Admiralty was bad through no fault of his, and he was persuaded to go to Egypt, which I think was a mistake. I stayed with him, and the microscope of home revealed him to me. His conceptions were magnificent and his decisions were like those of the Medes and Persians. Of all the awful people in the world nothing is so terrible as a vacillator. I am not sure the Devil isn't right when he says, "Tell a lie and stick to it." Lord Northbrook also in spite of intense opposition laid hold of my hand and led me forth in the paths I glory in, of Reform and Revolution. Stagnation, in my opinion, is the curse of life. I have no fellow-feeling with those placid souls who, like a duck-pond, torpid and quiescent, live the life of cabbages. I don't believe anybody can say, "Of such is the Kingdom of Heaven," because it is immortally shown that strife is the secret of a good life.

As with Lord Spencer, so was it with Lord Selborne. He again, as First Lord of the Admiralty, took the unusual course of kindly coming to Malta to see me when I commanded the Mediterranean fleet (the Boer War placed England in a very critical position at that time); and though there was a great strife with the Admiralty he chose me after my three years as Commander-in-Chief to be Second Sea Lord of the Admiralty and permitted me to unfold a scheme of education which came into being on the following Christmas Day without the alteration of a comma. More than that, he benevolently spared me from the Admiralty to become Commander-in-Chief at Portsmouth, to see that scheme carried out. Many letters have I that that step indicated the end of my naval career. I believe to that date it always has been so, but within a year I was First Sea Lord, and never did any First Lord hold more warmly the hand of his principal adviser than Lord Selborne held mine.

There are few people living to whom I am under a greater obligation than Admiral Sir Francis Bridgeman, G.C.B. This distinguished sailor aided me in the gradual building up of the Grand Fleet. As I have said before, it had to be done unostentatiously and by slow degrees, for fear of exciting the attention of the German Admiralty and too much embroiling myself with the Admirals whose fleets had to be denuded till they disappeared, so as to come under Admiral Sir Francis Bridgeman's command, with whom the Grand Fleet originated under the humble designation of the Home Fleet—a gathering and perpetuation of the old more or less stationary coast-guard ships scattered all round the United Kingdom and, as the old phrase was, "Grounding on their beef bones" as they swung with the tide at their anchors. In the Providence of God the animosities of the Admirals thus engendered caused the real success of the whole scheme—and what should have been as clear as crystal to the least observant onlooker was obscured by the fumes of anger exuding from these scandalized Admirals. I look back with astonishment at my Job-like conduct, but it had its compensations. I hope Sir Francis Bridgeman will forgive me for hauling him into this book— I have no other way of showing him my eternal gratitude; and it was with intense delight that I congratulated Mr. Churchill on obtaining his services to succeed Sir Arthur Wilson, the First Sea Lord, who had so magnificently adhered to the scheme I left.

Sir Arthur refused a Peerage, and he was a faithful and self-effacing friend in his room at the Admiralty those seven fateful months I was First Sea Lord during the war. It was peculiarly fortunate and providential that the two immediately succeeding First Sea Lords after my departure on January 25th, 1910, should have been the two great sailors they were—otherwise there would have been no Grand Fleet—they altered nothing, and the glacier moved along, resistless and crushing all the obstacles in its path, and now, after the war, it has passed on; the dead corpses of the foes of the scheme are disclosed, and we'll bury them without comment.

I began these talks by solemnly declaring that I would not mention a single living name—please let it stand—it shows what one's intention was; but one is really forced to stand up to such outstanding personalities as Sir Arthur Wilson and Sir Francis Bridgeman, and I again repeat with all the emphasis at my command that it would have been impossible to have conducted those eight great years of ceaseless reform, culminating in the production of the most incomparable fleet that ever existed, had not the two Political Administrations, four First Lords, and every member of the several Boards of Admiralty been, as I described them in public, united, determined, and progressive. Never for one instant did a single Board of Admiralty during that time lay on its oars. For to rest on our oars would not have been standing still; the malignant tide was fierce against us, and the younger Officers of the fleet responded splendidly.

On January 3rd, 1903, I wrote as follows in reply to some criticism of me as First Sea Lord:—

"Our Fleets are 50 per cent. more at sea, and we hit the target 50 per cent. more than we did two years ago.

"In the first year there were 2,000 more misses than hits!

"In the second year there were 2,000 more hits than misses!"

The very first thing I did when I returned to the Admiralty as First Sea Lord for those seven months in the first year of the war was instantly to get back Sir Percy Scott into the Fighting Arena. I had but one answer to all his detractors and to the opposition to his return:—

"He hits the target!"

He *also* was maliciously maligned. I don't mean to say that Sir Percy Scott indulges in soft soap towards his superiors. I don't think he ever poured hot water down anybody's back. Let us thank God he didn't!

I have repeatedly said (and I reiterate it whenever I get the chance) that Nelson was nothing if he was not insubordinate. Nelson's four immortal Big Fights are brilliant and everlasting testimonies to the virtues of Self-Assertion, Self-Reliance, and Contempt of Authority. But of Nelson and the Nelsonic attributes I treat in another place. (Ah! Lord Rosebery, if only you had written "Nelson's Last Phase"! I entreated you, but without avail!) (Again a repetition!) Nelson's *Life* not yet written! Southey's *Life*, meant only for schoolboys, still holds the field. W. T. Stead might have done it, for the sacred fire of Great Emotions was the calorific of Stead's Internal Combustion Engine. Suffice it to say of Sir Percy Scott that it was he and he alone who made the first start of the Fleet's hitting the enemy and not missing him. Why hasn't *he* been made a Viscount? But that is reserved for those in another sphere!

"The Tides—and Sir Frederick Treves."—One of my greatest benefactors (he saved my life. Six doctors wanted to operate on me—he wouldn't have it; the consequence—I'm better now than ever I was in my life) is Sir Frederick Treves, Surgeon, Orator, Writer, "Developer of the Powers of Observation." He, this morning, September 16th, 1919, gives me something to think about. It has relation to my dear and splendid friend Sir Charles

Parsons, President of the British Association and inventor of the Turbine, who said the other day at Bournemouth that our coal bids fair to fail and we must seek other sources of power. Considering that Sir Charles invented the Turbine—derided by everyone as a box of tricks, and it now monopolises 80 per cent. of the horse-power of the world—we ought to listen to him. His idea is to dig a twelve-mile hole into the earth to get hold of power. Now Sir Frederick in his letter this morning uses these words:

"*England is an Island.* We are surrounded on all sides with the greatest source of power in the world—the *Tides.*

"There is enough force in the Tides to light and heat the whole country, *and to run all its railways.* It is running to waste while we are bellowing for coal."

I know exactly what the Royal Society will say to Sir Frederick Treves. The Royal Society, not so many years ago, said through one of its most distinguished members that the aeroplane was a physical impossibility. When I said this to Sir Hiram Maxim he placed his thumb to his nose and extended his fingers; and, as I have remarked elsewhere, aeroplanes are now as plentiful as sparrows. So do not let us put Sir Frederick Treves in the waste paper basket. He's a great man. When Lord Lister and my dear friend Sir Thomas Smith were beholding him operating on King Edward at the time when his illness stopped his Coronation—even those two wonderful surgeons held their breath at Treves's astounding skill and confidence. He kept on, and saved King Edward's life. There was no "Not running risks" with him. He snatched his King from death. The others both thought Death had won, and they both exclaimed!

Sir Frederick won't see this until he reads it in his presentation copy of this book, or he wouldn't have it.

And then he is so choice in his educational ideas. Here's a lovely morsel, which I commend to Schoolmasters (Curse 'em! they ruined Osborne). Sir Frederick says:—

"Our present system of education is on a par with the Training of Performing Dogs, they're merely taught tricks! and Trick antics do not help a boy much in the serious business of life. There is no attempt to get at the mind of a boy, and still less any attempt to find out his particular abilities. The only thing is, Is he good at Mental Acrobatics? A very fine book on 'The New Education'17 was published in the Autumn of last year, 1918. It shows up the wasteful absurdities of the present Educational System. Of course, no attention has been paid to it, because it is so simple, so evident, and so human.... Years are spent in teaching a boy Latin Verses, but never a moment to teach him '*How to develop powers of Observation.*'"

I could tell my readers instances of Sir Frederick's powers in this last regard; and the medical students during the many years he was their Lecturer could all of them do Sir Frederick greater justice than I can.

"God bless Sir Frederick Treves!"

Of all the famous men I have known, Lord Kelvin had the greatest brain. He went to sea with me in many new ships that I commanded. Once, in a bleak March east wind at Sheerness I found him on deck on a high pedestal exposed to the piercing blast watching his wonderful compass, and he had only a very thin coat on. I said: "For goodness sake, Sir William, come down and put on a great coat." He said: "No, thank you, I am quite warm. I've got several vests on." His theory was that it was much warmer wearing many thin vests than one thick one, as the interstices of one were filled up by the next one, and so on. I explained this afterwards, as I sat one day at lunch next to the Emperor of Russia, when he asked me to explain my youth and good health, and I hoped that he would follow Lord Kelvin's example, as I did. Lord Kelvin got this idea of a number of thin vests instead of one thick one from the Chinese, who, in many ways, are our superiors.

For instance, a Chinaman, like an ancient Greek or Roman, maintains that the liver is the seat of the human affections. We believe that the heart is. So a Chinese always offers his hand and his liver to the young lady of his choice. Neither do they ever kiss each other in China. Confucius stopped it because the lips are the most susceptible portion of the human body to infection. When two Chinese meet, they rub their knees with their hands, and say "Ah" with a deep breath. A dear friend of mine went to the Viceroy of Nankin to enquire how his newly-raised Army was getting on with the huge consignment of magnificent rifles sent out from England for its use. The Chinese Viceroy told my friend he was immensely pleased with these rifles, and the reports made to him showed extraordinary accuracy, as the troops hit the target every time. The Viceroy sent my friend up in a Chinese gunboat to see the Army. When my friend landed he was received by the Inspector-General of Musketry, who was a peacock feather Mandarin, and taken to see the soldiers firing. To my friend's amazement the soldiers were firing at the targets placed only a few hundred yards off, and he explained to the Mandarin that these wonderful rifles fitted with telescopic sights were meant for long ranges, and their accuracy was wonderful. The Mandarin replied to him: "Look here! my orders from the Viceroy are that every man in the army should hit the target, because these rifles are so wonderfully good, and so they do, and the Viceroy is very pleased at my reports." And he added: "You know, we go back 2,000 years before your people in our knowledge of the world."

Lord Kelvin had a wonderful gift of being able to pursue abstruse investigations in the hubbub of a drawing room full of visitors. He would produce a large green book out of a gamekeeper's pocket he had at the back of his coat, and suddenly go ahead with figures. I had an interesting episode once. Sir William Thomson, as he then was, had come with me for the first voyage of a new big cruiser that I commanded. I had arranged for various responsible persons to report to me at 8 a.m. how various parts of the ship were behaving. One of them reported that a rivet was loose, and there was a slight leak. I said casually: "I wonder how much water would come in if the rivet came out altogether." Sir William was sitting next me at breakfast, very much enjoying eggs and bacon, and he asked the Officer: "How big is the rivet?" and whereabouts it was, etc. The Officer left, and Sir William went on with his eggs and bacon, and I talked to Sir Nathaniel Barnaby on the other side of me, who was the designer of the ship that we were in. Presently, Sir William, in a mild voice, never having ceased his eggs and bacon, said so much water would come in. Sir N. Barnaby thereupon worked it out on paper and said to Sir William: "You made a good guess." He replied: "I didn't guess. I worked it out."

The Midshipmen idolised Lord Kelvin, and they were very intimate with him. I heard one of them, who was four-foot-nothing, explain to Sir William how to make a magnet. Sir William listened to the Midshipman's lecture on magnetism with the greatest deference, and gave the little boy no idea of what a little ass he was to be talking to the greatest man on earth on the subject of magnetism. The same little boy took the time for him in observing the lighthouse flashes, and Sir William wrote a splendid letter to *The Times* pointing out that the intervals of darkness should be the exception, and the flashes of light the rule, in a lighthouse, whereupon the Chief Engineer of the Lighthouse Department traversed Sir William's facts. The little boy came up to Sir William and asked him if he had read the letter, and he hadn't, so he told him of it and then asked Sir William if he would like him to write to *The Times* to corroborate him. Sir William thanked him sweetly, but said he would take no notice, as they would alter the flashes, and so they did.

This little boy was splendid. He played me a Machiavellian trick. We had an ass one night as Officer of the Watch, and in the middle watch I was nearly jerked out of my cot by a heavy squall striking the ship. I rushed up on deck (raining torrents) and we got in what was left of the sails, and I came down soaked through and bitterly cold, and on the main deck I met my young friend, the little Midshipman, with a smoking hot bowl of cocoa. I never enjoyed anything more in my life, and I blessed the little boy, but it suddenly occurred to me that he was as dry as a bone. I said: "How is it you are dressed?" He said: "I am Midshipman of the watch." I said: "The devil you are! How is it you aren't wet?" "Well, sir," he said, "I thought I should be best doing my duty by going below and making you a bowl of cocoa." I felt I had sold myself, like Esau, for a mess of pottage. He was a splendid boy, and he wrote me periodically till he died. He was left a fortune. He was turned out of the Navy for knocking his Captain down. I received a telegram to say that he was ill and delirious and talking of me only, and almost immediately afterwards a telegram came to say he was dead.

Sir Nathaniel Barnaby, the eminent Director of Naval Construction at the Admiralty, was also a great man, but he never had recognition. He was not self-assertive. He was as meek as Moses, and he was a saint. It was he conceived the wonder of the time—the "Inflexible"; and I was her first Captain. He went out in her with me to the Mediterranean. We had an awful gale in the Bay of Biscay. Sir Nathaniel nearly died with sea-sickness. I was cheering him up, and he whispered in reply: "Fools build houses for wise men to live in. Wise men build ships for fools to go in."

If ever there was a great Christian, he was. After he retired he devoted his whole life to Sunday schools, not only in this country, but in America. There was some great scheme, of which he gave me particulars at the time, of a vast association of all Sunday schools wherever the English tongue is spoken. Perhaps it is in being now—I don't know; but it was a fine conception that on some specified day throughout the world every child should join in some hymn and prayer for that great idea of John Bright's—the Commonwealth of Free Nations, all speaking the same grand old English tongue. I was too busy ever to follow that up, as I would have liked to have done, and been his missionary.

A letter which he wrote to me in 1910, and a much earlier note of mine to him, which he enclosed with it, are interesting, and I give them here:

Letter from Sir Nathaniel Barnaby, K.C.B. (formerly Chief Constructor of the Navy) to Lord Fisher.

MORAY HOUSE,
Lewisham, S.E.
15th January, 1910

MY DEAR ADMIRAL,

I suppose the enclosed brief note must have been written by you to me over a quarter of a century ago. You were meditating "Dreadnoughts" even then and finding in me the opposition on the ground of "the degradation of our other Ironclads" through the introduction of the "18-knot 'Nonsuch.'"

I have said to you before that I love a man who knows his own mind, and insists on getting his way. I have therefore no complaint to make.

In a note dated two days earlier I see you say, "Bother the money! if we are all agreed that will be forthcoming."

And they accuse you of cheeseparing and starving the Navy!

It was I that stood for economy—see enclosed, on the principal events affecting and indicating Naval Policy, 1866–1884, drawn up by me for Mr. Campbell-Bannerman.

See also the other side of me in a letter to the Peace Society People, and see a little hymn written for children to "Russian National Anthem" and now widely sung.

With sincere respect and good wishes,

Yours always,
(Signed) NATHANIEL BARNABY.

Please return your note to me; nothing else.

SIR JOHN FISHER AT THE HAGUE PEACE CONFERENCE, MAY, 1899.

This was the old letter of mine which he enclosed:—

From Lord Fisher to Sir N. Barnaby in 1883.

January 25th.

I have delayed sending you this letter hoping to find copy of a brief article I wrote on H.M. Ironclad "Nonsuch" of 18 knots, after seeing your design A; I can't find it, and have written for the original, which I will send for your amusement. I don't think your argument is a sound one as to the "degradation of our other ironclads by the construction of an 18-knotter." Isn't the principle right to make each succeeding ironclad an improvement and as perfect as you can?

THERE IS NO PROGRESS IN UNIFORMITY!!

We've had enough of the "Admiral" class of ship. Now try your hand on a "Nonsuch" (of vast speed!).

In violent haste,
Ever yours,
(Sgd.)   J. A. F.

"Build few, and build fast,

Each one better than the last."

Two of Sir Nathaniel Barnaby's great successors in that arduous and always thankless post of Director of Naval Construction are Sir Philip Watts and Sir Eustace Tennyson-D'Eyncourt. These two great men have each of them done such service as should have brought them far greater honour than as yet they have received. The "Dreadnought" could not have been born but for Sir Philip Watts. I commend to all who wish to have a succinct account of the ships of the British Navy that formed the line of battle on the outbreak of war on the 4th August, 1914, to read the paper delivered by Sir Philip Watts at the Spring Meeting of the Naval Architects on the 9th April, 1919, when a very excellent Sea Officer with more brains than most people I have met presided—being the Marquis of Bristol. And it was a great delight to me that he commanded the "Renown," my favourite ship, to bring to England King Alfonso—an equally admired hero of mine. If ever there was a brave man it is King Alfonso.

My other scientific hero besides Sir Philip Watts is Sir Eustace D'Eyncourt. He also was the practical means, besides his wonderful professional genius, of bringing forth what are known as the "Hush Hush" ships on account of the mystery surrounding their construction; and notwithstanding the armchair "Know-alls" who have done their best to blast their reputation, they achieved—the five of them—a phenomenal success. Sir Eustace D'Eyncourt also gave us those incomparable Monitors, with their bulges under water, which were "given away" through the unmitigated folly of the Censors, who permitted a newspaper correspondent to describe how he had seen men, like St. Peter, walking on the water—they were walking on the protuberance which extended under the surface as the absolute protection against submarines; and when an old first-class cruiser called the "Grafton" had been so made submarine-proof, the captain of her, after receiving a torpedo fired at him at right angles and hitting him amidships, reported to the Admiralty that she went faster than before, simply because her hull proper had not been touched; the submarine had only blown away the submarine obstruction that Sir Eustace had fitted to her. Has he been made a lord? Personally I should say the tanks could never have existed without him; of that I am quite sure. Sir Philip Watts and Sir Eustace D'Eyncourt are enshrined in my heart.

Previously in this chapter I mentioned Mr. Gladstone. I sat next to him at dinner once. At the other side of him was a very beautiful woman, but she was struck dumb by awe of Mr. Gladstone, so he turned round to me and asked me if I had ever been in China. Yes, I had. And he asked me who were the best missionaries. I said the Roman Catholics were the most successful as they wore the Chinese dress, were untrammelled by families, so they got better amongst the people in the interior, but furthermore in their chapels they represented our Saviour and His Apostles with pigtails and dressed as Chinamen. Yes, he said, he remembered that, and he told me the name of the Head of the Roman Catholic Mission, whose name I had forgotten, and said to me that the Pope considered he had gone too far in that respect, and had recalled him. That had happened some twenty years previously, and I had forgotten all about it. Someone said what a pity that all that is now being said is being lost. Mr. Gladstone said: "Nothing is lost. Science will one day take off the walls of this room what we have been saying." This was years before the gramophone and the dictaphone and the telephone. He told us a great deal about Abraham and pigs, and why Abraham was so dead against them, and how he, Gladstone, had been driven by Daniel O'Connell in a four-in-hand, and how the Bishops in his early days were so much handsomer than now. One Bishop he specially named was called "The Beauty of Holiness." When he left, he asked me to walk home with him, which I did. Mrs. Gladstone said, seated inside the brougham which was waiting at the door: "Come in, William." He said: "No, I am going to walk with this young man." It was midnight, and Piccadilly was quite alive. He was living with Lady Frederick Cavendish, I think, at Carlton Gardens. We were nearly run over, as he was regardless of the traffic. I remember his saying: "Do right, and you can never suffer for it." I thought of that when, in my own case later on, it was "Athanasius contra Mundum." I was urged only to attack one vested interest at a time, but I said, "No, if you kick everyone's shins at the same time they won't trouble about their neighbours," and it succeeded; but alas! I gave up one thing, which was the real democratic pith and marrow, the Free Education of the Naval Officer, and a competence from the moment of entry, and open to all. King Edward said to me about this: "You're a Socialist." I said that a white shirt doesn't imply the best brain. We have forty million to select from, and we restrict our selection to about one-fortieth of the population.

I here relate an episode which made a deep impression on me and one never effaced. At the time of Gladstone's death I was looking at his picture in a shop window. Two working men were doing the same. The one said to the other: "That man died poor, but could have died rich, had he used his knowledge as Prime Minister to make investments quite lawfully; but he didn't!"

It really is a very fine thing in the public men of this nation.

I have always worshipped Abraham Lincoln. I have elsewhere related how he never argued with Judge or Jury or anyone else, but always told a story, thus following that great and inestimable example in Holy Writ: "And without a parable spake he not unto them." But one wishes it were more known how great were his simple views. His sole idea of a Christian Church was to preach the Saviour's condensed statement "to love God and your Neighbour!" He said that summed up all religion. He gloried in having been himself a hired labourer and believed in a system which allowed labourers "to strike" when they wanted to, and did not oblige them to labour whether you pay them or not. He said: "I do not believe in a law to prevent a man getting rich (that would do more harm than good), so while we do not propose any war upon Capital we do wish to allow the humblest an equal chance to get rich with everybody else. I want every man to have a chance to better his condition." And what Lincoln says of diligence is very good: "The leading rule for the man of every calling is DILIGENCE! Whatever piece of business you have in hand, before stopping do all the labour pertaining to it which can be done."

That most moving account of Lincoln's simple eloquence at the graves of Gettysburg is a most touching episode. The thousands listening to him never uttered a sound. There was a dead silence, when he stopped speaking. He left thinking himself a failure. It was the success of his life. A great orator just before him had moved the multitude to cheer unboundedly! but after Lincoln their feelings made them dumb.

While on personalities, I should like to say a little on one of the best friends I ever had and in my opinion the greatest of all journalists. Lord Morley once told me that he had never known the equal of W. T. Stead in his astounding gift of catching the popular feeling. He was absolute integrity and he feared no man. I myself have heard him tackle a Prime Minister like a terrier a rat. I have known him go to a packed meeting and scathe the whole mob of them. He never thought of money; he only thought of truth. He might have been a rich man if he hadn't told the truth. I know it. When he was over sixty he performed a journalistic feat that was wondrous. By King Edward's positive orders a cordon was arranged round the battle-cruiser "Indomitable," arriving late at night at Cowes with the Prince of Wales on board, to prevent the Press being a nuisance. Stead, in a small boat, dropped down with the tide from ahead and swarmed up a rope ladder under the bows, about 30 feet high and then along a sort of greasy pole, known to sailors as the lower boom, talked to one of the Officers, who naturally supposed he couldn't be there without permission; and the *Daily Mail* the next morning had the most perfect digest I have ever read of perhaps one of the most wonderful passages ever made. This big battle cruiser encumbered with the heaviest guns known, and with hundreds and hundreds of tons of armour on her side, beat the "Mauretania," the greyhound of the seas, built of gingerbread, carrying no cargo, and shaped for no other purpose than for speed and luxury.

Of course no other paper had a word.

Stead always told me he would die in his boots. Strife was his portion, he said. I am not sure that my friend Arnold White would not have shot him at sight in the Boer War. Stead was a pro-Boer, and so was I. I simply loved Botha, and Botha gave me great words. He said: "English was the business language of the globe"—that's good! Of course every genius has a strain of queerness. Does not the poet say: "Great wits to madness often are allied?" I remember a book which had a great circulation, entitled "The Insanity of Genius." I very nearly wrote a letter to *The Times* only I was afraid they might think *me* mad, and I was afraid that Admiral Fitzgerald might not think me modest (see his letter in *The Times* of Sept. 8th, 1919). This was my letter to *The Times*:—

"Genius is not insanity, it only means the man is before his time. That's all."

That was the whole of the letter.

There was a very great scientist (he is a very great friend of mine and he discovered something I can't remember the name of) who said: "A man must be mad to think of flying machines!" and he lived to see them as plentiful as sparrows.

Without saying a word to me or even letting me know, in a few hasty hours Stead wrote in the "Review of Reviews" in February, 1910, the most extraordinarily accurate *résumé* of every date and name connected with my career. It would have taken any other man a month. However, he made one great mistake in it. He only spoke in it, like all other things that have been said of me, of "The full corn in the ear!" What really is a man's life is the endurance and the adversity and the non-recognition and the humiliating slights and the fighting morning, noon and night, of early life. That brings fortune. I like that word "fortune." Those inspired men who translated the Great Bible never said a thing "happened," they always said it "fortuned."

I here insert a letter kindly lent me by Lord Esher. As it was written on the spur of the moment and out of the abundance of the heart, I give it verbatim. Esher loved Stead as much as I did. I knew it, and that's why I wrote to him. We felt a common affliction:—

April 22, 1912. HOTEL EXCELSIOR, NAPLES.

This loss of dear old Stead numbs me! Cromwell and Martin Luther rolled into one. And such a big heart. Such great emotions. You must write something. *All I've read quite inadequate.* The telegrams here say he was to the forefront with the women and children, putting them in the boats! *I can see him!* and probably singing "Hallelujah," and encouraging the ship's band to play cheerfully. He told me he would die in his boots. So he has. *And a fine death.* As a boy he had threepence a week pocket money. One penny bought Shakespeare in weekly parts, the other two pennies to his God for Missions. And the result was he became editor of a big newspaper at 22! And he was a Missionary himself all his life. Fearless even when alone, believing in his God—the God of truth—and his enemies always rued it when they fought him. He was an exploder of "gas-bags" and the terror of liars. He was called a "wild man" because he said "Two keels to one." He was at Berlin—the High Personage said to him: "Don't be frightened!" Stead replied to the All Highest: "Oh, no! we won't! *for every Dreadnought you build we will build two!*" *That* was the genesis of the cry "Two keels to one." I have a note of it made at the time for my "Reflections." But, my dear friend, put your concise pen to paper for our Cromwellian Saint. He deserves it.

Yours always,
FISHER.

"You cannot do anyone more good than by trying unsuccessfully to do him an injury," was one of the aphorisms of Lord Dalling (Sir Henry Bulwer); and it occurred to me forcibly on one occasion when I went to stay with my very great friend, Henry Labouchere (the proprietor of *Truth*). On the way I had been reading a peculiarly venomous attack on me in his paper; and when he greeted me as affectionately as ever, I showed it to him, saying: "Don't put your arm on my shoulder! Read that damned thing there!" Labouchere glanced at it and replied, "Where would you have been if I hadn't persistently maligned you?"

When I was with him at his villa at Florence, he used to smoke the most beastly cigarettes at ten a penny, yet he left over a million sterling, and was generous to absurdity to those he loved.

He had none but Italian servants; he told me he was always extremely polite to them for the knife came so easy to them. He said he didn't realise this until, after he had had some words with an English friend, his Italian gardener, who had overheard the altercation, asked Labouchere if he would like him (the gardener) to deal with his friend, and he tapped the stiletto in his waistband.

His own wit was as ready as his gardener's stiletto. On one occasion he was at Cologne railway station, and the Custom House Officer was turning his portmanteau inside out. Labouchere had a telegraph form in his pocket; he wrote out a telegram with a stylographic pen and handed it to the official who was standing behind the Custom House Officer and told him it was a Government telegram. This was the telegram:

PRINCE   BISMARCK,
BERLIN.

Can't dine with you to-night. Missed train through a damned ass of a Custom House Officer. Will let you have his name.

LABOUCHERE, Cologne.

They offered him a special train. Labouchere had never seen Bismarck in his life. This was the occasion on which Labouchere was reprimanded by the Foreign Office for his delay in taking up his appointment as attaché at St. Petersburg. His excuse was that the money allowed him only permitted his travelling by railway as far as Cologne; the rest of the way he walked.

This book would be incomplete if I did not draw attention to the great debt the nation owes to three men yet unmentioned in this volume.

Mr. George Lambert, M.P., twice refused office and sacrificed his political prospects and with a glorious victory sustained the whole Government effort to kick him out of Parliament; but he conquered with a magnificent majority of over two thousand! Why?

Because after serving for over seven years in the Admiralty he could speak of his own knowledge that the War administration and the fighting Sea Policy were shamefully effete.

The Recording Angel will mark down opposite Mr. Lambert's name: "Well done, thou good and faithful servant!" But may he also have his reward here and now, as many years of good work here below may lie between him and Heaven as yet.

Commodore Hugh Paget Sinclair is another "Stalwart" of the War. His business was to provide the officers and men to man the Fleet—imagine the stupendous task that was his!

We never wanted for Officer or Man!

He is now Director of Naval Intelligence; and may his ascent in the Navy be what is his splendid due!

Sir Alfred Yarrow I select for mention, for without him Mesopotamia would have been a bigger crime than it was, and throughout all ages it will be branded for gross and culpable and criminal ineptitude. If I was asked to name the Capturer of Bagdad I would unhesitatingly reply it was Sir Alfred Yarrow.

The Navy has not had its due credit for the Capture of Bagdad. If Sir Alfred Yarrow with his usual astounding push, and without regard to red tape or thanks or recognition, had not sent those splendid light-draught gunboats of his to Mesopotamia, packed up in bits like portmanteaux, then Bagdad would not have been ours. The Viceroy of India sent us (acting on the advice he had received) the wrong draught of water. We ignored the Viceroy and all his crew. It took *eighteen* days to get this pressing vital business through the Government Departments concerned. It took us *one* day to accomplish the whole procedure, with Sir Alfred Yarrow, and we chucked all the Departments. So 24 light-draught gunboats grew up like Jonah's Gourd, which came up in a night (Jonah, iv, 10).

*   *   *   *   *

I append a memorandum compiled from the Official papers:—

History of Provision of 24 Light-draught Gunboats for Mesopotamia.

*   *   *   *   *

Note.—These Vessels played a great part in the capture of Bagdad.

*   *   *   *   *

January 9th, 1915.—Telegram from Viceroy to India Office that Admiralty be asked to provide 4 gunboats—draught 4½ feet for Tigris.18

January 11th, 1915.—India Office asked Admiralty to meet Viceroy's wishes.

January 29th, 1915.19—Admiralty Departments suggested various types. War Staff proposed 3 from Egypt be sent.

January 29th, 1915.—Lord Fisher ordered 24 light-draught gunboats. In order to save time, Captain [now Rear-Admiral Sir S. S.] Hall, R.N., (Lord Fisher's Secretary) was directed by Lord Fisher "*to co-operate with Mr. Yarrow20 and carry the operation through without reference to Admiralty Departments or any other Departments.*"

January 29th, 1915.—*Conference held. Design settled.*21

January 30th, 1915.—{Captain Hall toured the country for likely
February 1st, 1915.—{firms to construct the 24 gunboats.

February 2nd, 1915.22—Proposals made for placing orders approved by Lord Fisher and First Lord, and orders were placed as follows:—

12 Small by Yarrow.
 4 Large by Barclay Curle.
 2 Large by Lobnitz.
 2 Large by Ailsa Shipbuilding Co.
 2 Large by Wood Skinner.
 2 Large by Sunderland Shipbuilding Co.

February 8th, 1915.—Captain Hall was appointed Commodore-in-Charge of the Submarine Service, but was directed by Lord Fisher to continue supervision of the provision of 24 gunboats.

Sir Alfred Yarrow ought (like Mr. Schwab) to have been made a Duke, and I wrote to Sir John Jellicoe, when he was First Sea Lord, and told him so.

The history of the Flotillas of light-draught gunboats built both for Mesopotamia and the Danube will ever be associated with the good service done by Sir Alfred Yarrow, and for which he was only made a Baronet. Those built for the Tigris led our Army to Bagdad and far beyond, and were at times unsupported far ahead of the military force; and without any question whatever without them the Mesopotamian muddle could never have emerged into a glorious victory. The speed with which these vessels were constructed and despatched in small parcels to Mesopotamia and there put together in an extemporary dockyard arranged by Sir Alfred Yarrow's staff was as much a feature as any other part of their production. It necessitated masses of natives of different religious persuasions being gathered together to assist the skilled artizans in bolting the pieces together and launching them on the Tigris. Their differing hours of prayer were a disturbing element in the rapidity of the construction; but my splendid friend the foreman from the Scotstoun Yard of Messrs. Yarrow contrived a prayer compromise. The Danube Flotilla arranged for with a number of other builders was equally remarkable; and Commodore (now Admiral) Bartolomé wrote me a commendatory letter of their good service there.

I must also mention Commodore (now Admiral) Sir S. S. Hall, but for whose continual journeys from shipyard to shipyard these vessels would never have been delivered on the scene of action in the time required.

Within six months all these Flotillas were thought of—designed—built— and in service, and nothing gave me intenser delight than the visit I paid to these craft as they were all built and then taken to pieces for transit to their destination in packages that any motor car could have transported.

The world at large can have little conception of the remarkability of those comparatively large hulls with good speed and practically drawing but a few inches of water—the propellers (which were too large in diameter for the depth of water) being made by an ingenious device to revolve in a well above the water-line, the water being drawn up by suction. I thought to myself as I viewed these miracles of ingenuity and rapidity: "England can never succumb."

CHAPTER XVI
THINGS THAT PLEASE ME

"I have culled a Garland of Flowers—

Mine is the string that binds them."

*　　　*　　　*　　　*　　　*

Thou shalt not kill, but needst not strive

Officiously to keep alive!

(When catching Submarines).

*　　　*　　　*　　　*　　　*

Seest thou a man diligent in business—he shall stand before Kings—he shall
not stand before mean men.

*　　　*　　　*　　　*　　　*

God who cannot be unjust,

Heedeth all who on Him trust.

Them who call on Him for aid,

Anguish shall not make afraid.

Trust him then in life. In death

He can give thee Living Breath!

After death the Life now thine

He can make the Life Divine.

*　　　*　　　*　　　*　　　*

I never bother to bother about anyone who doesn't bother to bother about
me!

*　　　*　　　*　　　*　　　*

[*Portrait by J. Mallia & Co., Valetta.*

COMMANDER-IN-CHIEF OF THE MEDITERRANEAN FLEET, 1899–1902.

"Put on the impenetrable armour of contempt and fortitude."

  *   *   *   *   *

When danger threatens and the foeman nigh,

"*God and our Navy!*" is the Nation's cry.

But, the danger over and the Country righted,

God is forgotten and the Sailor slighted.

  *   *   *   *   *

Never fight a Chimney Sweep; some of the soot comes off on you.

  *   *   *   *   *

Pas de Culte sans mystère.

  *   *   *   *   *

Ode to an Apple—

Newton saw an apple fall,
Eve an apple did enthral;
It played the devil with us all,
The Devil making Eve to fall.

*   *   *   *   *

"Liberty of Conscience" means doing wrong but not worrying about it afterwards.

*   *   *   *   *

"Tact" is insulting a man without his knowing it.

*   *   *   *   *

Even a man's faults may reflect his virtues.

*   *   *   *   *

Sincerity is the road to Heaven.

*   *   *   *   *

I thought it would be a good thing to be a missionary, but I thought it would be better to be First Sea Lord.

*   *   *   *   *

Think in Oceans—shoot at sight.

*   *   *   *   *

Big conceptions and Quick Decisions.

*   *   *   *   *

Napoleonic in Audacity.
Cromwellian in Thoroughness.
Nelsonic in Execution.

*   *   *   *   *

"Surprise" the pith and marrow of war!

*   *   *   *   *

Audacity and Imagination beget surprise.

*   *   *   *   *

Rashness in war is Prudence.

*   *   *   *   *

Prudence in war is Imbecility.

*   *   *   *   *

Hit first! Hit hard! Keep on hitting!! (The 3 H's).

*   *   *   *   *

The 3 Requisites for Success—Ruthless, Relentless, Remorseless (The 3 R's).

*   *   *   *   *

BUSINESS—Call on a Business man in Business hours only on Business. Transact your Business and go about your Business, in order to give him time to finish his Business, and you time to mind your own Business. [I had this printed on cards, one of which was handed to every caller on me at the Admiralty.]

*   *   *   *   *

The Nelsonic Attributes—

(*a*) Self Reliance.
(*b*) Power of Initiative.
(*c*) Fearlessness of Responsibility.
(*d*) Fertility of Resource.

*   *   *   *   *

Originality never yet led to Preferment.

*   *   *   *   *

Mediocrity is the Road to Honour.

*   *   *   *   *

Repetition is the Soul of Journalism.

*   *   *   *   *

No difficulty baffles great zeal.

*   *   *   *   *

The Pavement of Life is strewn with Orange Peel.

*   *   *   *   *

Inconsistency is the bugbear of Silly Asses.

*   *   *   *   *

Never Deny: Never Explain: Never Apologise.

*   *   *   *   *

"To defy Power that seems omnipotent ...

Never to change, nor falter, nor repent."

(SHELLEY.)

*   *   *   *   *

Cardinal Rampolla got his Hat at a younger age than any preceding Cardinal. Asked to account for his phenomenal success, he replied:—It's due to 3 things:

$$I \text{ never} \begin{Bmatrix} \text{asked for} \\ \text{refused} \\ \text{resigned} \end{Bmatrix} \text{anything.}$$

*   *   *   *   *

The best scale for an experiment is 12 inches to a foot.

*   *   *   *   *

Dread Nought is over 80 times in the Bible ("Fear Not"). So I took as my motto "Fear God and Dread Nought."

*   *   *   *   *

Moltke wrote as follows:

"A clever military leader will succeed in many cases in choosing defensive positions of such an offensive nature from a strategic point of view that the opponent is compelled to attack us in them."

*   *   *   *   *

In looking through a packet of ancient papers I find some youthful thoughts of my own and some others which evidently I thought very choice.

"Anything said before a lecture muddles it."

"Anything after weakens it!"

*   *   *   *   *

"There is nothing you can't have if you want it enough."

*   *   *   *   *

The following extract is from Blake:

"He who bends to himself a joy,

Does the winged life destroy;

But he who kisses the joy as it flies

Lives in Eternity's Sunrise."

*   *   *   *   *

Dean Swift satirized the vulgar exclusiveness of those who desired the infinite meadows of Heaven only to be frequented by the religious sect they adorned on earth:

"We are God's chosen few!

All others will be damned!

There is no place in Heaven for you,

We can't have Heaven crammed!"

*   *   *   *   *

Lord Dalling (Sir Henry Bulwer) codified his life in axioms and phrases. His intimate friend, Sir Drummond Wolff, says so. (By the way, Wolff's father was a marvellous Bible scholar. I heard him preach the sermon of my life: it was extempore, on "The Resurrection." A great friend of his told me that Wolff did really know the Bible by heart.) These are Lord Dalling's sayings; he quotes Talleyrand for one of his rules of life:

"Acknowledge the receipt of a book from the author at once: this relieves you of the necessity of saying whether you have read it."

Again this is excellent:

"You cannot do anyone more good than by trying unsuccessfully to do him an injury." (Mr. Labouchere gave me the same reason for attacking me in his paper *Truth*.)

"Nothing is so foolish as to be wise out of season."

"The best trait in a man's character is an anxiety to serve those who have obliged him once and can do so no more."

*   *   *   *   *

Nelson's Ipsissima Verba.

"Do not imagine I am one of those hot-brained people who fight at an immense disadvantage without an adequate object ... in a week's time I shall get reinforcements and the enemy will get none, and then I must annihilate him."

It was not "Victory" that Nelson ever desired. It was "Annihilation!"

*   *   *   *   *

Moses, Gideon and Cromwell.

Moses and Gideon were each of them summoned straight from their simple daily task to go and help their fellow countrymen, and both were able to perform the task allotted to them in spite of their first great doubts of their fitness for the work. The figure of Moses looms through the Ages as gigantic as the Pyramids, and nearer home and in a lesser sphere stands our English Cromwell, the Great Protector!

"I would have been glad," said Cromwell, "to have lived on my woodside or kept a flock of sheep rather than have undertaken a government like this." And yet in the end he had undertaken it because he said he "had hoped he might prevent some imminent evil."

*   *   *   *   *

Suffragettes.

The nine Muses were all women.
The three Graces were all women.

*   *   *   *   *

A great philosopher has stated that a woman can be classed under two categories:

1. A mother, a mistress and a friend; or,

2. A comrade and queen and child.

A woman is really rooted in physical reality, and all the above six attributes of the philosopher always live in her.

Thus the Song of Solomon produced a passionate commodity, but it required the Mary Magdalene of the Gospel to express the *summum bonum* of a woman of "Greatly Loving."

In the first prayer book of A.D. 1549 there was a Collect for her! No other woman had a Collect except the Virgin Mary.

Emotion, self-surrender, selflessness, immortal courage, wondrous physical beauty! Mary Magdalene was a great human reality. It is quite obvious she was no debauchee or her Beauty would have failed, nor could she have been a "hardened" sinner or she would have scoffed!

What was her history? What caused her lapse? Who was her Betrayer?

"Her sins, which are many, are forgiven; for she loved much. Verily I say unto you, Wheresoever this Gospel shall be preached in the whole world, there shall also this, that this woman hath done, be told for a memorial of her."

And is it not very striking that St. Peter, who dictated St. Mark's Gospel, records in the 16th chapter, verse 9, of St. Mark, that the first person in the world to whom the Saviour showed Himself after His Resurrection was Mary Magdalene?

"Now when Jesus was risen early the first day of the week, He appeared *first* to Mary Magdalene, out of whom he had cast seven devils. And she went and told them that had been with Him as they mourned and wept. And they, when they heard that He was alive and had been seen of her, believed not."

*   *   *   *   *

A Sun-Dial that I Love.

Que Dieu éclaire les heures que je perds.
(May God light up the hours that I fail to light.)

*   *   *   *   *

Though hidden yet from all our eyes,

He sees the Gideon who shall rise

To save us and His sword.

EPILOGUE
MOUNT PISGAH

IT is stated that the historian, Lecky, O.M. (I assisted at the operation of his receiving the Order of Merit) gave more thought and time to the book of his last years, "The Map of Life," than to any other of all his works, and it is said that for three years he kept on revising the last of its chapters.

The book was derided to me by a literary friend of great eminence as being "The Pap of Life!" I read its last chapters with great avidity. If for nothing else, the book is worthy of immortality for the reason that it so emphasises those great words of Dryden as being appropriate to the close of a busied life—

"Not Heaven itself upon the past has Power,

What has been has been, and I have had my hour."

Whenever (as I often do) I pass Dryden's bust in Westminster Abbey I invariably thank him for those lines.

Mr. Lecky urges his readers to leave the active scenes of life in good time and not to "Lag superfluous on the Stage" (I believe Mr. Gladstone recommended this also, but didn't do it!).

To illustrate Mr. Lecky we have that great and splendid Trio of Translation to Heaven at the very zenith of their powers. Elijah was hurrying along (that great, hairy, weird old man) so that Elisha could hardly keep pace with him, and he is suddenly caught up in a Chariot of Fire to Heaven! I ask, "Was not Nelson's leaving this earth quite a similar glorious departure?"

"Partial firing continued until 4.30 p.m. when a victory having been reported to Admiral Lord Viscount Nelson, K.B., and Commander-in-Chief, he THEN died of his Wound."

Moses (with whom I am now more particularly concerned) also left this life in a similar glorious way, for God was his companion when his Spirit left this Earth, and it markedly is recorded of Moses that—

"His eye was not dim,
Nor his natural force abated!"

Mr. Lecky doesn't quote my three men above. I consider them superior to Noah, Daniel and Job, who are the three named in Scripture as being so dear to the pious man. Ezekiel, chapter xiv., verse 14.

I reiterate that the advice of the derided Lecky seems to me excellent, to leave active life at one's zenith, and thus anticipate senility.

The Archbishop of Seville is a lovely story by Cervantes. All Spain came to hear him preach. Indeed he had to preach every day, the crowds were so great, and he said to his faithful Secretary: "Tell me when you notice me waning, for a man never knows it himself." The Secretary did so, and the Archbishop gave him the sack! Yes! The Archbishop had passed the Rubicon, and this dismissal was the proof. Having this fear, I left Office on my birthday in 1910, though for a few short months in 1914 I enjoyed the "dusky hues of glorious war," and exceedingly delighted myself in those seven months in arranging a new Armada against Germany of 612 vessels, and in sending Admiral von Spee and all his ships to the bottom of the sea.

The following much-prized lines were sent me on the Annihilation of Admiral von Spee's Squadron off the Falkland Islands on December 8th, 1914. He had sunk Admiral Cradock's Squadron five weeks before. The "Dreadnought" Battle Cruisers, "Inflexible" and "Invincible," sent to sink von Spee, made a passage of 14,000 miles without a hitch and arrived just a few hours before von Spee. It was a timely arrangement:—

From the President of Magdalen College, Oxford, Sir Herbert Warren (Professor of Poetry).

Merserat Ex-spe Spem, rediit spes, mergitur Ex-spes.

"Von Spee sent the 'Good Hope' to the bottom: hope revived; he is sunk himself, without hope."

From Mr. Godley, the Public Orator at Oxford University.

Hoc tibi Piscator Patria debet opus.

"Your country owes this exploit to you, O Fisher!"

But that Great Providence, that shapes our course, rough hew it how we will, ordained my departure from the conduct of the War. Amongst the masses of regretful letters at my departure I choose one from an Admiral then 88 years old, who satisfies the great Dr. Weir Mitchell's dictum of the clear brain becoming clearer with age. This Admiral annexed a Continent for England, abounding in riches in New Guinea; but he got no thanks; and England gave away his gift. But his name lives there. I conclude with his letter:—

DEAR OLD FISHER,

It is marvellous how all variations of our lives are unravelled by Divine Inspiration that cannot err.

"No one can 'hustle' Providence."
(That's one of your sayings!)
Think of Moses!

"He was the truest warrior that ever buckled sword.

He the most gifted Poet that ever breathed a word:

And never Earth's Philosopher traced with his golden pen,

On the Deathless Page, truths half so sage as he wrote down for men;

Yet no man knows his sepulchre, and no man saw it e'er,

For the Angels of God up-turned the sod and laid the Dead Man there."

Moses saved his people. He prepared them for the conquest in which he was to take no part. He was the meekest man on earth, yet he could be the most ruthless!

Doubtless you saved England at the Falkland Islands.

Doubtless you prepared our Fleet for this war! (Nothing to boast of! You the clay in the hands of the Potter!) And it seems likely that some Joshua will reap what you have sown! Yet history will put it right.

"O lonely grave in Moab's land! O dark Beth-Peor's hill! Speak to these curious hearts of ours and teach them to be still!"

Ever faithfully yours,
(Signed) J. MORESBY.

FOOTNOTES

1 "This one thing I do, forgetting those things which are behind, and reaching forth unto those things which are before, I press toward the mark."—*Phil.* iii. 13, 14.

2 Sir Julian Corbett, the author of the wonderful "Seven Years' War," wrote to me in past vituperative years as follows:

"Yesterday I was asked if it were *really* true that you (Sir John Fisher) had sold the country to Germany! I was able to assure the questioner that the report was at least exaggerated. It is often my fortune to be able to quiet minds that have been seriously disturbed by the unprecedented slanders that have been the reward of your unprecedented work."

3 See letters at end of this chapter.

4 On hearing of von Tirpitz's dismissal I perpetrated the following letter, which a newspaper contrived to print in one of its editions. I can't say why, but it didn't appear any more, nor was it copied by any other paper!

DEAR OLD TIRPS,

We are both in the same boat! What a time we've been colleagues, old boy! However, we did you in the eye over the Battle Cruisers and I know you've said you'll never forgive me for it when bang went the "Blucher" and von Spee and all his host!

Cheer up, old chap! Say "Resurgam"! You're the one German sailor who understands War! Kill your enemy without being killed yourself. *I don't blame you for the submarine business.* I'd have done the same myself, only our idiots in England wouldn't believe it when I told 'em!

Well! So long!

Yours till hell freezes,
FISHER.
29/3/16.

I say! Are you sure if you had tripped out with your whole High Sea Fleet before the Russian ice thawed and brought over those half-a-million soldiers from Hamburg to frighten our old women that you could have got back un-Jellicoed?

5 "A Naval Lieutenant, 1914–1918," by Etienne, 1919, pp. 48 *et seq.*

6 *Note.*—These are the names of the three first great Battle Cruisers of the Dreadnought type.

7 On January 2, 1915, Russia asked for a demonstration against the Turks in order to relieve the pressure they were putting on the Russian forces in the Caucasus. Next day the War Office cabled a promise, through the Foreign Office, that this should be done. Before he sent the cable Lord Kitchener wrote to Mr. Churchill: "The only place that a demonstration might have some effect in stopping reinforcements going East would be the Dardanelles."

8 "The dramatic scene which followed may one day furnish material for the greatest historical picture of the war. Lord Fisher sat and listened to the men who knew nothing about it and heard one after another pass opinion in favour of a venture to which he was opposed. He rose abruptly from the table and made as if to leave the room.

"The tall figure of Lord Kitchener rose and followed him. The two stood by the window for some time in conversation and then both took their seats again. In Lord Fisher's own words: 'I reluctantly gave in to Lord Kitchener and resumed my seat.'

"Mr. Asquith saw that drama enacted, and Mr. Asquith knew that it arose out of Lord Fisher's opposition to the scheme under discussion. But he allowed his colleagues on the Council to reach their conclusions without drawing from the expert his opinion for their guidance. The monstrous decision was therefore taken without it. But they all knew it—such a scene could not occur without everyone knowing the cause."

9 It must be emphasised here, as well as in regard to Lord Kitchener's statement to the War Council dated May 14th, 1915, that Lord Fisher considered that it would be both improper and unseemly for him to enter into an altercation either at the War Council or elsewhere with his chief Mr. Churchill, the First Lord. Silence or resignation was the right course.

10 This was the Armada of 612 vessels authorised by Mr. Lloyd George as Chancellor of the Exchequer.

11 At my entreaty a far better man went, Admiral Sir Reginald Henderson, G.C.B. He is a splendid seaman and he devised a splendid scheme.

12 This was written in December, 1908, and our Fleet and ships were always dogged in the war by them.

13 There are statues of Franklin and of Robert Falconer Scott in Waterloo Place; but neither of these displayed his heroism in naval action. They were each peaceable seekers—but what on earth good accrues from going to the North and South Poles I never could understand—no one is going there when they can go to Monte Carlo!

14 In the following selections, words between square brackets are not part of the original letters.

15 N.B.—These very motor boats here described sank two battleships of the Bolshevists only the other day. *See* Chapter IV.—F. 21/9/19.

16 *Then after this came the 15-inch gun; then the 18-inch gun, actually used at sea in the War; and then the 20-inch gun, ready to be built and go into the "Incomparable" of 40,000 tons and 40 knots speed, on May 22nd, 1915—F. 21/9/19.*

17 "The New Teaching," edited by John Adams. Hodder and Stoughton.

18 This shows how badly advised the Navy was by the India Office, *as under 3 feet was vital,* and the order was given accordingly.

19 Eighteen days going through Departments.

20 Mr. Yarrow had technical charge of the whole business and was the sole designer—and there was no paper work whatever.

21 All this action on the same day.

22 All the rest of the required action taken in 4 days.

9 789357 389587